BATTLE IN IRAQ

Josephine Hammond was born in London but brought up in West Africa. A graduate of University College, London, she taught languages for many years and now runs her own business in Pembrokeshire. She is the author of several short stories and poems and has also published magazine and newspaper articles. This is her first book.

BATTLE IN IRAQ

Letters and Diaries of the First World War

J. M. HAMMOND

The Radcliffe Press

LONDON • NEW YORK

Published in 2009 by The Radcliffe Press
6 Salem Road, London W2 4BU

Distributed in the United States and Canada Exclusively by
Palgrave Macmillan, 175 Fifth Avenue, New York NY 10010

ISBN 978 1 84511 963 8

A full CIP record is available from the Library of Congress

Library of Congress Catalog card: available

Printed and bound in Great Britain by CPI, Antony Rowe, Chippenham.
Copy-edited and typeset by Oxford Publishing Services, Oxford.

FSC
Mixed Sources
Product group from well-managed forests and other controlled sources
Cert no. SGS-COC-2953
www.fsc.org
© 1996 Forest Stewardship Council

Contents

Illustrations

Maps

Illustrations

This book is dedicated to the thousands of men of the merchant navy who gave their lives for their country in two world wars. I wish to express my grateful thanks to my husband, Captain Andrew Hammond for his patience and for his advice on all things nautical and to my son Joseph Hammond for his help on the initial idea for the jacket illustration.

School photograph. William Reed is in the third row from the front and sixth from the left.

Prologue

Ah, make the most of what we yet may spend,
Before we too into the Dust descend;
Dust into Dust, and under Dust, to lie,
Sans Wine, sans Song, sans Singer and – sans End!
(*Rubáiyát of Omar Khayyam*, verse 23)

An old leather jewellery case started it all. It was waiting at the back of my mother's wardrobe, left over from the days of elegant travel, when suitcases were made of leather and were so heavy that you needed a porter to help even before you had filled them with belongings. This particular brown leather case was small, about eighteen inches wide. The exterior was scratched, scuffed and battered looking. Several ancient half torn travel labels decorated its surface. It looked as if it had been round the world several times and could tell tales of adventure and exploration.

When I opened it, I was instantly transported back to my childhood, to our house in Africa and the room in which the case had been kept. The case had the same spicy, dusty smell I remembered from the desk in that room – a mixture of polish, sunshine and the Sahara dust the harmattan wind blew through the house. The case was lined with fabric stained with age and use, and it contained the germ of an idea.

The story held in the case was one I had known vaguely all my life. Although he died long before I was born my mother used to talk about her father, William Louis Reed, and tell us of his heroism and generosity; and here was the proof. In the case I found his diaries, closely written and almost indecipherable.

Throughout my childhood I had every so often peered into the interior of the case taking things out and turning them over in my hand. There was a fine blue box with gold tooling round the edges and the letters DSO marked at the centre of the lid. There were other medals too, as well as certificates, photos and newspaper cuttings, all yellowing and curled at the corners. I had never bothered to stop to read the detail. The sunshine, my bicycle or a new friend had always called too urgently.

Somewhere in the back of my mind I had always known there was a story there, but while my mother was alive I felt it belonged to her and was for her to write or not as she chose. Now that I have inherited it, I feel free to write it.

The first diary, which was covered in a wine-coloured leather binding, tells of my grandfather William's travels and work in Persia, as well as how he became involved in the war. The second diary, bound in khaki canvas with a brown leather edging, looks as if it might have been an army issue book. It speaks of his daily life in a Turkish prison camp. The leather case also contained letters from the Admiralty to my great-grandmother, as well as my grandfather's official report to the Admiralty of what happened to his ship, the *Julnar*, as it steamed up the Tigris. The once white paper, now stained the colour of tea, but the words were as clear as the day they were first posted. Reading the letters to William's mother I began to imagine what effect they might have had on her when she first opened them.

At the bottom of the case, on paper so worn that it was tissue thin, was a hand-written poem about the exploits of the *Julnar* and how it had meant so much to so many people. There was also a copy of the *Basrah Times*, possibly the only one still in existence. It started me on a journey through the Imperial War Museum, the Royal Geographical Society, the National Maritime Museum, Lloyds of London, the National Archives, the Middle East Centre at St Antony's College, Oxford, and the British Library with its many eye witness accounts and recent histories. It was a story I had to tell.

The Worldly Hope men set their Hearts upon
Turns Ashes – or it prospers;
And anon, like Snow upon the Desert's
Dusty Face
Lighting a little Hour or two – is gone.
(*Rubáiyát of Omar Khayyám*, verse 14)

On the front page of the *Basrah Times* lying at the bottom of my grandfather's suitcase was the following proclamation to the people of the Wilayat of Baghdad.

> In the name of my King and in the name of the peoples over whom he rules I address you as follows:
>
> Our Military operations have as their object the defeat of the enemy and the driving of him from these territories. In order to complete this task I am charged with absolute and supreme control of all regions in which British troops operate; but our armies do not come into your cities and lands as conquerors or enemies, but as liberators.
>
> Since the days of Hulagu your citizens have been subject to the tyranny of strangers, your palaces have fallen into ruins, your gardens have sunken in desolation and your forefathers and yourselves have groaned in bondage. Your sons have been carried off to wars not of your seeking; your wealth has been stripped from you by unjust men and squandered in distant places.
>
> Since the days of Midhat, the Turks have talked of reforms; yet do not the ruins and wastes of today testify to the vanity of those promises?
>
> It is the wish not only of my King and his peoples, but it is also the wish of the great Nations with whom he is in alliance, that you should prosper even as in the past when

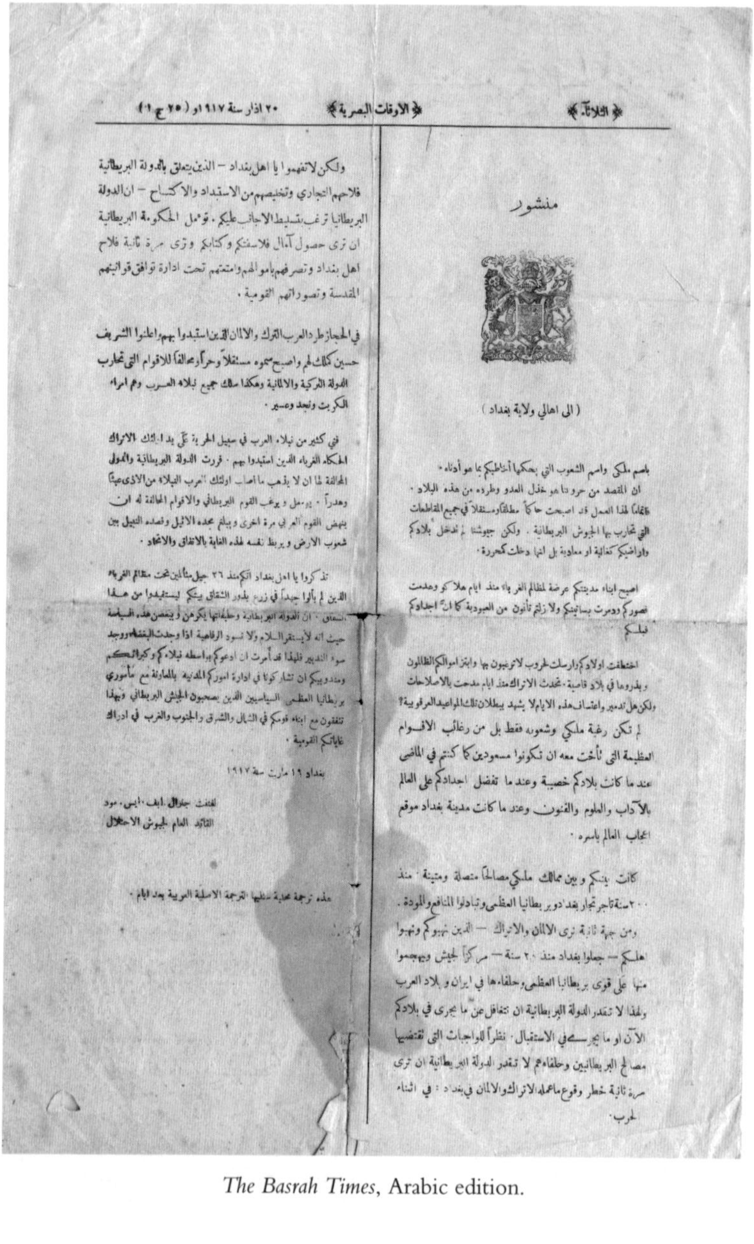

الثلاثاء — الاوقات البصرية — ٢٠ اذار سنة ٩١٧ او (٢٥ ج ١)

منشور

(الى اهالي ولاية بغداد)

باسم ملكي واسم الشعوب التي يحكمها أخاطبكم بما هو أدناه ·

ان المقصد من حروبنا هو خذل العدو وطرده من هذه البلاد · فاتماماً لهذا العمل قد اصبحت حاكماً مطلقاً ومستقلاً في جميع المقاطعات التي تحارب بها الجيوش البريطانية . ولكن جيوشنا لم تدخل بلادكم واراضيكم كغالية او معادية بل انها دخلت كمحررة ·

اصبح ابناء مدينتكم عرضة لمظالم الغرباء منذ ايام هلاكو وهدمت قصوركم ودمرت بساتينكم ولا زلتم تأنون من العبودية كما ان اجدادكم قبلكم

اختطفت اولادكم وارسلت لحروب لا ترغبون بها وابتز اموالكم الظالمون وبذروها في بلاد قاصية · تحدث الاتراك منذ ايام مدحت بالاصلاحات ولكن هل تدمير واعتساف هذه الايام لا يشهد ببطلان تلك المواعيد العرقوبية؟

لم تكن رغبة ملكي وشعوبه فقط بل من رغائب الاقوام العظيمة التي تأخت معه ان تكونوا مسعودين كما كنتم في الماضي عند ما كانت بلادكم خصبة وعند ما تفضل اجدادكم على العالم بالآداب والعلوم والفنون وعند ما كانت مدينة بغداد موقع اعجاب العالم باسره ·

كانت بينكم وبين ممالك ملكي مصالحاً متصلة ومتينة · منذ ٢٠٠ سنة تاجر تجار بغداد وبريطانيا العظمى وتبادلوا المنافع والمودة . ومن جهة ثانية نرى الالمان والاتراك — الذين نهبوكم ونهبوا اهلكم — جعلوا بغداد منذ ٢٠ سنة — مركزاً لجيش ويهجموا منها على قوى بريطانيا العظمى وحلفاءها في ايران و بلاد العرب ولهذا لا تقدر الدولة البريطانية ان تتغافل عن ما يجرى في بلادكم الآن او ما يجرى في الاستقبال · نظراً للواجبات التي تقتضيها مصالح البريطانيين وحلفاءهم لا تقدر الدولة البريطانية ان ترى مرة ثانية خطر وقوع ماعمله الاتراك والالمان في بغداد : في اثناء الحرب·

ولكن لا تفهموا يا اهل بغداد — الذين يتعلق بالدولة البريطانية فلاحهم التجاري وتخليصهم من الاستبداد والاكتساح — ان الدولة البريطانيا ترغب بتسليط الاجانب عليكم · تؤمل الحكومة البريطانية ان ترى حصول آمال فلاسفتكم وكتابكم وترى مرة ثانية فلاح اهل بغداد وتصرفهم باموالهم وامتعتهم تحت ادارة توافق قوانينهم المقدسة وتصوراتهم القومية ·

في الحجاز طرد العرب الترك والالمان الذين استبدوا بهم واعلنوا الشريف حسين كملك لهم واصبح سموه مستقلاً وحراً وحالفاً للاقوام التي تحارب الدولة التركية والالمانية وهكذا سلك جميع نبلاء العرب وهم امراء الكويت ونجد وعسير ·

في كثير من نبلاء العرب في سبيل الحرية على يد اولئك الاتراك الحكام الغرباء الذين استبدوا بهم · قررت الدولة البريطانية والدول الحالفة لها ان لا يذهب ما اصاب اولئك العرب النبلاء من الاذى عبثاً وهدراً · يؤمل و يرغب القوم البريطاني والاقوام الحالفة له ان ينهض القوم العربي مرة اخرى و يبلغ مجده الاثيل وقصده النبيل بين شعوب الارض و يربط نفسه لهذه الغاية بالاتفاق والاتحاد ·

تذكروا يا اهل بغداد انكم منذ ٢٦ جيل متألمين تحت مظالم الغرباء الذين لم يألوا جهداً في زرع بذور الشقاق بينكم ليستفيدوا من هذا الشقاق · ان الدولة البريطانية وحلفاءها يكرهون و يمقتون هذه السياسة حيث انه لا يستقر السلام ولا تسود الرفاهية اذا وجدت البغضاء ووجد سوء التدبير فلهذا قد أمرت ان ادعوكم بواسطة نبلائكم وكبرائكم ومندوبيكم ان تشاركونا في ادارة اموركم المدنية بالمعاونة مع مأموري بريطانيا العظمى السياسيين الذين يصحبون الجيش البريطاني وبهذا تتفقون مع ابناء قومكم في الشمال والشرق والجنوب والغرب في ادراك غاياتكم القومية ·

بغداد ١٩ مارت سنة ١٩١٧

لفتنت جنرال . ايف . ايس . مود
القائد العام لجيوش الاحتلال

هذه ترجمة محلية ستليها الترجمة الاصلية العربية بعد ايام ·

The Basrah Times, Arabic edition.

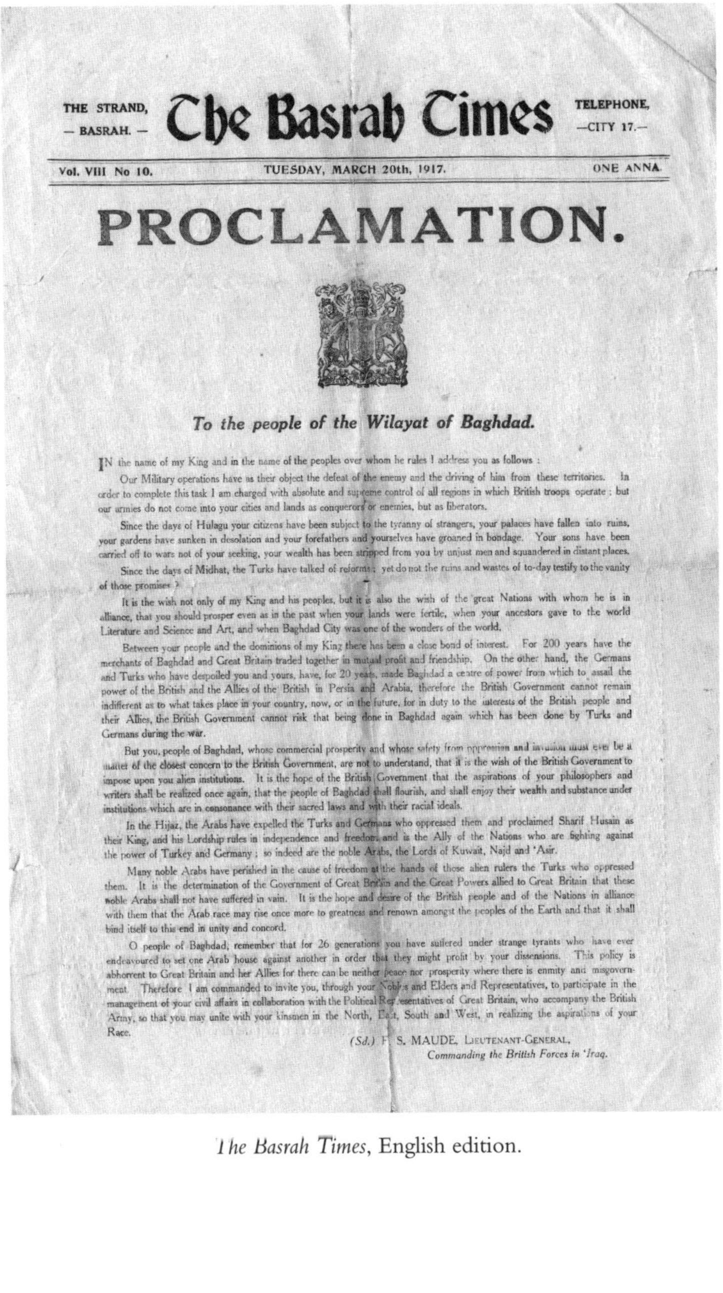

THE STRAND, — BASRAH. — **The Basrah Times** TELEPHONE, —CITY 17.—

Vol. VIII No 10. TUESDAY, MARCH 20th, 1917. ONE ANNA.

PROCLAMATION.

To the people of the Wilayat of Baghdad.

IN the name of my King and in the name of the peoples over whom he rules I address you as follows :

Our Military operations have as their object the defeat of the enemy and the driving of him from these territories. In order to complete this task I am charged with absolute and supreme control of all regions in which British troops operate ; but our armies do not come into your cities and lands as conquerors or enemies, but as liberators.

Since the days of Hulagu your citizens have been subject to the tyranny of strangers, your palaces have fallen into ruins, your gardens have sunken in desolation and your forefathers and yourselves have groaned in bondage. Your sons have been carried off to wars not of your seeking, your wealth has been stripped from you by unjust men and squandered in distant places.

Since the days of Midhat, the Turks have talked of reforms ; yet do not the ruins and wastes of to-day testify to the vanity of those promises ?

It is the wish not only of my King and his peoples, but it is also the wish of the great Nations with whom he is in alliance, that you should prosper even as in the past when your lands were fertile, when your ancestors gave to the world Literature and Science and Art, and when Baghdad City was one of the wonders of the world.

Between your people and the dominions of my King there has been a close bond of interest. For 200 years have the merchants of Baghdad and Great Britain traded together in mutual profit and friendship. On the other hand, the Germans and Turks who have despoiled you and yours, have, for 20 years, made Baghdad a centre of power from which to assail the power of the British and the Allies of the British in Persia and Arabia, therefore the British Government cannot remain indifferent as to what takes place in your country, now, or in the future, for in duty to the interests of the British people and their Allies, the British Government cannot risk that being done in Baghdad again which has been done by Turks and Germans during the war.

But you, people of Baghdad, whose commercial prosperity and whose safety from oppression and invasion must ever be a matter of the closest concern to the British Government, are not to understand, that it is the wish of the British Government to impose upon you alien institutions. It is the hope of the British Government that the aspirations of your philosophers and writers shall be realized once again, that the people of Baghdad shall flourish, and shall enjoy their wealth and substance under institutions which are in consonance with their sacred laws and with their racial ideals.

In the Hijaz, the Arabs have expelled the Turks and Germans who oppressed them and proclaimed Sharif Husain as their King, and his Lordship rules in independence and freedom, and is the Ally of the Nations who are fighting against the power of Turkey and Germany ; so indeed are the noble Arabs, the Lords of Kuwait, Najd and 'Asir.

Many noble Arabs have perished in the cause of freedom at the hands of those alien rulers the Turks who oppressed them. It is the determination of the Government of Great Britain and the Great Powers allied to Great Britain that these noble Arabs shall not have suffered in vain. It is the hope and desire of the British people and of the Nations in alliance with them that the Arab race may rise once more to greatness and renown amongst the peoples of the Earth and that it shall bind itself to this end in unity and concord.

O people of Baghdad, remember that for 26 generations you have suffered under strange tyrants who have ever endeavoured to set one Arab house against another in order that they might profit by your dissensions. This policy is abhorrent to Great Britain and her Allies for there can be neither peace nor prosperity where there is enmity and misgovernment. Therefore I am commanded to invite you, through your Nobles and Elders and Representatives, to participate in the management of your civil affairs in collaboration with the Political Representatives of Great Britain, who accompany the British Army, so that you may unite with your kinsmen in the North, East, South and West, in realizing the aspirations of your Race.

(Sd.) F. S. MAUDE, LIEUTENANT-GENERAL,
Commanding the British Forces in 'Iraq.

The Basrah Times, English edition.

your lands were fertile, when your ancestors gave to the world Literature, Science and Art, and when Baghdad City was one of the wonders of the world.

Between your people and the dominions of my King there has been a close bond of interest. For 200 years have the merchants of Baghdad and Great Britain traded together in mutual profit and friendship. On the other hand, the Germans and Turks who have despoiled you and yours, have, for 20 years, made Baghdad a centre of power from which to assail the power of the British and the allies of the British in Persia and Arabia, therefore the British Government cannot remain indifferent as to what takes place in your country, now, or in the future, for in duty to the interests of the British people and their Allies, the British Government cannot risk that being done in Baghdad again which has been done by Turks and Germans during the war.

But you, people of Baghdad, whose commercial prosperity and whose safety from oppression and invasion must ever be a matter of the closest concern to the British Government, are not to understand, that it is the wish of the British Government to impose upon you alien institutions. It is the hope of the British Government that the aspirations of your philosophers and writers shall be realized once again, that the people of Baghdad shall flourish, and shall enjoy their wealth and substance under institutions which are in consonance with their sacred laws and with their racial ideals.

In the Hijaz, the Arabs have expelled the Turks and Germans who oppressed them and proclaimed Sharif Husain as their King, and his Lordship rules in independence and freedom and is the Ally of the Nations who are fighting against the power of Turkey and Germany; so indeed are the noble Arabs, the Lords of Kuwait, Najd and ‘Asir.

Many noble Arabs have perished in the cause of freedom

at the hands of those alien rulers the Turks who oppressed them. It is the determination of the Government of Great Britain and the Great Powers allied to Great Britain that these noble Arabs shall not have suffered in vain. It is the hope and desire of the British people and of the Nations in alliance with them that the Arab race may rise once more to greatness and renown amongst the peoples of the Earth and that it shall bind itself to this end in unity and concord.

O people of Baghdad, remember that for 26 generations you have suffered under strange tyrants who have ever endeavoured to set one Arab house against another in order that they might profit by your dissensions. This policy is abhorrent to Great Britain and her Allies for there can be neither peace nor prosperity where there is enmity and misgovernment. Therefore I am commanded to invite you, through your Nobles and Elders and Representatives, to participate in the management of your civil affairs in collaboration with the Political Representatives of Great Britain, who accompany the British Army, so that you may unite with your kinsmen in the North, East, South and West, in realizing the aspirations of your Race.

(Sd.) F. S. MAUDE, Lieutenant-General
Commanding the British Forces in Iraq
Basrah Times, Tuesday 20 March 1917

1

Where it all Began

Think, in this batter'd Caravanserai
Whose Doorways are alternate Night and Day,
How Sultan after Sultan with his Pomp
Abode his Hour or two, and went his way.
(*Rubáiyát of Omar Khayyam*, verse 16)

The *Basrah Times* came into production shortly after the British took Basra from the Turks on 23 November 1914, and when, three years later, the British also took Baghdad, they distributed the newspaper there as well. Later, the famous scholar-traveller, Gertrude Bell, and the chief political officer, Sir Percy Cox, launched a special Arab edition of the newspaper they called *The Arab*. When it came out in Baghdad, then as now the capital city, Maude's proclamation was on the front page. However, by that time my grandfather's adventures on the Tigris were already over.

Frederick Stanley Maude had taken over command from General Townshend, who, through incompetent handling of the campaign in Mesopotamia in general and in Kut in particular, had singularly failed to cover himself in the glory he had anticipated. However, three months after his proclamation was published Maude died, either of cholera or typhoid. Gertrude Bell commented that bowing out at that point was the best thing he could have done because only under great duress had he signed the proclamation that Sir Mark Sykes had drafted in London; he would never have supported the idea of independence and home rule for the Arab nations that became British policy.

Basra was liberated from the Turks before Baghdad. The occupying British forces intended the *Basrah Times* for both troops and the local civilian population and to this end it was brought out in English and Arabic. The proclamation announced definitively that the British forces had also taken Baghdad and made clear the difference between the British invaders and those whom they had chased out, the Turks. According to the proclamation, the British were not there to exploit but to protect, collaborate and nurture.

Under the terms of the Sykes-Picot Agreement, concluded during the First World War, the French and British drew the boundaries of Iraq as we know it today, which roughly corresponded to what was once known as Mesopotamia, the Greek word for 'between rivers'. Many readers will be familiar with Agatha Christie's *Murder in Mesopotamia*, which was where she met Max Mallowan, her second husband and 13 years her junior. At the time Mallowan was an archaeologist working with Leonard Wooley, whom Agatha Christie knew and accompanied to Mesopotamia. While Mallowan directed excavations at Tall Arpachiyah in Iraq in 1933 and wrote a scholarly work called *Early Mesopotamia and Iran*, she wrote her famous murder mysteries, setting many of them in the exotic locations she visited in the Middle East.

It is believed that Mesopotamia was where the world's first cities originated and, consequently, the first civilizations. The word civilization comes from the Latin *civis* meaning citizen. It was only when people started to move away from the hunter-gatherer way of life, and develop more sustainable methods of agriculture, that they could settle in large groups or cities. Only then was it possible for our modern way of life to begin, with its associated

Proclamation Day: hoisting the Union Jack at Basra.

legal, economic and political systems. City life also afforded greater protection from wild animals.

Farming started in the north of the country in about 10,000 BC. As the population increased so people began to move south, at least to the limits of dry land, for, being dominated by the Tigris and Euphrates, the south was and is marshy. This meant that food production had to be organized more efficiently. The Sumerians, who were the first people to rule the lands between the mighty rivers, developed the wheel, the plough, the sailing boat, irrigation and arithmetic. They were also spiritual and philosophical; they introduced the dichotomies of the human and divine, and of heaven and hell, and it was they who first narrated the biblical story of the flood.

The first city is said to have been near Baghdad at Ur (Ur of the Chaldees in the Bible), Abraham's birthplace. Babylon, Arbil and Uruk, near Nasiriya in modern Iraq, were nearby. Mount Ararat, on which Noah's Ark settled, albeit on the Turkish–

Armenian border, is also associated with this area. Ararat is believed to be the Hebrew equivalent of Urartu, the Assyro–Babylonian name of a kingdom that flourished between the Aras and Tigris rivers from the ninth to seventh centuries BC. The story of the flood, of saving one righteous man along with the creatures of the earth, is derived from the *Epic of Gilgamesh*, which the Sumerians are thought to have written in about 3000 BC. The Jews were held captive as exiles in Babylon and took the story to their hearts. It was here that the 300-foot high Tower of Babel was built. It was probably a ziggurat, a form of stepped pyramid, which the Jews, who came from a more primitive culture, saw as reaching up to heaven; the many languages were those of the slaves who built it. Kurnah, on the Shatt al-Arab, lays claim to be the site of the Garden of Eden. However, a quote from *The Times History of the War*, said to have been spoken by an English soldier encamped there during the First World War, makes one wonder: ''Ere, Bill, if this is the Garden of Eden I wonder what Adam & Eve did with these 'ere mosquitoes a-buzzin' around them.'

The cities were vast, even by modern-day standards. They were home to hundreds of thousands of people. They existed as independent city-states and were constantly fluctuating between falling out and forming new alliances among themselves, but despite numerous wars and conflicts, the cultures were highly developed. The first writing – a cuneiform script on clay tablets – originated in this part of the world and was used, for the most part, to compile lists of property, goods bought and sold, or receipts and debts, in other words all the trappings of an organized and bureaucratic society. The arts also thrived and, with the clay tablets used to record the deeds of kings, history came to be valued for its own sake.

Cuneiform writing was very different from the hieroglyphics used in Egypt. A wedge-shaped stylus would be employed to mark the soft clay with symbols. These were a combination of whole words and phonetic signs. The script began with picto-graphic images, but with clay an unsuitable medium the pictures became stylized into wedge-shaped combinations of lines before eventually taking on a totally abstract form. Many hundreds of tablets survive because, unlike the papyrus or leather that was used for writing in other cultures, the material is not perishable.

The tablets provide a wealth of information about the culture and way of life in that period. In fact, *The Epic of Gilgamesh* was written on clay tablets, so they had a use quite apart from keeping administrative accounts, or recording the deeds of kings and historical events, as I have already mentioned. It is possible to date the texts because the tablets were grouped in chronological order, with the actual date identified by the name of the ruler.

In 1780 BC Hammurabi united Mesopotamia as one country under his rule and set out 282 laws on an eight-foot stele. Many of these laws were surprisingly democratic and supported the rights of ordinary people. However, the stability of the region was eventually disturbed when, approximately seven centuries later, the Assyrians, led by Tiglath-Pileser I, started to conquer lands as far afield as the Mediterranean, slaughtering every male inhabitant in every town or city they took and establishing their capital at Nineveh. After the counterattack, which resulted from the Babylonians, Elamites and Medes (the ancestors of the Kurds) forming an alliance against the Assyrians, Babylon became the seat of power. Nebuchadnezzar II then ruled over what was, with the Hanging Gardens of Babylon, the greatest city in the ancient world and it was he who attacked Jerusalem and forced the Jews into exile.

The Babylonians divided each month or phase of the moon into four periods of seven days. The seventh was kept as a day for propitiating the gods. The day of the full moon was even more special and was called *Shabbatum*. The word *sabat* in modern Arabic means seven, while *Shabbat* in Hebrew means rest. The Babylonians, who were keen astronomers, developed the zodiac, dividing the belt round the earth where the sun, moon and stars were thought to reside into 360 degrees. Consequently, all circles were similarly divided.

In 538 BC, the Persians in turn conquered the Babylonians. Under Persian rule the Jews were free to go home, but many chose to stay and there has been a significant Jewish population in Iraq ever since, or at least until Saddam Hussein began to persecute them and throw them out in the twentieth century. The Assyrians, also a significant section of the population in Iraq, became Christians in the very early days of Christianity and have been persecuted ever after. These Catholics are of the Chaldean rite and use Aramaic, the language of Christ, in their prayers and rituals. They can trace their origins in Iraq back to the time of Christ. They too were a significant minority. In modern times they fought the Kurds and had to flee in 1991, but many returned to Iraq afterwards to rebuild their churches and their lives. They are now under serious threat from the Islamic majority and are once more having to flee their homeland.

Mesopotamia continued under Persian rule until Alexander the Great destroyed the Persian Empire in 331 BC. After this the next great influence on the country was Islam. It was soon after the conversion to Islam in the seventh century AD that the name Iraq was used, which means 'the country that is firmly rooted'. The Abbasid dynasty ruled Iraq and its empire stretched from Tunisia to the borders of China, covering most of modern-day Pakistan. Following the death of Mohammed in 632, the Abbasids inherited the caliphate from its founders, the early Muslims, and they became the spiritual as well as secular rulers. The Abbasid caliphs were descended from Abbas the uncle of Mohammed rather than from the prophet himself. Under the Abbasid rulers Iraq and the capital they built, Baghdad, flourished. Iraq became a major centre for arts and sciences with Baghdad as the capital. In the ninth and tenth centuries Baghdad ranked alongside Constantinople as one of the greatest centres for commerce in the world. It was around this time that the *1001 Nights* was written with stories about the great caliph Harun al-Rashid, Sinbad, Aladdin and Sheherazade, as well as many others.

Centres of learning continued to flourish. One of the greatest medieval doctors was Ibn Sina whose books were still in use in the sixteenth century in Europe, where he was known as Avicenna. A mathematician from Baghdad wrote the first book on algebra; the word algebra comes from the Arabic and literally means reduction. Tablets have been found that date back 4000 years and contain a full mathematics text prefiguring the theories of Pythagoras. The University of Baghdad was famous for its study of philosophy, politics, history and religion, as well as translations of many classical texts from Europe, China and India.

However, all this lasted a mere 200 years. In 1258 Genghis Khan's grandson, Hulagu, led the Mongol hordes across from Central Asia, destroying every town and city in their wake and slaughtering three-quarters of a million people. Baghdad was also sacked. A century later, under Tamerlaine, the Mongols came back to restore their former empire, but now all that remains of them is the pyramid of skulls they constructed at Tikrit, a village now infamous for being the home of Saddam Hussein.

Tikrit has another famous son, Saladin, whose name means defender of the faith. Saladin is celebrated as the greatest warrior of the Arab world, partly because it was he who defeated the Christians in the third Crusade and took the city of Jerusalem. Born in 1138 he became ruler of Egypt in 1171 where he built the citadel; he also built the first *madrasahs* or religious schools. He went on to unite all Islam under his rule and in 1187 took back Jerusalem from the Crusaders. Not only was his extraordinary courage celebrated throughout the Christian and Islamic worlds, but he was also renowned for his chivalrous behaviour as a soldier and admired as a just ruler. When he died there was not enough money in his coffers for his funeral expenses because he had given so much to the poor. Saddam Hussein referred to him frequently in speeches but conveniently seemed to forget that Saladin had in fact been a Kurd.

Baghdad did not recover from the devastation the Mongols had wreaked for several hundred years and in 1534 Suleiman the Magnificent, the Turkish sultan, captured the city without a fight.

For the next two centuries Iraq was the ball in an elaborate game of ping-pong played between the Persians and Turks. By the eighteenth century it was once again becoming an important centre for trade, but the Turks under Midhat Pasha, who eventually gained the upper hand, found that the British, in the shape of the British East India Company, had been there first and had set up a trading post at Basra at the conjunction of the Tigris and Euphrates rivers.

Turkish rule at this time meant that Iraq was part of the Ottoman Empire, which Osman I established and which lasted from the fourteenth until the early years of the twentieth century. The Ottoman Empire stretched from the Adriatic to Aden and from Morocco to the Persian Gulf, covering North Africa, Asia and Europe as far west as Vienna. The Turkish influence failed to promote expansion, agriculture or trade and Iraq never regained its former cultural glory.

One of the earliest English travellers to visit the Persian Gulf was Sir Ralph Fitch, who came there in 1583 during the reign of Queen Elizabeth I with a view to trading. The Portuguese captured him, along with his two companions, and sent them to Goa, thus also making them among the earliest Englishmen to set foot in India. His work eventually resulted in the formation of the East India Company.

The first British victory in the Gulf was on 19 January 1622 when a force laid siege to and captured a Portuguese fort on Kish Island opposite Hormuz. The British then made a treaty with the Persians, or Iranians, to keep two men-of-war constantly in the area to defend and police the Gulf. The number of warships was later increased to five and from that time onwards British seamen patrolled and protected the area. The Turks only controlled Basra and the town of Fao at the entrance to the Shatt al-Arab, south of which lay the region of Al-Hasa and the peninsula of Qatar and, beyond that, the Pirate Coast. Britain had treaties with the chiefs of this area agreeing to keep the peace at sea and refrain from piracy. The pirates had been plundering the highly prized pearls that were one of the major exports of the area. As *The Times History of the War* (1916) explained, 'The pirates have been turned from their evil ways by the maritime truce imposed by the British Government; their strongholds remain unchanged in appearance. … A century ago the British subdued these nests of wild corsairs.'

In 1618 the British flag flew for the first time in the Gulf at Jask on one of the East India Company's trading vessels. The company traded with Jask for three or four years but there was constant trouble with the Portuguese who held Hormuz. The Portuguese joined forces with the Shah of Persia and attacked. The British continued to defend the Gulf with warships under the terms of a treaty made after the action was over. After the sacking of Hormuz a British factory or warehouse was established at Bunder Abbas. The British helped the Arabs fight off others, especially the Dutch and Portuguese; they were respected and feared and the British Indian Navy carried out a survey of the Gulf in 1785. The British produced charts and lights for the area, but their greatest achievement at that time was probably the suppression of piracy.

The two commodities that were important, and had been for centuries, were dates and pearls; in fact, so important were they that Bahrain was once known as the pearl island. Tempted by the promise of wealth and power, the emperor of Germany, William II, came onto the scene. On a visit to Constantinople in 1889, he instigated what became known as the Berlin-Byzantium-Baghdad Scheme, which involved persuading the Turks to enter into an alliance that would enable him to gain a foothold in the Gulf. His aims were both economic and political, for he had visions of Germany controlling the fertile plains of the Tigris and Euphrates and once more becoming the breadbasket of the world, as it had been before the Mongol hordes destroyed the ancient irrigation system. Even more than this, however, the Germans wanted to make Iraq the jewel in their crown in the way that India was for Britain. After establishing a firm called Wonkhaus to trade in mother of pearl and shells, they set up a vice-consulate at Bushire at a time when there were only six German nationals in the region. Control of a port in the Gulf waters would have given them a stepping off place to India. Oil too was becoming increasingly important. So keen were they to achieve their aim that as hostilities were breaking out the Germans tried to buy the allegiance of the Arab population by showing themselves as favourable to Islam and the British as the infidels against whom the Arabs, Turks and Germans should unite in jihad or holy war.

Britain, however, continued to keep tight control commercially and strategically, fighting many battles to protect its interests and to prevent any other flag flying over this useful staging post for India. To quote again *The Times History of the War* (1916), 'The British claim to paramountcy in the Gulf thus rests on a long sequence of events by which, at a heavy expenditure of blood and treasure, we made it a haven of peace.'

The Germans and Turks continued to trade in the area alongside the British. In 1903 the Germans built the Baghdad Railway, which began at Konia in Turkey, went through Aleppo, on to Mosul and Baghdad, and eventually connected the capital with Basra, its main trading port. By allowing its own concession to lapse, Britain had missed a golden opportunity here. In 1909 the Anglo-Persian Oil Company acquired the concession to exploit the oil reserves in Iran on the other side of the Shatt al-Arab, and this gave both countries access to the sea. The Turks attacked many of the installations and when war was declared between Germany and Britain, it came as no surprise when the Turks threw in their lot with the Germans against the country that had foiled all their attempts to take control in Iraq.

2

Journey in Persia

While the Rose blows along the River Brink,
With old Khayyam the Ruby Vintage drink:
And when the angel with his darker Draught
Draws up to Thee – take that, and do not shrink.
(*Rubáiyát of Omar Khayyám*, verse 48)

My grandfather, William Louis Reed was born in London in 1884. He was the youngest child of four, having a brother and two sisters. I never met him. He died many years before I was born. I never met his older brother Sydney either, but I have vivid memories of his two sisters because we used to visit them whenever we were in London when I was a child.

Auntie Kit was married to Bert and they lived not far from the area of London, St Johns, where they all grew up. Their garden fascinated me. Coming from Africa, I was used to gardens that were wide open and partly wild. This narrow, little oblong of perfect tidiness and symmetry set in rows of identical houses and gardens was a wonder to me. Auntie Kit and Uncle Bert had one daughter, Eileen, who was my mother's only cousin. Edie's house was very similar but she lived alone.

Both Kit and Edie spent the war years in London with all the hardships that that involved. Edie's young man had been killed at the front and after the war she never married. Young men were in fairly short supply after the horrors of the trenches.

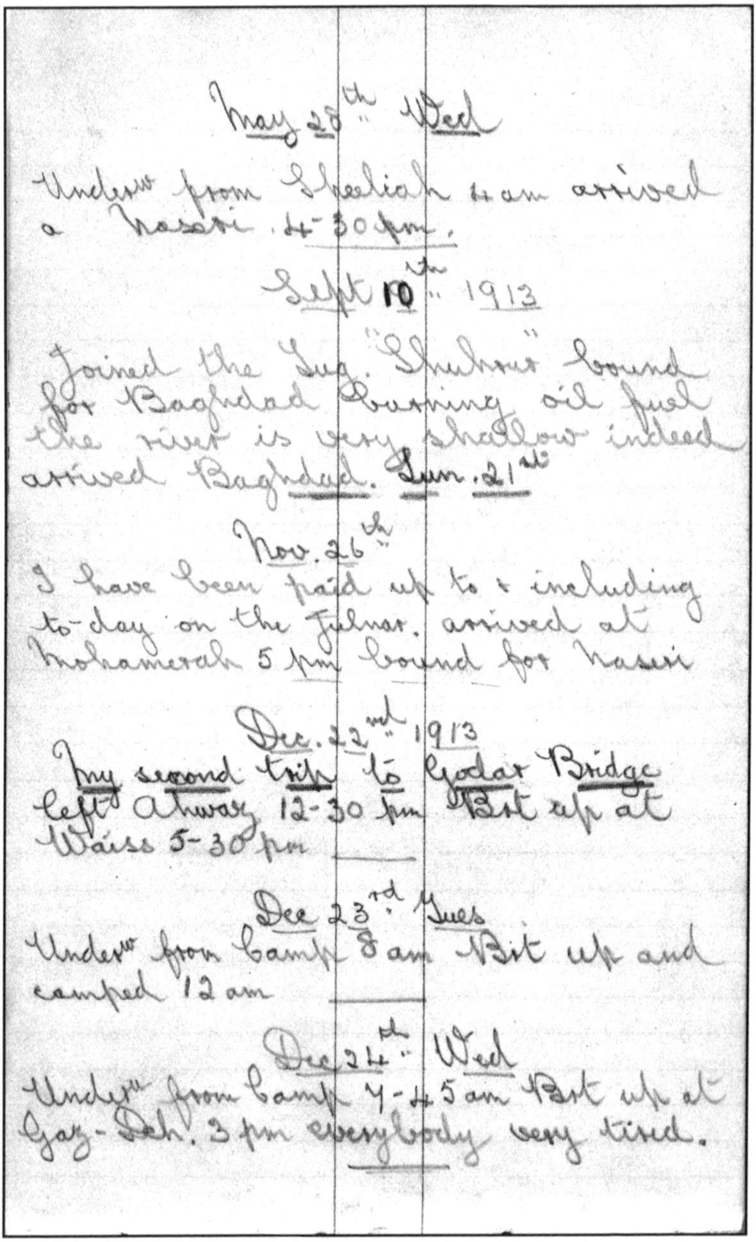
May 28th Wed

Underw from Sheliah 4 am arrived a Nasri 4-30 pm.

Sept 10th 1913

Joined the Tug "Shushan" bound for Baghdad burning oil fuel the river is very shallow indeed arrived Baghdad. Sun. 21st

Nov. 26th

I have been paid up to & including to-day on the Julnar. arrived at Mohamerah 5 pm bound for Nasri

Dec. 22nd 1913

My second trip to Godar Bridge

Left Athwaz 12-30 pm Bit up at Waiss 5-30 pm

Dec 23rd Tues

Underw from camp 8 am Bit up and camped 12 am

Dec 24th Wed

Underw from camp 7-45 am Bit up at Gaz-Deh. 3 pm everybody very tired.

Extracts from diary between late May and Xmas Eve 1913.

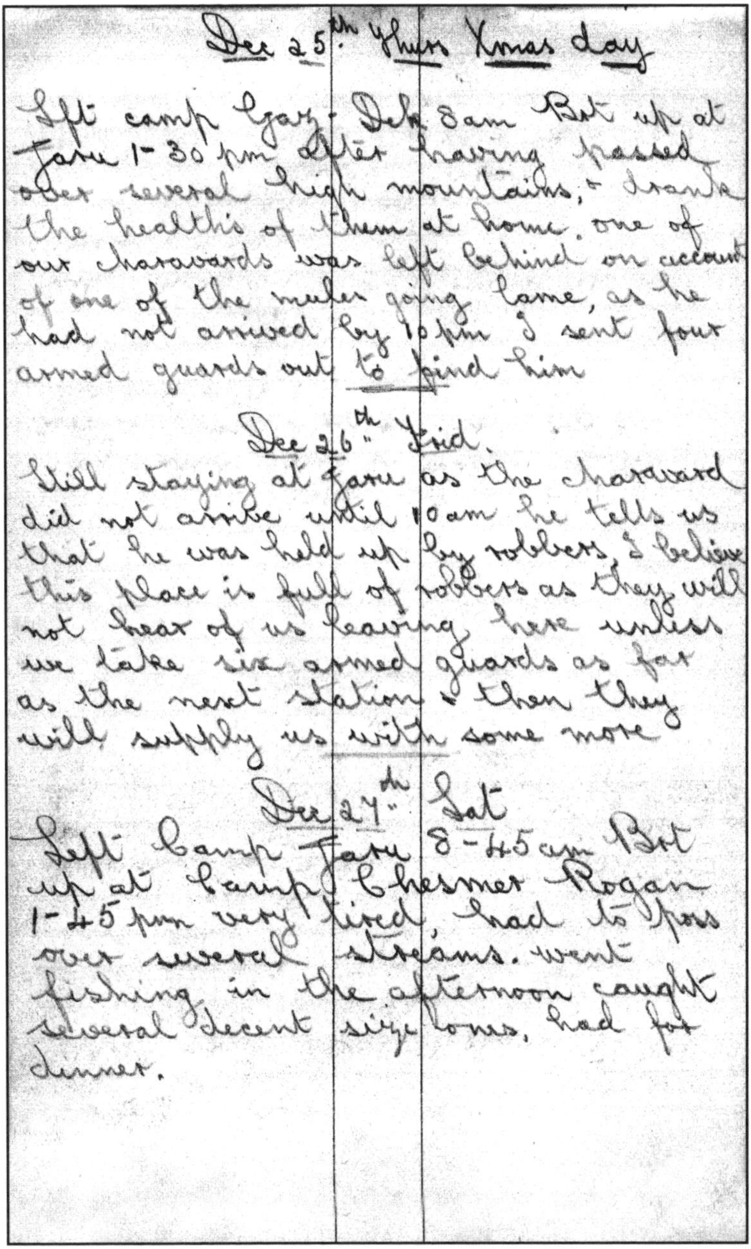

Dec 25th Thurs Xmas day

Left camp Gaz-Dek 8am Got up at Jaru 1-30 pm after having passed over several high mountains, & drank the healths of them at home. one of our charvards was left behind on account of one of the mules going lame, as he had not arrived by 10 pm I sent four armed guards out to find him

Dec 26th Frid.

Still staying at Jaru as the charvard did not arrive until 10 am he tells us that he was held up by robbers, I believe this place is full of robbers as they will not hear of us leaving here unless we take six armed guards as far as the next station & then they will supply us with some more

Dec 27th Sat

Left Camp Jaru 8-45 am Got up at Camp Chesmer Rogan 1-45 pm very tired, had to pass over several streams. went fishing in the afternoon caught several decent size ones, had for dinner.

Xmas Day and its aftermath

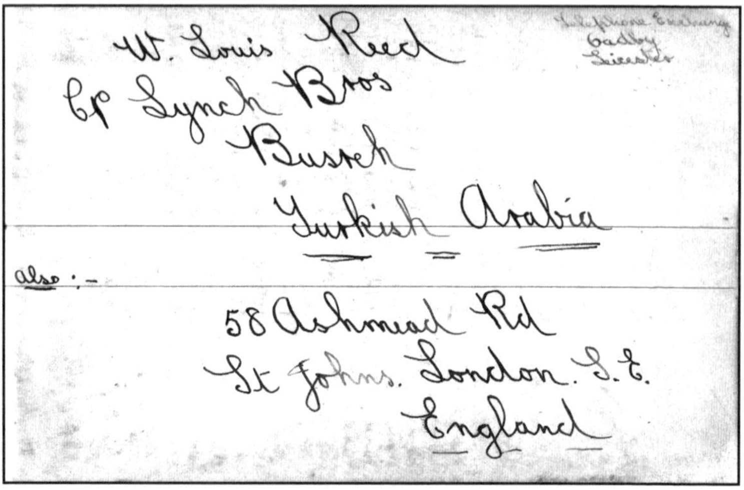

Further extracts from the diaries.

The funny thing was that while Kit was short and round, cosy looking with apple cheeks, Edie was tall and rather gaunt. They were as unalike as sisters could be. As a child I preferred going to Edie's house because she had a set of flat irons graded in size – the little tiny one would have been for collars and cuffs and the big one for sheets. They were no longer used as the efficiency of electric irons had made them redundant. She also had a set of saucepans, of which some were so small that they were almost doll like, and I enjoyed playing with those. But best of all were the sandwiches she made us. It was in the days before Mother's Pride had taken over the bread market, so she used real bread with a good golden, crispy crust. She always buttered the end of the loaf as she went along and then cut the thinnest slices I have ever seen, every one absolutely straight. She then sprinkled a slice with sugar and put another one on top of it to make perfect sugar sandwiches.

The family lived in the area of southeast London near Woolwich and Greenwich. It was here that the shipbuilders, Rennie & Co. of Greenwich, built and fitted the engines of the first steamers that the Euphrates and Tigris Steam Navigation Company used on the Tigris. The first of these vessels to arrive was sent from London to Basra in numbered pieces. In the old Lynch dockyard at Margil, like Edie's perfect bread slices, the pieces were then fitted together. The components for the very first steamer arrived on New Year's Day 1862.

My grandfather, William Louis Reed, signed his articles of agreement on 5 August 1909 at the age of 25. He had trained as a marine engineer with Rennie & Company and the articles of agreement he signed were with the Euphrates and Tigris Steam Navigation Company Ltd. He was to serve as an engineering officer on its ships and his duties started in Basra. The company was part of Lynch Brothers, which had been running ships on the two rivers under the aegis of the British government since 1841, following an agreement with the Pasha of Baghdad allowing Captain Lynch of the Indian Marine to navigate the Euphrates. Captain Lynch also had a letter from the vizir dated 1861 confirming his right to navigate the Tigris under the British flag. William was to get to know this river intimately.

Ships first began to ply their trade on the two great rivers of Mesopotamia in 1836 when John Laird of Liverpool built two steamers named after the rivers on which they were to work. The first voyage they made was on 16 March, but the following May the *Tigris* was wrecked in a terrible storm and two crew members were drowned, one being Lieutenant Lynch, brother of Henry Blosse Lynch. Henry took the *Euphrates* upriver on a journey of exploration. It was the first steamship ever to go to Baghdad and in 1838 he took it up from Kurnah to Fallujah and then through canals to cross the desert between the Euphrates and Tigris. In terms of speed and reliability, Lynch Brothers surpassed all its rivals on the river.

William's diaries began in Iran, which at that time was known as Persia. In 1901, for the princely sum of £20,000, a British subject, Mr W. K. D'Arcy, acquired the concession to exploit petroliferous areas throughout the Persian Empire. The cost of the exploration nearly bankrupted him, so he sold his interest to the Burmah Oil Company, which in turn created the Anglo-Persian Oil Company as a subsidiary. Calouste Gulbenkian, an Armenian by birth, was put in charge of the project and became known as Mr 10 per cent. It took seven years of drilling before the oil started to flow and Persia, as agreed in the concession, earned only 16 per cent of the revenue from its own oil.

Being desperate for cash, the Persian government made a habit of selling concessions to foreigners. The British even had the concession to trade tobacco throughout Persia – and this was a land in which every man, woman and even some children used tobacco heavily. With the Board of Admiralty converting to oil for fuelling its ships, it became imperative to protect supplies, so, at Winston Churchill's request, the British government bought shares in the Anglo-Persian Oil Company to the tune of £2,200,000. This would give Britain control of its own fuel supplies. Also, with new motorcars starting to roll off assembly lines in Europe and America and their use becoming more and more widespread, a great thirst for oil was being created in the Western world.

At the beginning of the twentieth century Russia, which had a monopoly on road building, exerted a strong influence on Persia. For example, Cossacks had taken over Persia's military training and even established a brigade under the direct command of the tsar. Eventually, being in need of a loan, the shah agreed to pay all customs receipts to the tsar for a period of 75 years. When rebellion and calls for a parliament were creating turmoil in the cities, Russian troops were brought in to restore order and quell the fledgling democracy. Before and during the First World War Russians, Germans, Turks and English jostled for control and influence in Persia.

Mr Henry Blosse Lynch was a senior partner in the company started by his brother Thomas and known as Lynch Brothers. They grew up on their family estate in Partry, County Mayo. Henry joined the Indian Navy, helped survey the Gulf and learnt both Arabic and Persian. Thomas travelled extensively throughout the region and at one time served as consul-general for Persia in London. The two brothers became so integral to Persian and Mesopotamian shipping, diplomacy and business that Henry was awarded the highest Order of the Lion and the Sun while Thomas was made a Knight of the Order of the Lion and the Sun. Henry died in Paris in 1873 and Thomas in London in 1891.

In late summer 1889 Henry Lynch, from the next generation of the family, explored the region of Luristan in Persia and delivered a paper to the Royal Geographic Society describing the area in detail. In his journey from Shustar to Ispahan to establish a trade route, he followed the course of the Karun River. The route subsequently became known as Lynch Road, partly because the company eventually built it and partly because it became the company's main route to the oilfields at Maidan. From Mohammerah on the Shatt al-Arab the river was navigable as far as Ahwaz. Here there were some ferocious rapids so the rest of the journey had to be made by land: it was a slow and arduous trek. Only one year later, in June 1890, a 35-ton stern-wheel steamer, the *Shushan*, was the first ship to cross the rapids and get as far as Shustar where it moored up. This was then established as a fortnightly service in conjunction with steamers of the Euphrates and Tigris Steam Navigation Company on the lower river. Later William was to sail on the *Shushan* several times.

The *Shushan* was so named after the town in southwest Persia also known as Susa. The story of Esther unfolded here as did that of Nehemiah. It is 200 miles east of Babylon and was the winter capital of the Elamites as far back as 2200 BC. Prosperity came to Susa with the reign of Cyrus in 538 BC. Then Darius I extended the Persian Empire from the Nile to the Indus. The ruins of the ancient palace can still be seen. Daniel is thought by some to have faced the lions in their den in Susa and eventually to have died and been buried there.

Xerxes ruled here from 485 to 465 BC. He banished his wife, Vashti, for disobedience and married Esther, the beautiful adopted daughter of Mordecai, a rich Jewish merchant. She used her position as the king's favourite to influence him so that he would save Mordecai from those plotting against him and keep her people, the Israelites, safe.

Nehemiah was a high official in the court of Artaxerxes who ruled from 464 to 423 BC. Artaxerxes appointed Nehemiah as governor of Judea where Nehemiah was able to re-establish the city of Jerusalem and to bring stability to the returning exiles.

The city of Susa, excavated in 1851, covered 5000 acres, which were divided into four parts. There was the citadel mound, the palace area, the business and residential area and the flat land west of the river. The palace itself, which was 123 acres, contained courtyards, gardens, stairways, arched gateways and a throne room. Among the ruins of the city a stone cube was found that had numbers engraved on it. In the story of Esther, Hamman who was plotting against Mordecai cast lots or 'pur' to decide his fate. Mordecai was saved and the Jewish feast of Purim is to this day a celebration of his escape from death.

When Captain Samuel Plant, master of the *Shushan* visited it, the ruins of the palace gave some sense of the massive construction it once was. There were traces of magnificent fluted columns that must have reached 50 feet in height and been 15 to 20 feet in girth. Only the massive plinths remained intact and these were covered with cuneiform inscriptions. Daniel's tomb was in the centre of a room specially built with a high dome some way from the palace. The sarcophagus was a coffer of dark wood shaped like an altar carved and covered with inscriptions standing directly under the dome from which hung all manner of religious symbols. Iron and brass railings surrounded it.

It was here that William came to work, in the land of the ancient Persian Empire, of the Medes and the Elamites, of the kings Cyrus and Darius and Xerxes. It was the land of the great Sassanian and Achaemenian dynasties and later of Omar Khayyam, the poet, mathematician, astronomer and philosopher who died in 1123.

The first entry in William's diary was on 7 February 1912. He had left Ahwaz in Persia, modern-day Iran, at midday and arrived at 6 p.m. They had covered a distance of about 25 miles. He travelled to Ahwaz on a paddle steamer called the *Mejidieh*, 463 tons of steel built in Glasgow with a 150 hp engine. The skipper of the vessel was a man who later became his friend, Captain Charles Cowley. Ahwaz lies in an area of flat cultivated land but there were swamps further up the river and, of course, the rapids. William was on his way up the 'Persian Roads' to repair the Godar Bridge, a vital element of the Lynch Road. This bridge was at Godar-i-Balutak and it crossed the Karun River 2320 feet above sea level in the Zagros mountains.

The Karun River rises in the mountains of Zerdeh Kuh and, being fed by glacier water, runs southeast to Dopulum. From here it turns southwest and then northwest to Shustar where it goes south to Mahammerah, ending its journey in the Shatt al-Arab. The main tributaries are the Ab-i-Bazuft and the Ab-i-Bors. North of Shustar the Shur-i-Labahri taints the Karun with salt water. In the mountains the water is swift and deep and glass green in colour. William found it good to bathe in at Godar, but too cold at Bazuft.

From Ali Magrib William and the work party had to march the rest of the way, camping overnight. The journey was difficult because the terrain was mountainous and often stony. The route they took was the same one established as a trade route for the benefit of the Anglo-Persian Oil Company and explored by Henry Blosse Lynch.

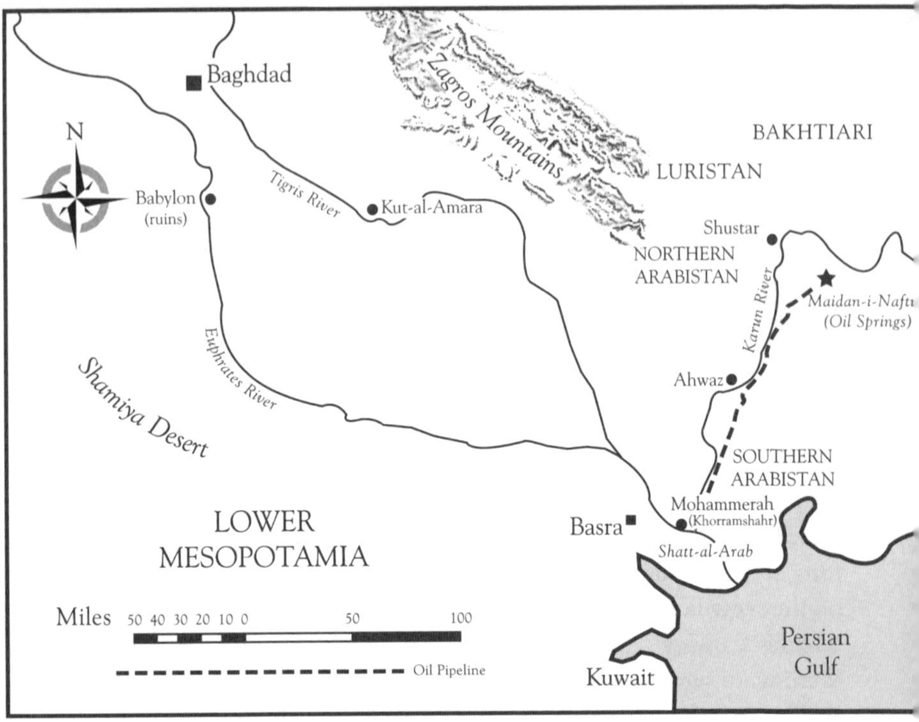

Oil pipeline and Karun River.

The road building concession was originally awarded to the Imperial Bank of Persia, but when in 1889 it failed to complete work on time, it passed to the Persian Transport Company. When, in its turn, it failed to complete the project, Lynch Brothers was brought in. The concession the Shah of Persia signed in 1902 was to last ten years and a caution of £10,000 was paid against failure to complete on time.

Changes were made to the concession to allow for the harshness and difficulty of the work. Instead of a levelled road it was to be a caravan route in the mountainous areas or where the terrain was particularly hazardous. Tolls were to be levied at the rate of ten krans for the full length of the road or two krans for each stage. As for animals – 'passage of quadrupeds, each four-footed animal passing that road loaded or empty 15 shahis, if the four-footed animals did not complete the whole distance they had to pay three shahis for each stage.'

The main factor in the failure to finish constructing the road from Sultanabad to Mohammerah via Khoramabad, Dizful and Shustar was the chronic unrest in the province of Luristan. The representative of the Persian Transport Company spoke of 'unruly and lawless tribes who refuse to bow or to submit to the authority of central government, and this is no new thing, for it dates back to olden times'.

Lynch Brothers encountered the same problems. In 1904 marauding tribesmen attacked Lieutenant Lorimer, the consul at Ahwaz, and his companion Colonel Douglas. In an attempt to establish order 400 Cossacks were sent in as a punitive force. In December 1910 a company report to the foreign office stated that the road was 'overrun by the robber chieftain Naib Hussein, and the country south of Sultanabad and west of Isfahan was infested by raiding bands of Lurs'. The consul at Mohammerah suggested placing an engineer permanently in the area to deter the robbers. 'Having an engineer on the spot might cause difficulties to vanish,' he asserted; William's companion on his journey, Mr Sotham, was the man appointed. In 1912, the year of William's journey, the London newspaper the *Financier* carried a report saying that the Kuhgelu and Kashgai tribes were looting any caravans that attempted to make their way along the road.

The concession was due to expire in 1912 but the project was still unfinished so Lynch Brothers began lengthy negotiations with the Persian government to be granted an extension. The Persians were reluctant to admit that there was a problem that they had neither the will nor the means to contain so they prevaricated. Meanwhile, there was a famine in Luristan despite the increased prosperity that the road should have brought. The tribes were still growing only food sufficient for their needs and not cash crops that they could now export up the road. In 1912, the year that William's diaries began, regular caravan traffic was becoming established. Some merchants tried to send caravans to Khoramabad. When a few small ones got through safely, a big caravan was formed which was promptly looted. An extension to the concession was finally granted in 1914 but by then war was stopping further progress.

Friday 9 February 1912

Left camp 9 a.m. Brought up at Gaz-Deh at 1 p.m. with a terrible thirst; drank two bottles of beer; the march was rather interesting having to pass over some high hills.

The mountain range was made up of a succession of parallel rocky ridges and valleys, each higher than the last. It went up to 6000 feet and each wall of rock was a step to a higher level. They jutted out above the valley, deep elephant-grey, looking like vast castles in the air. Places where Crusaders might fight honourably and knights rescue fair maidens.

Monday 12 February 1912

Left camp 8.15 a.m. Brought up at camp at 1.30; the road was most stony and rough. Had to pass over several streams.

Wednesday 14 February 1912

Raining heavens hard too wet to proceed. Mr Sotham and I hanging on to tent poles to stop them from being blown down, great sport.

The weather varied between very hot and very cool. In the winter, snow often blocked the passes for three months at a time.

Thursday 15 February 1912

Tents and everything too wet to proceed spent day drying gear.

After the gentle undulations of the terrain beyond Shustar and Gergir the party went through a valley of oaks where the water ran under green shade. From here the journey became difficult as they crossed rough and stony ground with crumbled broken rock.

The track wound among boulders making it hard for loaded mules to get through.

Friday 16 February 1912

Left camp 8 a.m. Brought up at camp 12.15 p.m. (Malimir) very hungry ate half a duck and four boiled eggs.

The weather was again very wet and forced them to stay where they were for several days and to keep to their tents. The party was expecting a visit from Abdullah Khan who did not appear on the Saturday as planned, but arrived the next day.

Sunday 18 February 1912

Too wet to proceed. Khans visited us in the afternoon all went for a shoot together, shot three hares started raining and blowing lasted all night.

The road passes through the region of Luristan and through Bakhtiari country, named after the tribes of the same name. The area was not very populous, for most of the people were nomadic, but the Bakhtiari were settled and there were two branches to their tribe – the Haft Lang and the Chehar Lang. The princes (or Ilkham) of Bakhtiar had their seat at Kalah-i-tul. Their family name was Khan but we can only speculate whether the brothers who were so friendly to William and the rest of the working party were of the same family. The princes kept a tight hold on the country to protect it from brigands, punishing harshly anyone found committing highway robbery.

The Bakhtiari were Aryan in type not Semitic. The men used to shave the backs of their heads but wore the hair at the front long and flowing to the shoulder. They wore round felt hats and shirts of blue calico that reached their knees with a brown abba or cloak thrown around the shoulders. The women wore loose blue trousers or short coloured petticoats and draped tops coloured red and blue. Instead of veils they wore gaily coloured scarves. Bright eyes shone from nut-brown faces creased with weather and smiles. They lived in huts made of mud and reed.

All this William saw at Malamir. The plain of Malamir is not far from Kalah-i-tul and is 2750 feet above sea level. It was an areas in which the temperature dropped dramatically at night and there were cool breezes in the morning. The rock was mostly limestone and the broad valley was dotted with abrupt conical hills and hummocks. White gypsum lay exposed while the upper slopes were made up of rubble and pebbles. The plain was fertile and beautiful.

A lake at the north end of the plain is thought to be the possible site of the great ancient fire temples of the Sassanian cities of Aidij and Sosirate. Ardashir, the grandson of Sasan, founded the Sassanian dynasty, which ruled the Persian Empire from AD 224 to 651. The dynasty had a fondness for grandiose architecture. During this time Zoroastrianism became the state religion and it still flourishes in some areas. Central to the practice of the faith, which sees life as a struggle between good and evil, is fire. It is believed to be a purifier and so is essential to their rituals. Cleanliness is highly prized and every ritual takes place in front of a living flame. In the fire temples, the holy of holies, the flames were kept bright day and night.

At the eastern side of the plain is a cleft of rock with inscriptions and bas-relief, first discovered by Henry Layard, who lived for many months at a time with the Bakhtiari chieftain, and the Russian Baron de Bode. Some inscriptions from Malamir can be seen in the British Museum.

From a lofty cave on the western wall of the valley there is a wide view over the plain towards the lake and mountains, great bastions of rock with perpendicular faces and giant maidenhair ferns clinging to the surfaces, damp and oozing from the spring beneath. In the cave are two niches where one can discern a sculptured figure and more inscriptions. The northern mountainside contains two more niches with carved figures that are better preserved.

Water from the spring flowed to a village and, leading to the cave, were the rough and stony remnants of a very old roadway, littered with the remains of ancient buildings or ruined vaults from the Sassanian era. There was also a sacred ruin. The bas-reliefs and inscriptions in the cave were from the Achaemenian period, which lasted from the death of Cyrus the Great in 529 BC until Alexander the Great killed and defeated Darius III in war in 330 BC. The writing in the inscriptions is a Persian version of the cuneiform script, but when William saw it it had not yet been deciphered. A causeway paved with large hewn stones supported by transverse slabs climbed up the winding terraces of the eastern wall of the plain of Malamir. The Rah-i-Sultan, or Sultan's Way, dated back to an era beyond the period of the Atabegs.

Monday 19 February 1912

Rained and blew hard all night. Too wet to go any further this morning. If it clears up shall proceed this afternoon. Left much to my regret at 12 noon. Climbed to the top of a very high mountain which took about one hour, after reaching the top found that the muleteers had camped at the bottom so there was nothing to do but climb down again. Then to cap it all, before we could finish pitching the tents a thunder storm came on and you should have seen the water rushing through the tents about four inches deep. So there was only one thing to do that was to turn into bed. Then how it rained and blew is beyond words. Two of the tents were blown down but thank goodness mine stood the test.

Mr Sotham left me at the top of the mountain and said he was going to ride to Godar but I'm sorry to say that he was caught in the thunderstorm and lost the road. After being in this terrible position for about five hours, they saw somebody strike a match. They made for the spot and found that it was two muleteers that had been overtaken by the storm and they had to force one of them to show them the way to the (Godar) bridge. As it was pitch dark they couldn't see a hand before you, had they not seen the light they would very probably have died of exposure as it was thundering and raining heavens hard, to say the least of various wild beasts, leopards, wild cats etc.

The mountains were home to many varieties of wild animals. William named a few in his diary such as hares and ibex. There were also squirrels, foxes, wild pigs and goats, eagles, snakes, scorpions and, more dangerously hyenas, lynx, bears, panthers and leopards. While near the river and on the plains there were lions. The following day William woke early at 5.30 a.m., keen to make a start on the road to the bridge. The muleteers would not budge.

Tuesday 20 February 1912

Got up at about 5.30 a.m. and tried my damness [*sic*] to get the muleteers to proceed but no fear they wouldn't budge until about 10.30 a.m. Climbed the mountain again after having cursed everybody in camp. Arrived at Godar bridge about 6 p.m. after travelling over a very rough road. Lynch road they call it, but I failed to see where the road comes in, most stony and rough. Then much to our disgust the muleteers stopped on the road so we were stuck at the bridge without tents or anything. So we all, Mr Sotham, two Persians and I slept on the floor of a tent that was already here, which belonged to one of our masons. We never took our clothes off or anything, simply laid down and slept.

Wednesday 21 February 1912

Muleteers arrive at noon. Mr Sotham fined each muleteer 5/- besides this he locked them up for four days with only dry bread to eat. Had a decent lunch today, the first for two days. We ate a chicken and partridge each besides a large plate of rice. Spent the day pitching tents. What oh for a good sleep tonight.

The Godar Bridge is situated in the lush, verdant valley of Godar-i-Balutak. To the north can be seen the high mountains where the river narrows. Lofty hills to the south and east are covered with loam and overgrown with oaks. The two ridges surrounding the valley are bare at the top and harsh compared with the gently rolling hills between. At this point the left bank of the Karun is very high. Near Deh-i-Diz, where there was a fort, the land had been ploughed. The plain was also at times dotted with black tents belonging to the Ilyat, one of the nomadic tribes.

Before the bridge that William was working on was built, there was only a rope bridge for crossing the river. Herbert A. Richards was the first white man to come to Mohammerah and he arrived there in 1889 as a consular official. In 1896 he travelled up the Karun River to report on the proposed site of the new bridge and describes how rough the going was. At one point it took two hours for his party to cover 200 yards. Their mules kept falling down and after one had rolled into the river on its back, the muleteers took the loads off them and carried them to where the going was easier.

At Godar-i-Balutak, the proposed site of the bridge, great oaks clothed the hills and the river was swift and turbulent. The span at the site was 107 feet and the river banks were very high, making it unlikely that floods would wash the bridge away. The existing rope bridge had a deep sag, going down vertically six or eight feet. The only alternative to the bridge was to cross by precarious rafts of animal skins inflated and tied together with sticks on top. The bridge that William was repairing had been proposed by the Khans and approved by Herbert Richards's report, but there were still traces to be seen of the old rope bridge and the toll house beside it.

Richards had travelled on the *Shushan* from above the rapids to Shustar and made the journey many times in the course of his work. The ship had a major problem. It was starting to run out of fuel. The supply of wood was now short because so many trees had been cut and it was out of the question to import coal; it would have been far too costly. Richards had an idea. He knew that the Persians used oil that they obtained from the ground to fuel their lamps but its whereabouts was a closely guarded secret. Many of the ancient Zoroastrian fire temples were kept burning with oil or gas that came naturally out of the ground. The priests held on very carefully to their knowledge of where these deposits of oil were.

Oil was known about from earliest times and used for medicines, heating, cooking, sacred fires and waterproofing. Alexander the Great used it to provide heat and light in his tent during the siege of Persia in 331 BC. The Persian king fighting him had summoned 1200 blacksmiths to construct iron horses on wheels that were filled with black oil, then lit and run at the enemy; they called it Greek fire. To the priests of the Zoroastrian faith it was essential for the eternal flames in their fire temples.

Richards's initial enquiries at first met with a complete blank. People either did not know or did not want to tell, but then came a breakthrough. One day, as he sat over his tiffin, a man came to him saying that he knew where the oil was and could take Richards to the place. There and then they laid their plan. Richards announced that he was going on a shooting trip, a regular activity that was unlikely to arouse suspicion. They even let it be known that they were going in quite the opposite direction to the one they intended.

The ruse worked and they set off without arousing any undue interest. They walked through precipitous mountains and chasms until they were about 25 miles from Shustar. The mountains overlooked a peaceful valley of opium poppy fields, pomegranates and mulberry trees and in the rivulets and creeks of the mountains oil floated in black iridescent swirls that glittered in the sunlight. Suddenly, looking down at the valley they saw people running towards them brandishing weapons. Richards feared the worst, but it turned out to be a dispute between the villagers and local chief who was demanding taxes. His men had rounded up all the villagers' animals in lieu of payment. The villagers retaliated and in the ensuing chaos the animals all headed straight back home, so the chief and his men had to leave empty handed. Richards and his 'hunting' party were unhurt and went home in peace.

On his return to Shustar, Richards negotiated with the priests and they agreed to supply oil to the *Shushan*, which became the first ship on the river to be fuelled in this way. The source Richards found was the same that W. K. D'Arcy later discovered. He saw its enormous possibilities and importance as he had seen at first hand the development of the fledgling motorcar industry with its endless need for oil. He also knew that oil was beginning to be used to fuel ships, so he and the Anglo-Persian Oil Company began to pump the black gold commercially. As is often the way, D'Arcy, as a pioneer of the industry made little money and eventually went bankrupt. It was those who followed him, especially Gulbenkian, who made fortunes. Oil has proved to be a blessing and a curse to the region ever since, for it drives the politics of the Middle East and its relationship with the West. The year of William's journey to repair the bridge at Godar, 1912, was also the year that oil first began to flow commercially in Iran. The following year 80,000 tons was being extracted.

After his arrival at Godar on 21 February, William spent the next few days settling into camp and starting work on the bridge. He and Mr Sotham had some fine meals of ibex and hare, both of which William found very tasty. The first part of the work was to set up their equipment. They had to construct their own forge and vice bench and make a ladle for pouring lead. The work entailed chipping paint and rust and building a new framework for bracing the bridge. The floor was stripped and painted in sections so that the bridge could still be used. He also managed to get a letter home with one of the gang who was returning to Ahwaz. Communications were not good. When they discovered that the condition of the bridge was much worse than anticipated, they sent a telegram to London. A runner had to take it to Ahwaz to send, which meant that he had to travel night and day. And yet, despite the difficulties, the mail did get through, as the next two entries show.

Saturday 9 March 1912

Weather grand, very warm, riveting wind bracings, girders drilling holes in rock for carrying rag bolts (4¾") for wind bracings, drilling holes in rocker plates found today that in all there is something like five hundred ¾" holes to be drilled. Mr Sotham received a letter today from Tehran re bridge. He answered same and sent one to Ispahan.

Wednesday 13 March 1912

Weather grand, thousands of sheep and goats passed over the bridge this morning, continued drilling rocker plates finished drilling and riveting girders for wind bracings also drilling rock for rag bolts, received mail from home today. One letter from Ma, one from Edie also one from Syd.

There was another major worry for the group in this isolated spot.

Thursday 14 March 1912

Things here begin to look very queer, the Kugalloos' are on the warpath again. Mr Sotham has sent to Deh Diz for more guards, also sent a telegram to London re situation.

All must have been well because we do not hear about the 'Kugalloos' again. The Kuhgelu, as they were in fact called, were a nomadic tribe whose area was the southern end of the foothills near the Gulf. They moved with the seasons and were about 100,000 in number. They were known to be wild and lawless.

Wild ibex would wander around and the group received visits from the friendly Khans who had taken them shooting. Yousif Khan brought presents of sweets, fruit and Turkish cigarettes. These and letters from home continued to be the things that kept up their morale. With their work being outdoors, the weather was a constant obsession and seemed very changeable. It certainly rained a great deal, swelling the rivers and sometimes making it impossible to carry on working.

Saturday 30 March 1912

Weather still rotten, worse than yesterday raining in torrents all day long. The river has risen about 50ft in 24 hours. Impossible to do any work on the bridge.

But by the Sunday it had cleared up again.

Sunday 31 March 1912

The river here is a sight of a lifetime when in flood.

This was one Sunday when the Sabbath was observed, a constant concern throughout the diary. Monday 1 April was William's twenty-eighth birthday, but he made no mention of it. He restricted his comments for that day to describing the work in progress. The group continued diligently with the repairs. It seems that the bridge had been in a very poor condition. The routine was only varied by occasional letters from home and even more occasional visits.

Tuesday 16 April 1912

Weather grand thousands of sheep and goats. Continued drilling holes in existing saddle ready to take top half of rocker. Commenced to work on sag but found this was impossible instead of pulling the girders up, had all the strain on the main cable and commenced to bend same. Mr Sotham wired London, estimates 3 months to correct sag as it would mean entirely stripping the bridge, continued working on bracings for Ahwaz pier. Received mail from home. We had a very surprising visit today from Lord Lamington, Colonel Woodcock, Mr Charters and Mr Hodson who were on their way to Tehran. All had dinner in our tent, must say I found Lord Lamington very decent.

Lord Lamington had at one time been president of a committee set up to support the ill-fated rebellion and struggle for democracy in Persia. He had been assistant private secretary to Lord Salisbury in 1885 and became Conservative MP for St Pancras shortly thereafter. He also served as governor of Bombay for a while. His main interest was the welfare of both the empire and Eastern people. He worked tirelessly to promote a better understanding between East and West. Four days before he visited William and Mr Sotham, he and his companion Captain Williams had been attacked and robbed. Both had been slightly wounded by flying bullets.

A Mr Bagge and a Mr Blain arrived on 2 May to stay for a while. By Saturday 4 May the bridge was finished and the party had to make its way back across country.

Saturday 4 May 1912
Weather grand completed Ahwaz pier. Mr Bagge and Mr Blain still staying with us. Finished all work on bridge thank God.

Monday 6 May 1912
Weather grand, left camp 9 a.m. had great trouble in proceeding on account of meeting the tribes hundreds of them, the road being very narrow. Camped at a ruined village at 12.15 p.m.

Tuesday 7 May 1912
Weather grand up with the moon proceeded at 1.30 a.m. so as to avoid the sun and meeting the tribes, camped at Malamir at 7.45 a.m.

Wednesday 8 May 1912
Weather very dull left Malamir 3.30 a.m. Kalah-i-tul at 8.30 a.m. met Capt and Mrs Gray (British consul at Ahwaz) there stayed with them for an hour, had some tea and cake etc. then proceeded to Allah Corshed where we arrived at 12 a.m. very tired had a rest for a little while then had a swim and felt quite refreshed. Had two riflemen guards.

Thursday 9 May 1912
Weather grand left Allah Corshed 3.45 a.m. arrived at Kersallah at 8.45 a.m. Very nice quiet place had a fine swim.

Friday 10 May 1912
Weather grand much warmer than at the bridge. Left camp at 1.50 a.m. arrived at Ramez (a capital) 9.30 a.m. Everybody tired out, a most rough march very stony. Found Yousif Khan here, he will not hear of me buying anything to eat he is cooking and supplying all the grub which I need not say is grand.

Saturday 11 May 1912
Weather very dull resting here today as Yousif Khan said he was going to pay me a visit. He called this morning we had a very jolly time together, he is still feeding us, had a grand lunch of Persian plough and various native drinks. Also had a visit from Said Hussein our agent here so must call on him this evening. Called and had a very good time.

A meal in Persia is eaten sitting on rugs spread on the floor. Water for washing hands is offered first and the food is served on large metal trays. They might have eaten pilau rice flavoured with sultanas and onions. This would have had a sauce known as *dehn* to accompany it. The Persians consider *dehn* a great delicacy but the feringees, or foreigners, describe it as nothing more than rendered fat. Unleavened bread, which the colonials called 'slapjacks' but that we might recognize as pitta bread or chapattis, was part of the staple diet; the meal might end with *bahamias*, a kind of sweetened biscuit. The drink offered would be goats' milk or *libba*, a type of buttermilk.

William continued on his way to Ahwaz, travelling overnight and resting and swimming in the day. On arrival at Ahwaz he had to wait around for a telegram from London. He also paid the wages to all the workmen. He then joined the *Shushan* to make the journey to Shustar.

The *Shushan* was first commissioned in 1884, the year William was born, for the Nile expedition to relieve General Gordon in Khartoum; he had been under siege for 317 days. Help arrived too late, Gordon was killed and his head displayed on a pike.

The *Shushan* was a 35 ton stern-wheel river steamer, 150 feet in length and with a draught of only 2½ feet. It had three separate rudders that worked simultaneously. According to its captain, Samuel Cornell Plant, it was a pretty vessel. His memoirs, written in 1891, were found among his effects when he died in 1960. He was 24 years old at the time and the *Shushan* was his first command. He described the ship as having a long, black funnel and brass work that glistened like gold. The deckhouse was gaily painted and fitted with snowy white awnings to give shade on deck. There were only two Englishmen on board – Samuel and Mr Stanley Webber, the engineer.

The rapids at Ahwaz were infamous, stretching for 2000 yards; a series of five separate lines of sandstone boulders and mud ran from bank to bank with only a very narrow channel through each one. They blocked access to the Karun River, so a horse-drawn tram would carry passengers from one river to the other. The plan was for the *Shushan* to shoot the rapids and to establish a dual ferry service. Passengers would be able to sail up to Ahwaz and then transfer to the *Shushan* on the far side of the rapids to continue their journey to the furthest navigable point on the Karun River.

Extra hands were employed and many stout manila ropes; 250 men lined the bank ready to take the ropes and tow the boat out of trouble if need be. The women and children of Ahwaz came to watch. Samuel ordered a full head of steam to ensure that the boat had enough power to get through the immensely powerful torrent of water that gushed past the boulders towards them. An 11-gun salute from the shore heralded their departure as they set off upstream. In places the channels through the rocks were less than 20 yards wide and the power of the water threatened to wash them away at any moment, but they made it. The crowd of men lining the bank erupted into excited cheering while the women began a shrill ululation of joy. The children scampered up and down shouting and clamouring.

The first journey did not end there. Captain Plant and his engineer Webber went on to explore the river to find out how far navigation was possible. They had to proceed very slowly using a measuring pole to test its depth. The river passed through flat uninteresting country. It had high steep banks and was very sinuous. It was also a Mecca for mosquitoes and sandflies. At one point the river divided into three, so the *Shushan* explored each one – the Shateit, the Diz and the Abu Gerger. The Shateit and Gerger unite lower down.

The Gerger had an artificial canal along some of its length that flowed through a 100-foot-deep gorge cut through solid sandstone rock. There were remains there of an ancient weir and sluices and, half a mile further on, was a dam called Pul-i-Bulaiti. This dam was also a viaduct; to either side of it were passes and tunnels through which water gushed to drive nearby flourmills.

The Shateit follows the river's natural course. The bridge of Valerian that spans it is a magnificent structure of granite blocks and sluices topped by a stone bridge 570 yards long with 41 arches. Legend has it that the emperor of Rome, Valerian, built it while a prisoner of the Sassanian king over 1800 years ago.

All proved difficult to navigate as they had such extremely sharp bends, but the Diz ran through dense jungle, where some of the wildest most lawless tribes lived. Eventually, a route was established to Shuliah, which was the port for Shustar – according to Samuel, a most insanitary, smelly place where the streets ran with raw sewage, which William's diary confirms.

The banks of the river teemed with wild life including many snipe, which were not only good for hunting but also good to eat. Samuel and his engineer did a great deal of hunting including bagging a lion or two. They also noticed that just north of Shustar the creeks and pools were often coated with slicks of oil.

Friday 17 May 1912

Weather grand left for Shustar at 4 a.m. Brought up at Derrkersen 5.30 p.m. met Cole, Elliott and Dr Dias had dinner and game of bridge.

Saturday 18 May 1912

Arrived at Shuliah at 5.30 a.m. not enough water to go right up to Shustar so Capt. Regan and I went over by mules about a two hours journey stayed at our office till after lunch and went and visited the water mills most pretty the sight of a lifetime but Shustar itself is about the most dirty place on God's earth. I had a touch of fever here but soon got over it and returned to Shuliah at about 7.30 p.m.

The Karun rises in the mountains at 1300 feet and was the only navigable river at that time. It was so winding and tortuous that a boat had to travel 26 miles to make 12 miles overland and at times it was so narrow that two vessels could not pass each other. The current was very swift but at low water season when there was no more melted snow to feed it, it became extremely shallow with draught limited to three feet. The *Shushan* with William aboard stayed at Shuliah for several days during which time the temperature climbed to 111°F in the shade. Sheds were checked, as well as pumps and when all tasks were completed they returned to Ahwaz where social life involved dinners and games of bridge.

Saturday 25 May 1912

Weather grand. I am laid up with typhoid, must keep smiling.

There was no further entry until 26 June.

Saturday 26 June 1912

Laid up with typhoid. Up today for first time. Started to eat solid food. Weather grand beginning to pick up a little. Had a telegram from Dad.

William was unable to eat anything and survived on liquids. He tossed and turned sweating profusely in the searing heat. Not only was he running a high fever but the weather was at its hottest at this time of year. On 12 July, during his convalescence, he recorded a temperature of 127°F degrees in the shade. He managed to enjoy this time despite everything, for he described dinners out, tennis parties and having photographs taken in Lynch's garden. When he was fit again he set off for Mohammerah and Maaghil where he met up with his father, my great grandfather on 19 July. He does not say how his father got there, but William was given some holiday so was able to spend time with him. On 5 August William found himself back at work, this time in Iraq, on board the *Mejidieh*, with Captain Cowley once more. The two men were pleased to see each other. He joined the ship at Basra from where they went upriver to Baghdad.

Basra was a wealthy bustling port reputed to be the home of Sinbad the sailor. Houses with carved latticework windows overlooked a bazaar fragrant with spices and perfumes, coffee, tea and freshly-baked bread. Pyramids of coloured vegetables and fruit burst upon the eye. Dates from gardens surrounding the town were on sale everywhere.

After this there was a long gap in the diary entries until 4 March 1913 when he joined the *Malamir* as chief engineer to replace Mr Gostling who had six months leave. This took him back to Iran. The diary picked up again in May 1913.

Saturday 24 May 1913

Left Ahwaz and joined the *Shushan* as [I] am having a trip to Shustar. Left at 6 a.m. Rawlings and Tomlinson are also with us. Anchored for night at 9 p.m.

Sunday 25 May 1913

Underway 4 a.m. Brought up at Shuliah 6 p.m.

Monday 26 May 1913

In the morning we all went out bird nesting and shooting. Abdullah Khan invited us in to dinner sent horses out for us, so Capt. Regan and I rode in at full gallop. Spent the evening with him, sleeping at his house.

Tuesday 27 May 1913

Left in the morning at 5 a.m. as we had arranged overnight to float back to Shuliah on a raft which was quite a treat, the journey taking about three hours. We both are feeling very sore after our ride of yesterday. Abdullah Khan came and had dinner with us this evening. Today has been very hot indeed.

William moved from ship to ship, according to orders, for the remainder of the year. It is during this time that he took his first trip on the *Julnar*, leaving it on 26 November 1913. December found him once more heading for the Godar Bridge. The journey did not go smoothly.

Thursday 25 December 1913 Christmas Day

Left camp Gaz-Deh 8 a.m. Brought up at Jaru 1.30 p.m. after having passed over several high mountains and drank the healths of them at home. One of our charavards was left behind on account of one of the mules going lame, as he had not arrived by 10 p.m. I sent four armed guards out to find him.

Friday 26 December 1913

Still staying at Jaru as the charavard did not arrive until 10 a.m. He tells us that he was held up by robbers. I believe this place is full of robbers as they will not hear of us leaving here unless we take six armed guards as far as the next station and then they will supply us with some more.

Saturday 27 December 1913

Left Camp Jaru 8.45 a.m. Brought up at Camp Chesmer Rogan 1.45 p.m. very tired. Had to pass over several streams. Went fishing in the afternoon caught several decent size ones, had for dinner.

The journey lasted three more days over rough stony ground. Fishing provided supper on several more evenings and he found a great deal of change since his last visit with a fine new caravanserai at Kul-a-Tul. The weather was a trial with heavy rain frequently preventing travel, while at Malamir it was so cold that when the party got up in the morning their tents were covered with frost. When they finally arrived at Godar Bridge the whole group was exhausted from the journey that day, the last of 1913.

Wednesday 31 December 1913

Left Malamir 8 a.m. Arrived at Godar Bridge 6 p.m. Oh, how tired I was, went straight to sleep, had to pass over a very high mountain on the road, everybody dead tired.

Thursday 1 January 1914

Today fixing tents properly the guard at the bridge charged the muleteers bridge fees, which I think is most unfair.

Preparations for the work to be done took up the next few days. These included cleaning out the storeroom and checking the stock. Needless to say a lot of gear had been stolen in the two years since he was last there. He then set about making the tools required, paint scrapers, buckets, screwdrivers and chisels.

Tuesday 6 January 1914

Have fixed up with a muleteer to take us to Amarat at 25 krans per mule 10 in number, there are five of us going including myself. Today received back the money that they charged for our last caravan bridge fees 180 kran.

Wednesday 7 January 1914

Left Godar Bridge 11.30 a.m. Brought up at Deh-Diz 4.30 p.m. a very nice journey. Had to pass through a forest it was worth five quid the whole road being very pretty. Had to clear the snow away before we could put our tents up, this is the first time I have been in the snow for about five years

There was a wide variety of plants to be seen in the mountains and valleys along the Karun River. Some areas were yellow with the flowers of St John's wort. There were myrtle trees as well as tamarisk and willows. So many walnut trees grew here that Persia at one time exported the wood to France for furniture. There were also briar roses, juniper, mulberry, hawthorn and maple. Ivy and cork trees grew in abundance. Deh-i-Diz nestled at the foot of the mountains surrounded by cultivated land and gardens.

Between 9 and 15 January 1914 heavy rain held the party up with 'nothing to do but to lay in bed all day', but when they finally got moving the following day there was heavy snow six inches deep making it a very arduous journey. Their arrival at Amarat Bridge was soon followed by further torrential rain that lasted all the following day as well. Ali and William went 'in search of bread, eggs, fowls' and started work on the Amarat Bridge.

Wednesday 14 January 1914

Finished clearing mud from bridge level, have made a step at the Ahwaz end of bridge, continued painting. Mirza and Oster Goolie arrived here today – received a letter from Mr Sotham telling me he expects to arrive here tomorrow, went fishing this evening caught about eight, one weighing 9 lbs. Advanced Mirza Razor 1000 kroners.

Friday 16 January 1914

Left Amarat Bridge 7.45am arrived at Godar Bridge 6.15 p.m. everybody dead tired, this journey is as a rule 2 days, had to pass over a high mountain.

Monday 19 January 1914

Cutting and screwing suspension rods as the turnbuckles sent from home are already too long for the centre of the bridge. We had a fire in the camp tonight one tent burnt down.

After the exertions of the previous day's journey and a day working in the open air for hours William retired to his tent and fell into an exhausted sleep. He was woken only a couple of hours later by shouting and a general hullabaloo. As his mind began to focus he realized that the glow that was lighting up the sky was from a fire and that the crackling he could hear was the flames leaping aloft. This was accompanied by a great deal of yelling and panic. He struggled out of his tent to find the whole camp in uproar and everyone rushing about. The tent at the centre of all this chaos was past all help. It was engulfed with flames and folding in on itself like a piece of tissue paper. He could see the men, whose only shelter it was, running back from the river bank with buckets of water. They threw these over the fire in a rush of adrenalin. Then stood, staring forlornly at the resulting soggy mess steaming in the night.

'Is anyone going to tell me what happened here?' he bellowed. The muleteers all ran for cover. It wasn't their problem. The men all stood still looking sheepish. 'Right. You, Braithwaite. I can usually trust you. Spill the beans, old man.'

'Well, Sir, it was like this. We had a few bevvies, you know. It's so cold here a man needs something to keep body and soul together. Smith and Johnson went back to their tent and me and Roles we dossed down in ours. The next thing I know there's bloody great flames a leaping all over.' At this point Johnson cut in to explain that he had lost his balance. 'I'm very sorry, Sir. I knocked over the tilly lamp that was right by the side of the tent … then it was all so quick. We didn't stand a chance.'

'Well, accidents happen but we are now going to have to have three men in tents designed for two. Who do you think is going to put up with you two?'

'We'll be fine, Sir,' replied Johnson. 'The others will see us right.' 'Fine, you organize it. I'm off to sleep. You can clear up the mess in the morning. You'll have to pay for that tent though.'

Monday 26 January 1914

Finished rag bolt run same with lead, continued re-screwing suspension rods. Mail in from Ahwaz this morning letter from Edie, Rachel, Kit and Bert and two Kentish Mercury's from Ma.

At Godar Bridge the work lasted until 5 February. Except for the fire, William's stay here went smoothly. Again it featured visits from his friends the Khan family as well as letters to and from home. His Christmas cards from home arrived on 31 January. Finally, on 5 February he was able to write: 'Everything finished simply waiting for mules, weather brighter.'

Friday 6 February 1914

Muleteers arrived this evening so am preparing everything for leaving tomorrow, have bricked the door of our stores, as every year they break the wooden door down and steal everything useful.

Saturday 7 February 1914

Left the Bridge 9 a.m. arrived at Malamir 6 p.m. dead tired, received a mail today.

William continued his journey through Kul-a-Tul and Allah Corshed. On 9 February he recorded that they had arrived at a very small Persian village called Ogand at 5 p.m. having set off at 6 a.m. They were all very tired; it must have been an arduous journey. William wrote, 'I think this is the longest journey I have ever done.' The party moved on the next morning resting at Ramez where they saw the company agent.

Thursday 12 February 1914

Left Ramez 12 noon commenced raining after we had been on the road about an hour and continued until we arrived at our station. Much too wet to pitch tents so I sent a man on ahead and he rented a Persian room where we stayed the night, arrived at camp at 5 p.m.

Saturday 14 February 1914

Left camp 9 a.m. had to pass over a very deep stream up to the horses' backs arrived at Ahwaz 6.30 p.m. very tired. On my arrival here was very sorry to hear that Capt. Rawlings died yesterday and that Capt. Butterworth of the Raithwaite Hall was murdered on his ship in Bussorah by two coolies.

Sunday 15 February 1914

Taking it easy.

After this the diary became quite scrappy for a while with only occasional entries.

Sunday 3 May 1914.

Miss Mitchel dined with Roles and I on the *Khalifah* serious thing happened Roles and I had our photos taken.

May 7 1914

I have been paid up to and including this day from the *Khalifah.*

1 June 1914

My hen hatching today brought out 12 chicks out of 15 eggs.

The next two entries concerned his request for leave, which the company promised for the following spring in their reply.

Sunday 26 July 1914

Great excitement last night, lots of firing. Arab robbers raided a village near here 3 killed.

4 August 1914

News tonight of war being declared on Germany by England.

Saturday 22 August 1914

Towed *Julnar* to Mohammerah by *Mejidieh* and *Bulbul* as England are on the eve of war with Turkey.

The news in October was purely personal as one friend Waggles got married and Roles was discharged for drunkenness and left by the mail for Karachi. And yet this was just as hostilities were really getting started between the Turks and the British.

Monday 26 October 1914

Received a letter from Baghdad office giving me six months notice to commence from October 19th. Everybody in the company has received the same.

This was a reference to orders to take part in the war effort. The British military forces commissioned all Lynch Brothers ships sailing under the Euphrates and Tigris Steam Navigation Company flag. As Britain went to war against Turkey, Sir Percy Cox, the chief political officer, issued a declaration to the Arab people that their religion and liberty would be respected and that they should maintain order in their own territories while ensuring that their subjects did nothing that could further the cause of the enemy and harm British interests.

Sunday 8 November 1914

HMS *Espiègle* fired on Turkish forts at Mohammerah about 6.30 p.m.

This was the beginning of hostilities between Turkey and Britain. It followed several weeks of threats and ultimatums as the Turks objected to the presence of British vessels in the Shatt al-Arab. HMS *Espiègle* was a twin screw sloop commanded by Vice-Admiral Nunn. The Admiralty pressed Lynch boats into service at about this time as the realization dawned on it just how vital river transport was going to be.

Monday 9 November 1914

Heavy firing heard this morning.

Sunday 15 November 1914

Heavy firing at Abadan today. Turks driven back.

The British force occupied the island of Abadan to protect the oil refineries and tanks as well as the pipeline that brought the oil there from Maidan-i-Naftun. HMS *Espiègle* also came there to join battle with a convoy of ships.

17 November 1914

Big battle at Mohammerah today. Turkish troops retreating.

Abadan and Mohammerah were in Persian territory. Both places were important for Britain's oil interests. The troops were landed at Sanniyeh, nine miles from Mohammerah, by the convoy. The fight was also on for control of Basra.

Friday 20 November 1914

Orders late Thursday night to proceed to Abadan landing troops.

After this he was sent to Iraq where he carried out the remainder of his duties in the war. So, at the end of 1914, William found himself in the land of the Garden of Eden, of Babylon and Nebuchadnezzar, where the prophet and scribe Ezra is said to be buried. He was in a land that nurtured the very beginnings of our culture. Here the stories of the *Thousand and One Nights* were played out. The characters from them are part of our folklore too. We all know of Aladdin, Ali Baba, Scheherazade and Harun al-Rashid the great caliph of Baghdad. While Basra was the home port of Sinbad the sailor. William sailed on the *Mejidieh* with Captain Charles Cowley who was something of a Sinbad himself. The two of them made a formidable team.

Sunday 22 November 1914

Taking troops to Basra landed them on the German wharf German agents and clerks taken prisoner by the English.

This was the day before the Union Jack was officially hoisted over the town of Basra although it had been captured on the 21st.

Thursday 3 December 1914

Orders this morning to proceed to Kurnah with troops. They are loading us with two 18 lb field guns. Left at 8 o'clock this evening.

From Basra, the British force pushed on to Kurnah where the retreating Turks had decided to make a stand. It had the advantage of being close enough to their sources of supplies, food and reinforcements. It was also not easy to attack from round the flank.

Friday 4 December 1914

Arrived at Kurnah 3.30 a.m. landed troops at once, fired the first shot from PS *Blosse Lynch* 10.30 a.m. fired in all 264 rounds. The HMS *Espiègle*, HMS *Lawrence*, *Mejidieh*, *Miner*, *Shaitan*, *Salimi*, *Malamir*, HMS *Odin*, *Louis Pelly* sorry to say that we had to retire at about 3.45 p.m.

The small vessels listed were all river boats or tugs drafted in to help with the war. Some were paddle steamers. Their main tasks were troop transport and running supplies but they had to be armed to defend themselves as the need arose and they were in the thick of this battle. The *Miner* was holed below the water line.

Saturday 5 December 1914

Left here 11.30 a.m. arrived at Basra 4 p.m. embarked the 2nd Battalion of the Norfolk regiment left again for Kurnah 10.45 p.m.

These were the reinforcements for the battle for Kurnah.

Sunday 6 December 1914

Arrived at Kurnah 4.40 a.m. landed troops. News this morning that the Turks have been reinforced. We are leaving for Basra (12.30 noon) for more troops. Arrived Basra 5 p.m. embarked mules and troops.

With this new batch of troops to add to those already there, the British now had a slightly superior force. The *Mejidieh*, with Cowley and William on board lined up to the port side of the *Espiègle* to help with the shelling of the Turkish positions. Lyddite was extensively used against the Turkish entrenchments.

Monday 7 December 1914

Big fight today a shell hit the tug *Shaitan*. One killed two wounded. So far no news as to how the war has gone.

On this occasion the launches had chugged upriver to Kurnah where a tremendous barrage of gunfire forced them to retreat. The *Shaitan* was caught in the cross-fire receiving a direct hit on its bridge that killed Lieutenant-Commander Elkes RNR. He too was a Lynch man.

Tuesday 8 December 1914

No news this morning bar that there are a lot of killed and wounded. The *Malamir* and *Salimi* are taking the wounded to Basra. Big fighting again today. We have fired about a 100 rounds, one piece of a shell from the Turkish guns fell onto our table while we were having tea. News in this evening that as there are so many wounded, the two boats are not enough, so the *Mejidieh* left for Basra this evening, the *Louis Pelly*' was riddled with bullets but thank goodness nobody killed.

Cowley and William proved to be a real thorn in the side of the Turkish forces. Between them they took their shallow draught paddle steamer close in to the banks where bigger craft could not go. They landed troops and ammunition right under the noses of the Turks, guns blazing all the while.

Wednesday 9 December 1914

Late last night the troops surrendered, we are to proceed up early this morning, as the Turkish troops were going to be disarmed. Had a walk round Kurnah. Left late in the evening for Basra with 1009 prisoners.

Subbi Bey, the Turkish commander, agreed an unconditional surrender with General Fry and the British flag was hoisted over the Garden of Eden, as Kurnah is believed to be. It was surrounded by still, green, glassy water, vast expanses of reed beds and marshy spaces were home to hoopoes, bee-eaters and kingfishers. Tall heron stalked the sedges where grebe and snake birds dived, while tortoises floated by like flat little boats. Not that it was quite what the troops expected of an earthly paradise as it was also home to massive clouds of sandflies and mosquitoes. The shimmering heat created mirages that cheated the mind's eye.

The soldiers had a rhyme that summed up their opinion:

> Is this the land of dear old Adam,
> And beautiful mother Eve?
> If so, dear reader, small blame to them
> For sinning and having to leave!
> I've tried to solve a riddle,
> You wish to know it? Well,
> If Kurnah's the Garden of Eden,
> Then where the dickens is Hell?

It fell to Cowley and William to transport the Turkish prisoners, including their commander Subbi Bey, back to Basra aboard the *Medjedieh*. They had already done their utmost to undermine the Turkish offensive by constantly landing troops and artillery for the British forces where it could do most harm. His undoubted British status protected William but the Turks saw Cowley as a local. He was the son of an Irishman who had been senior captain in the Euphrates and Tigris Steam Navigation Company, a position he himself was later to hold. He held British citizenship but his mother, Sushan Minas, was an Armenian who had escaped the massacre in Persia in which her parents had died. She and her brothers and sisters fled to Iraq where they made Baghdad their home. Apart from a brief spell of school and training in Liverpool and seagoing experience on a sailing ship, the *Pendragon*, Charles Cowley spent all his life in Iraq. To the Turks he was an Ottoman citizen and so a traitor. They had already accused him of piracy and threatened to take their revenge. Now Subbi Bey repeated the charge and swore that they would get him in the end as he went down river to the prison camp aboard Cowley's ship. William and Cowley could not take the threats seriously and took to hoisting the skull and crossbones on whichever boat they were working when it was in port.

After the battle at Kurnah Vice-Admiral Nunn invited the two friends on board HMS *Espiègle* for a celebratory dinner to thank them for the part they had both played in routing the Turks. They sat down to eat in the officers' mess at a large mahogany table laid with fine china, silver and crystal glasses. General Townshend, who was commanding the troops, was also a guest and the conversation naturally centred on the battle and hopes for success in the war. Many a glass was raised to toast that eventuality. General Townshend became quite muddled in his Napoleonic military theory, confusing his principal mass with his turning manoeuvres. Cowley and William complimented Nunn on his table and the delicious food they had eaten. 'I've brought my cook from Goa here. The Goans, you know, are a gentle people, very biddable. They only leave Goa to work as cooks or gardeners then go back and retire on the proceeds. Whole bally place must be chock full of cooks.'

'Well, he's done us proud tonight. Let's drink to the cooks of Goa,' replied William. And so yet another toast was drunk. At the end of the meal a bottle of fine port made its way leftwards around the table and a last toast was drunk to king and country. Cowley and William then made their way slightly unsteadily back to the *Medjedieh*. Later they received letters of appreciation from the Admiralty for their part in the battle of Kurnah.

Thursday 10 December 1914

Arrived at Basra 10 a.m. and took prisoners onto one of the BI boats. We fired in all 700 rounds.

Sunday 13 December 1914

News from Dad this morning at Basra, that Kit made me an uncle (a daughter) on October 25th.

This was the birth of my mother's cousin, Eileen.

Monday 21 December 1914

Yesterday towed the *Julnar* up to dock.

Thursday 24 December 1914 (Xmas Eve)

Left Maaghil for Kurnah 7 p.m. with horses.

Friday 25 December 1914 Xmas Day

Arrived Kurnah 10 a.m. left 12.30. Arrived Maaghil 4.10 p.m. drank freely.

Well it was Christmas after all!

Saturday 26 December 1914 Boxing Day

Left Maaghil 12.30. Brought up at Mohammerah 6 p.m.

Saturday 2 January 1915

Left Kurnah for Basra, the guns that were put on us yesterday were taken off again this morning.

The organization of the campaign in Mesopotamia was poor and extremely muddled. This description of guns being loaded and then immediately unloaded would seem to confirm that.

Saturday 23 January 1915

Sent home forty pounds to Ma by money order. I have got jaundice.

There is now another gap in the diary presumably because of his illness. However he evidently made a good recovery.

Monday 1 February 1915

Sent home thirty pounds to Ma. Rejoined the *Julnar* this afternoon.

Thursday 4 February 1915

Lord Hardinge Viceroy of India arrived at Basra.

As viceroy, Lord Hardinge had overall responsibility for the Indian army and the campaign in Mesopotamia. He was welcomed to Basra by the native Arab population. In reply to their welcoming speech he said:

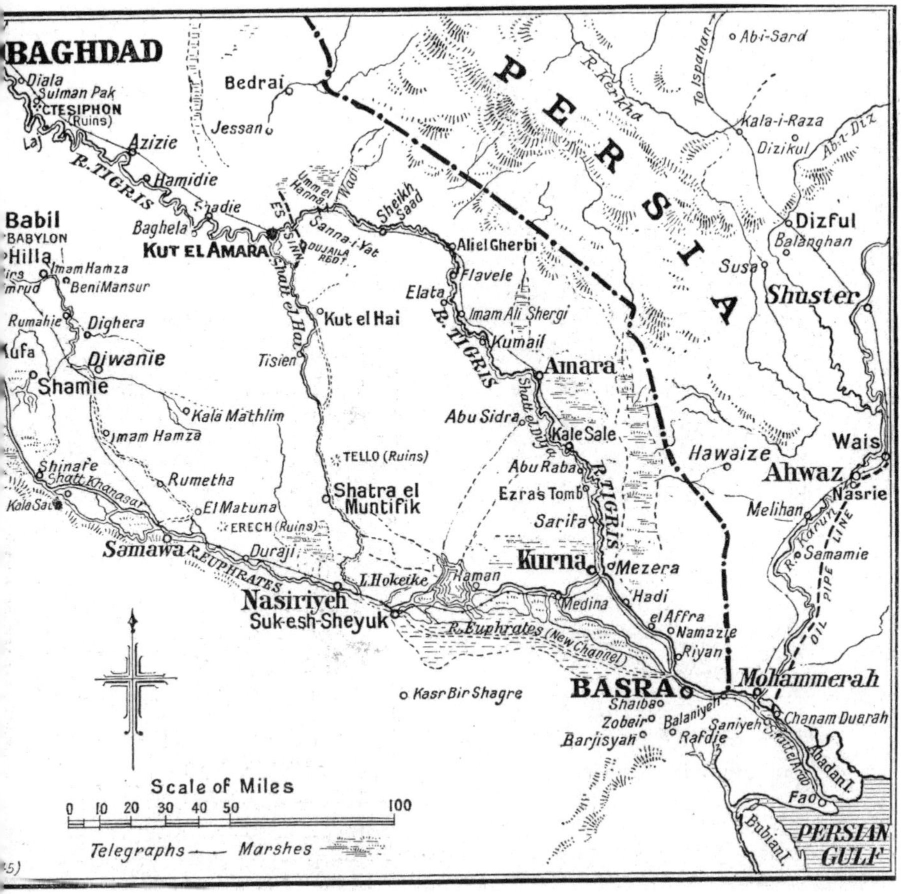

Lower Mesopotamia.

The British occupation has raised problems which require prompt consideration and settlement. I have come here to see local conditions for myself in order the better to judge what measures are necessary. You are aware that we are not engaged single-handed in this great struggle and we cannot lay down plans for the future without a full exchange of views with the other great powers, but I can hold out the assurance that the future will bring you a more benign rule.

Saturday 6 February 1915

Lord Hardinge passed here (Maaghil) on his way to Kurnah on board HMS *Lawrence*, Mr Thomas arrived this morning.

Saturday 10 April 1915

Dad left here (Basra) for home at 2 p.m. by the mail boat *Dumra.*

His father was visiting him as he was also in the merchant navy and his ship called in at Basra. The British India Steam Navigation Company owned the *Dumra*, which was built in 1894 of steel and weighed 1695 tons. It had two decks with an awning and electric light, so was a very modern ship for its day. It was a fast mail boat plying the Persian Gulf. William took the opportunity to send home more money with his father and on Sunday 9 May 1915 he was finally able to take leave.

Sunday 9 May 1915

Homeward bound by the SS *Kerman.*

Monday 17 May 1915

Went ashore today at Bushire with Capt. Waterlow, by sailing boat and had tiffin with Mr Malcolm, Strick's agent who is blind.

From here the ship sailed on to Bunder Abbas and headed for India. On arrival in Karachi, this was many years before partition so Pakistan did not exist as an independent state; William went ashore and took a garry ride around the town. He pronounced it to be 'quite a decent place'. He travelled on aboard the same ship via Aden where they arrived on 3 June. He and Captain Waterlow enjoyed a lunch at the Royal Hotel before rejoining the ship and sailing on. William's diary shows that they stopped at Port Said, went past both Malta and Gibraltar arriving off the English shoreline on 24 June.

Thursday 24 June 1915

Passed Deal 11.15 a.m. arrived Gravesend 5 p.m. left the ship and caught 7.45 p.m. train from Greenhithe arrived home about 10 p.m.

Wednesday 29 September 1915

Met Miss Gill for first time awfully nice girl.

Saturday 2 October 1915

Miss Gill and I had a fine time at the Music Hall.

Saturday 9 October 1915

Went to the Globe Theatre to see *Peg o' My Heart* very fine.

This was one of the most popular of the entertainments on the London stage. At the start of the war people stayed away from the theatres and many shows had to close down. However, by Christmas 1914 the gloom had lifted and the audiences came back. Soldiers on leave made up a large percentage of these audiences. They doubtless needed the escape from reality that laughter and light music could offer them. These entertainments became known as revues. The rest of the audience was female; consequently the only plays to gain any popularity were light romances. *Peg o' My Heart* was one of these.

Sunday 7 November 1915

Flo came home for the first time.

Thursday 13 November 1915

Went down to Flo's to tea. Said goodbye to her people, was very sorry to leave her, we seemed to have got on very well together. She was upset at parting and so was I.

We must assume that Flo is the same person as Miss Gill but that he is now on sufficiently intimate terms to call her by her first name. Who knows how their friendship might have developed if it had not been interrupted by war.

Saturday 12 November 1915

Left Tilbury by the SS *Arabia* for Basra 1 p.m. Dad, Syd and Uncle Ted came to see me off.

Syd was William's brother, twelve years his senior.

Monday 15 November 1915

Arrived Basra 8.30 a.m. and joined the *Julnar* after having had a very enjoyable journey out.

On board the *Julnar*, Cowley was once again the commanding officer. He was full of news of having had a narrow escape when the Turks finally attempted to take revenge. An assassin had boarded the ship and attacked the unconscious form in the bunk where Cowley normally slept. Luckily for him he was not there. The person in the bed, Captain Wingate, was seriously injured but survived his ordeal. The two friends, Cowley and William, being pleased to be working together again and relieved at Cowley's escape from death drank a celebratory whisky. By this time the British were firmly in control of a large part of Mesopotamia, from Basra right through to Kut-al-Amara. Sir Percy Cox, or Supposi Kokus as the Arabs called him, was installed as chief political officer. Gertrude Bell, the famous traveller, writer and Arabist, ably assisted him. Having been chased out of Kut the Turks were now entrenched at Ctesiphon further up the Tigris. The river was extremely difficult to navigate at this time of the year because water levels were low. Consequently, General Townshend's troops had been unable to chase the Turks up the river and march on into Baghdad as they would have liked.

Wednesday 15 November 1915

Left Basra 3 a.m. loaded with troops.

Against his better judgement but urged on by the War Office and his superiors, Townshend led his men to Ctesiphon with a view to advancing to Baghdad from there. The army was driven back to Kut-al-Amara where they were besieged by the Turks.

Tuesday 4 January 1916

Left Ali Gerby 10.45 a.m., with General Younghusband aboard. Order of leaving was *Blosse Lynch*, *Julnar* and two P boats astern. Anchored 2.30 p.m.

General Younghusband was one of the commanders of the military operation that took Kut. The advance on Sheikh Saad began that day. It was the first battle of many in the fight to relieve the besieged garrison at Kut-al-Amara and recapture the town.

Sir Francis Michie Shepherd, later ambassador to Persia, fought in the Tigris Corps. He describes going upriver to join the battle on barges lashed to 'P' boats. There were two attached on either side of each boat making it very difficult to steer the boats, especially on the tight bends of the sinuous Tigris River. They weaved and lurched along like a drunken man trying to walk a straight line. The men were packed like sardines on the barges. When the boats encountered a particularly tight bend all the men had to disembark with their baggage and walk across country to meet the boat again on the other side of the bend. The barges were not fitted with safety rails and every so often a man would fall overboard with a loud plop. Two men suffered concussion when they had the misfortune to fall between the barge and the 'P' boat.

Saturday 15 January 1916

Sheikh Saad have been laying here several days, a big battle took place here our wounded being about 4000.

By this time the *Julnar* had been drafted into service as a hospital ship. Like the other steamers used in this way there was totally inadequate provision for the situation and the wounded on board these ships suffered horrific privations, unnecessary illness and pain. William must have helped to transport the wounded to Basra and seen their appalling plight.

21–24 January 1916

Big battle at Orah. We had very heavy losses here. Rotten weather pouring with rain.

The men struggled through heavy rain and deep mud to no avail. In one regiment only one man, a young subaltern, came out alive and unharmed.

1 March 1916

I was operated on at Amara Hospital for two abscesses. Remained in hospital twelve days.

24 February 1916

Sent home forty pounds by money order to Ma.

28 February 1916

Mrs Gill died today.

These last entries are out of date order. I would guess that due to his illness and because he was very busy with his duties he had not filled in his diary. Mrs Gill must be the mother or grandmother of his girlfriend Flo. This is the last entry he made before history overtook him.

3

The Ottoman Empire

The Worldly Hope men
Set their Hearts upon
Turns ashes – or it prospers; and anon,
Like Snow upon the Desert's dusty Face
Lighting a little Hour or two – is gone.
(*Rubáiyát of Omar Khayyám*, verse 14)

The Ottomans were so-called originally because they were descendants of the first ruler of Turkey, Osman I. However, by the nineteenth century the name had become more a cultural definition or identity than a political definition. This is perhaps because the empire had spread so widely that most of its citizens were not Turkish in origin and were not Turkish speaking.

Early occupiers of the land we now know as Turkey were the Seljuks. These were a nomadic Turkmen tribe who spread from central Asia and southeast Russia to settle in Asia Minor and Anatolia during the tenth and eleventh centuries. They converted to Sunnite Islam and continued their invasion to Baghdad. Their dynasty ended when the Mongols conquered Turkey.

Osman I, an emir in Bythynia, began the conquest of neighbouring regions and founded the Ottoman dynasty in 1300 after defeating the Seljuks. He continued to expand his realm through wars, alliances and buying territory. Agreements with factions of the Byzantine Empire gave the Ottomans a foothold in Europe, notably Gallipoli. From here they moved into Thrace, Macedonia, Bulgaria and Serbia. When they took control in Egypt under the leadership of Bayezid, the caliph of Cairo awarded him the title of sultan.

In 1413 they pushed further into Europe and extended their influence south of the Danube; and in 1444 they defeated a Crusader army. People in the east looked upon the Crusaders as barbarian invaders and, compared with the great mathematical and astronomical texts of the Arab world, to say nothing of their medical knowledge, Western culture was certainly a lot more primitive.

Less than ten years later the Christian world experienced a great shock when, under Mehmud II, the Ottomans sacked Constantinople with terrible violence. This great city, containing as it did the basilica of Santa Sophia, had been one of the main centres of Christianity. The loss of Constantinople marked the end of the Byzantine Empire. From here the Ottomans moved on to Morea, Trebizond, Bosnia, Albania and the Crimea.

Christian youths from the Balkans were drafted into the army and converted to Islam to form the Janissary Corps, the sultan's most trusted troops who also acted as his personal bodyguards. All members of the government and army were regarded as the ruler's personal slaves and, along with the ruling class, were sworn to complete obedience to ensure the indivisibility of power.

Turkey pursued its ambitions further by taking on the mamelukes who had ruled Syria and Egypt since 1250. The mamelukes were slave soldiers who seized power and then governed the two countries through selecting a ruler from their own ranks. They drove the Mongols back and the Crusaders out of Syria. The Ottoman Turks conquered them in Syria but not in Egypt where they survived as a class and stayed to govern in the name of the Ottoman Empire until 1811. The conquest of the mamelukes brought Palestine and Algeria into the empire, which effectively doubled its size.

The Ottoman Empire's golden age was from 1520 to 1566. Süleyman I already presided over a vast empire, but he went on to conquer Hungary, annexe Tripoli and extend his power to Mesopotamia and the Persian Gulf. The Ottoman navy dominated the eastern Mediterranean. It eventually added the Caucasus and Azerbaijan to its long list of territories.

Like all empires, however, this one too began to decline, even while it was expanding. Decline was due to the weakness of the administrative and social structures. There was also a lack of political ability among the sultans who were hereditary rulers, fatally coupled with increasing power and rivalry in the ruling class. It was a rigid hierarchical society. The colour of clothing one was permitted to wear and the size and shape of one's hat denoted one's rank. Corruption was rife, even among the elite Janissary Corps. Once known for their honour and bravery as defenders of the faith, they sank so low as to use dead colleagues to make false claims to secure payments. Industries fell idle and the trade routes the Ottoman Empire controlled, such as the silk road to China, became disused with consequent losses to the economy. Improvements in navigation enabled commerce to use sea routes rather than overland transport. At the same time, powerful European states formed alliances to exclude Turkey from Europe's markets.

The Levant Company was established in London in 1581. It was more than just a commercial trading company, for it gave diplomats and consular staff the wherewithal to let Britain trade with and watch over the dealings of the Ottoman Empire. The Persians were a threat to the empire at this time. They were Shiite and not Sunni Muslims, so there was a religious element to the hostilities. At about this time the British and Dutch were vying with the Portuguese for control of the spice routes. Persia formed an alliance with them to curtail Portuguese attempts to establish an empire. Out of this was born the Muscovy Company, which a group of British traders set up to create an overland route from the Caspian Sea across Russia to import Persian silk. The trade route did not last long but it gave Britain a foothold in Persia from where it was able to control the Gulf region and have further influence in the Middle East.

In rural areas of the Ottoman Empire administration became weaker and more disorganized, leading to the formation of small feudal states. This helped to bring about unrest in the cities where food supplies were disrupted and many people were on the brink of starvation. Because technology failed to make its way from Europe to Turkey, the Europeans gained a massive advantage over the Ottomans. Only when Napoleon conquered Egypt did technology come to the Middle East. The French brought the printing press, scientists and artists. The Ottoman aristocracy made some attempts to modernize and adopt Western styles and ideas, but this led to a reactionary revolt within Turkey.

In 1808 local authorities in the various states of the empire openly opposed central government. Mahmud II carried out some modernization by bringing in a comprehensive education system and Westernizing the penal code and maritime law. The year 1821 saw a rebellion in Greece against Ottoman rule. The Egyptians supported the Turks, but when France, Britain and Russia came to the aid of Greece, the Ottomans were forced to retreat and peace negotiations were started. In 1829 Greek independence was proclaimed and a monarchy was established three years later. Famously, the poet Lord Byron fought on the Greek side and raised a great deal of sympathy for the cause. In 1853 Russia pursued its expansionist ambition and tried to take power in the Balkans. The Russians wanted to establish a protectorate over Orthodox Christians within the Turkish Empire. Once they besieged Moldavia and Walachia the Turkish forces retaliated and war broke out. Britain and France went to the aid of Turkey fighting mostly in the Crimea. By 1856 war was over, Russia had withdrawn but Turkey lost some territory.

Despite Mahmud II's modernizing measures, power became even more centralized. There were few checks on the ruler, but he did institute the first constitution in any Islamic country. These reforms did not, however, prevent Turkey's terrible massacres of Bulgarians and Armenians in 1875 and 1896. The Treaty of San Stefano led to further loss of territory in 1878. After another war with Russia over the Balkans, negotiations took place at the Congress of Berlin. The Treaty of San Stefano forced Turkey to give up Romania, Serbia, Montenegro, Bulgaria and Cyprus. Abdul Hamid held the rest by assuring Europe that the empire maintained peace within its own boundaries.

Being in a constant state of war did nothing to help the finances of the empire, which wasted money on magnificent palaces and misguided attempts to ape the West and in which corruption and bribery were rife. Sultan Abdul Hamid developed a pan-Islamic policy, but despite his modern outlook, he presided over horrific massacres in the Balkans and in Armenia, thus earning him the nickname of the 'Red Sultan'.

In 1908, trouble came from within in the shape of a revolt by a group known as the Young Turks, accompanied by further massacres of Armenians, especially Christian ones. Gertrude Bell's close friend Major Charles Doughty-Wylie rode out at the head of a small group of Turkish troops to quell the uprising in Mersin and Adana. His action saved hundreds of lives, though he later lost his own at Gallipoli. Abdul Hamid was ousted from power the following year. Mehmed V took over as sultan but he was more of a figurehead because real political power now lay in the hands of the Young Turks.

The Balkan wars, which immediately preceded the First World War, ensured that Turkey was regarded as a pariah state not fit to be part of Europe. Tsar Nicholas I called the Ottoman Empire the 'sick man of Europe' and the European powers now wanted to see the dismemberment of the empire.

Western attitudes to Turkey were formed over many centuries of conflict dating back to the Crusades. Knights returning from war told tales of Muslim vices, especially sodomy. Turks were seen as fierce warriors and cruel and ruthless in their treatment of prisoners. In the eighteenth century, Westerners began to look upon them with new eyes, as diplomats and businessmen instead of warriors. A fashion developed for all things exotic and eastern in dress and furnishings, for exotic pleasure and lust, which was evident in the paintings of Delacroix and Géricault. In the nineteenth century, though, the Turks again infuriated the West with their atrocious violence towards Christians in the Greek war of independence, the slaughter in Bulgaria and Bosnia and the campaign against the Armenians, which lasted from 1890 to 1914.

In 1914, as two large German warships sailed into the Bosporus, Turkey announced that it would be entering the First World War on the German side. Following their defeat, Sultan Mehmed V was overthrown and Mehmed VI took his place. He, however, the last of the Osmanli dynasty, was merely a pawn of the Allied powers and was deposed in 1922. During the war Mustafa Kemal had emerged as a hero to the Turks when he led their victory at Gallipoli. A republic was formed when the sultan was deposed and a new spirit swept the nation with Kemal as leader. One of his first reforms was to introduce surnames and for himself he took the name Atatürk, Mustafa Kemal. Under Kemal Atatürk, Mustafa Kemal the modern state of Turkey began to be formed and was once more rooted in its ancient home of Anatolia.

4

Kut or Bust

'Tis all a Chequer-Board of Nights and Days
Where Destiny with Men for Pieces plays:
Hither and thither moves,
And mates, and slays,
And one by one back in the Closet lays.
(*Rubáiyát of Omar Khayyám*, verse 49)

The Germans persuaded the Turks to come into the war on their side following years of propaganda and spending a great deal of gold. For them, the war in the east was a useful way of taking troops and equipment away from the main theatres of war in Europe, stretching British and allied resources to the limit. They also hoped to extend their influence in this area, creating an empire of their own. The Turks had been ruling Iraq for 400 years, so partnership with them gave the Germans instant access to the country and its valuable oil reserves.

Persians found their loyalties split. For years the Russians and British had been rivals for the concessions to trade in different products, including oil, and for influence in the country. They were confused to find the British and Russians allies against Germany. Some tribes threw in their lot with the Germans believing, with persuasion from Germany, that it was the best way to gain independence and get rid of the two rivals. Others took up arms for the Russians, hoping to curb English power, or for the English, hoping to be rid of the Russians. Still other tribes preferred the British imperialists to the other two. The Bakhtiari were pro-German because they were anti-Russian or pro-British because they were anti-Turk. Only the Sheikh of Mohammerah at the mouth of the Shatt al-Arab remained reliably loyal to Britain.

As Turkish and German ambitions became more pressing in the region Britain began to wake up from its long slumber of complacency and moved to protect the oilfields at Maidun-i-Naftun. The name means the plain of oil. This field lay in a cup in the hill 70 miles northeast of Ahwaz. This was the area where William Louis Reed had worked before the war. Pipes carry the oil for 142 miles to refineries at Abadan on the Shatt al-Arab, passing through Bakhtiari country and through the territory belonging to the Sheikh of Mohammerah.

The sheikh leased the land to the Anglo-Persian Oil Company and was responsible for the security of the pipeline and the safety of its employees. As William mentioned in his diary, armed guards provided protection during his journey and work along the Karun River. The sheikh was a shareholder in the company, a fact that no doubt helped him to remain loyal. The Khans, the leaders of the Bakhtiari tribes, were also shareholders and received a subsidy for guarding the company's works.

Hostilities with Turkey began on 29 October 1914 when the Turkish navy bombarded Russian Black Sea ports. This was a violation of international law; the British, French and Russian allies responded by withdrawing their ambassadors.

Management of the war in Mesopotamia was left to the British army in India. This was despite the Indian army having suffered a series of cutbacks in its finances, due in part to the loss of revenue from the recently abolished opium trade. To the troops, the war here was an annoying distraction and not their main focus of attention. In his book *The Long Road to Baghdad*, Edmund Candler, an eye-witness with the Tigris Corps, nowadays we would call him a war correspondent embedded with the troops, said, 'We wished that we were killing Germans, the real menace to civilization, and not these dupes, Arabs and Turks, whom they had drawn round them in a double coil of protection.' And yet those oilfields were vital to the war effort since the navy had gone over to oil to fuel its ships while Mesopotamia and the waters of the Gulf were the gateway to India.

In the autumn of 1914 hostilities began in earnest on 29 September when the sloop HMS *Espiègle*, under Vice-Admiral Nunn's command, entered the Shatt al-Arab, regarded as Turkish waters at that time because it was part of Ottoman territory. Its mission there was said to be purely precautionary. The navy was so unprepared for war in the Middle East and in desert regions that it spent the first few weeks dying all its tropical whites with a solution of permanganate of potash to turn them khaki.

News that the Turkish navy had requisitioned large stocks of coal and oil from Lynch Brothers and that there were two German raiders at large in the Indian Ocean had alarmed the British and sent them scurrying to protect their oil interests in this area and their route to India. The Turks protested and after several ultimatums they fired on the sloop as it anchored downstream from Abadan.

The *Ekbatana*'s German crew began filling disused vessels with sand, which they then sank to form a barrier to close off the entrance to the Karun River to British ships. Meanwhile, the Turks had refused the British government's request to honour their obligations of neutrality in Europe. HMS *Odin* had been waiting for just such an eventuality and went in to support *Espiègle*. The battle of Abadan was the first in the struggle for control of Iraq. Turkish forces entrenched opposite Abadan opened fire on the British ships. With the assistance of *Espiègle*, *Dalhousie* and *Lawrence*, *Odin* retaliated and the Turks fled.

British troops arrived from India to take control of Turkish Arabia. General Gorringe went to the Karun River to fight those tribes that appeared to be supporting the Turkish and German side. Since they were an undisciplined, disorganized force, he soon subdued them and secured the oilfields for Britain. A garrison was left to protect the precious fuel. The British quickly captured the port of Basra and then pushed inland up the Karun, Tigris and Euphrates rivers. The British Expeditionary Force had established control of a large 200-mile tract of Turkish territory, thus achieving the main objective of the campaign, which was to protect British oil wells. As we have seen, these were particularly important because the navy needed oil to fuel its warships. The British also hoped to win over the Arab population and strike a blow at Turkish power in Asia.

That many British troops were native Indians may not have helped the British cause with the Arabs. Almost two-thirds of the forces in Mesopotamia were Indian troops comprised of Sikhs, Punjabis, Pathans, Bhopalis and Ghurkhas. According to T. E. Lawrence, in his book *Seven Pillars of Wisdom*, Arabs were tolerant of Africans and reserved their racial prejudice for Indians. Whatever the reason, Arab locals could not necessarily be relied on for their support. Most were still under the sway of their Turkish masters and could not believe that their rule of 400 years would come to an end. Some simply supported either side on an opportunistic basis. It took time, several British victories in the area and the persuasive tongue of T. E. Lawrence to make the Arab tribes trust Britain.

It was Sir Percy Cox's idea to take Kut-al-Amara as a stepping stone to Baghdad and Lord Hardinge and General Nixon supported him. Eventually, Whitehall was also persuaded and agreed. It was not necessary to take Baghdad from a strategic point of view since the oilfields had already been secured, but it was the capital city and would restore pride and morale after the defeat at Gallipoli. It also ensured the British control of the Tigris. Since travel in this area was so difficult by land because of flooding in the rainy season and poor roads, the river was an important means of transport. If they controlled Baghdad as well as Basra and the river between they would have a commanding position.

However, this decision over stretched British resources, for the expeditionary force in Mesopotamia was under-manned, underequipped, especially for river transport, and under-financed. The need for river transport was recognized early on and, by the end of November, the navy had commandeered the steamers owned by one of the Lynch Brothers group, the Euphrates and Tigris Steamship Company. Many of the personnel, including my grandfather, William Louis Reed, became naval reservists and were given a Royal Navy rank. It was said that Mesopotamia was a difficult place in which to fight because, with the terrain in the delta of the two rivers consisting of swamp and marshland, 'there was too much water for soldiers and not enough for sailors'. In the spring, when the snow from the mountains of Persia melted and swelled the rivers, water would stretch as far as the eye could see. Every so often a village could be seen seeming to float on the water. The flotilla of boats plying the river in support of the army's movements on land comprised everything from navy war sloops to little fly-class boats, tugs, paddle steamers and bellums. The latter were long narrow boats steered by a paddle or pole in the manner of a punt; in peace time they would be gaily painted and used for transporting reclining passengers, much like a small exotic gondola. There were also maheilahs, which were larger and fitted with huge rudders, a cut-away prow, high forward sloping mast and lateen sail. Even the gufas were occasionally pressed into service. These cauldron shaped boats made of pitch and reeds had not changed since the time of Herodotus and moved only in curves.

The rush for Baghdad took place before enough transport was available to convey reinforcements to the front. The Indian army set out with 3000 mules and 1600 camels. However, there was no grazing for camels in Basra and in a land of floods, mud and rivers they were singularly inappropriate. Headquarters had not understood the need for river transport. One depleted division was sent in to attack the second capital of an empire that could command an army of 700,000 fighting men. But, in the arrogance of those times, it was thought that they were mere Turks against British Tommies.

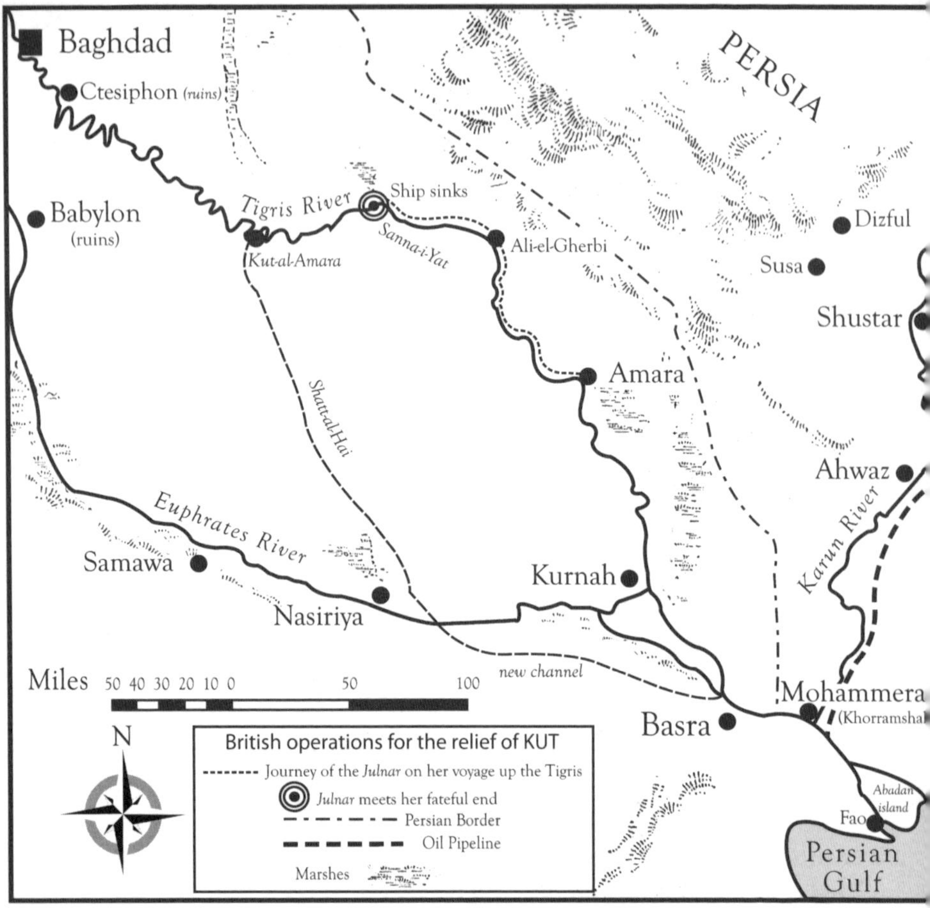

British operations along the Tigris.

The point of departure for the push to Baghdad was Kut-al-Amara, a small town on the Tigris at the furthermost point of British control. It was 100 miles south of Baghdad. Kut was also strategically important because it lay at the junction of the Shatt-al-Hai and Tigris. The Shatt-al-Hai connected the Tigris with the Euphrates. Control of Kut and Nasiriya meant control of both ends of the waterway connecting the Tigris and Euphrates. The Turks under the leadership of Nur-ud-Din had set themselves up in a formidable position. They straddled the river seven miles downstream of Kut with a division on each bank and a connecting bridge.

General Townshend was in charge of a force of 14,000 men.

He had already led several attacks on the Turks. Initially he met with success. His tactics were to take the Turkish left with his main force after feigning an attack on their right. Strong reserves were brought in by the enemy but the exhausted British troops, buoyed with adrenalin despite heat and thirst, flung themselves with gusto into a bayonet attack on open ground against the Turks, routing them completely and taking the town of Kut.

The Turks retreated to Ctesiphon where once more they set up a strong defensive position astride the Tigris. The ancient city of Ctesiphon had been the capital of the Parthian and Sassanian kings. Parthia, in northeast Persia near Khorosan in modern Iran, consisted of a feudal confederacy of kingdoms, first under the Achaemenians, then the Seleucids who controlled a great empire between 250 BC and AD 224, at which point the Sassanians conquered it. Its fearless cavalry and mounted archers defeated the Roman army at Carrhae, now Haran in Turkey, in 53 BC. The Romans led by the emperor Trajan finally captured Ctesiphon in AD 115. The remains of the palace of Khosrow I, who ruled from AD 531 to 579, incorporate the largest known brickwork vault with a span of over 82 feet (25 metres). The city witnessed the fall of great empires and great men. It was here that Alexander the Great is thought to have contracted the illness that ended his life and here too that the Roman emperor Julian was killed in battle against the Persians in AD 63. It was in its turn reduced to ruins by a jihad perpetrated by the new religion of Islam in the seventh century when the Arabs captured it in AD 637. All that remains of it now is an arch staring out over the empty desert.

Ctesiphon is only 18 miles short of Baghdad; with another victory under Townshend's belt it would only be a day's march from there to Baghdad and the advance began on 19 November. As the battle raged, the Turkish trenches were captured and recaptured several times, but after the fourth day the Turks received reinforcements. General Townshend was now in an impossible situation. Nine miles from his shipping and sources of

A street in Kut.

supplies, facing superior forces of fresh troops while his own were exhausted from days of fighting and with casualties numbering more than 4500, he was forced to fall back to Kut-al-Amara. The navy supported the army throughout the retreat by shepherding the river craft under heavy fire from Turkish guns and snipers. The *Shaitan* was grounded and sank, the *Comet* and *Firefly* were lost, the former destroyed by fire and the latter captured.

The army arrived back in Kut on 2 December with over 1500

prisoners and wounded. The inadequacy of the medical backup let the latter down badly. General Townshend decided to stand his ground at Kut and wait for reinforcements from Basra. Kut was a town of 600 houses, some shops, a mosque, cafés and a small bazaar.

Meanwhile, the Turks had amassed further reinforcements and were now besieging the town. They also pushed down the line to take up a position across the route of any relief force. There was very little fighting going on in the other parts of the country so the whole Mesopotamian campaign became concentrated in the effort to remove the Turks from Kut and to take Baghdad. It became an obsession – Kut and Baghdad or bust. The one beneficial effect of the siege was to make Whitehall and the Indian army headquarters at Simla realize that the campaign could not be carried out on the cheap, especially when news broke that Turkish troops no longer required in the Dardanelles were heading for Mesopotamia. They also finally woke up to the idea that river transport was absolutely essential.

The Turks were entrenched in six different positions along the river but they were so close together that they might as well have been one. The Turks also had the advantage of the terrain around them. This was swampy or at times flooded. The flat alluvial riverbanks were a maze of irrigation channels. It was vital to try to keep control of the river, which was essential for transport.

The third division of the British Expeditionary Force was already entrenched at Ali el Gherbi about 70 miles from Kut. This was reinforced by infantry and guns from Basra. In January 1916, while General Townshend was pinned down with his men in Kut, a large body of troops was quickly concentrated in the area under the command of General Aylmer to force the Turks out of their positions and relieve the garrison. This force was known as the Tigris Corps and it came from the sixth cavalry brigade. Major-General Keary commanded the third division while the seventh division was the responsibility of Major-General Younghusband. The force comprised 25,000 men altogether, some of whom were brought over from France, while fresh troops also came in from Egypt and India. Due to the difficulties of the journey, units were split up and new scratch units formed. Everything was done in haste and in a great muddle because it was believed that the men in the garrison at Kut-al-Amara could not hold out for long. Meanwhile, the garrison was on full rations and confident of being relieved.

The force in Mesopotamia was now much bigger than had originally been planned. Consequently, there were not enough river steamers for transport and supplies. There were no hospital steamers, very few field ambulances and the artillery was weak. Aylmer wanted to postpone his attack but could not because of the pressure from General Townshend who even sent messages asking 'if they were on the right river?' The general was anxious about his food supplies and ammunition. He believed that they did not have enough to last beyond mid-January. He sent constant messages urging an early attack. It was also thought that Turkish reinforcements were on the way and it would be beneficial to attack before they arrived.

General Townshend had several reasons to sit tight in Kut. First, he believed that as long as the British held Kut, the Turks could not get their ships, barges, stores and munitions down the river from Baghdad to attack Amara and make further advances. It would also allow time for British reinforcements to come upriver from Basra and for the Russian Allies under General Baratoff to move towards Baghdad. He also believed that by making a stand at Kut he was holding territory gained in the past year at the cost of so much blood. As the siege began to bite he buoyed the troops up with fine speeches:

> Our duty stands out clear and simple. It is our duty to Empire, to our beloved King and country, to stand here and hold up the Turkish advance as we are doing now, and with the help of all, heart and soul together, we will make this defence to be remembered in history as a glorious one.

Lynch Brothers had hastily built the fort and blockhouses at Kut prior to the siege. It was never anticipated that they would be put to such use. The town contained many other buildings that the army commandeered, including the Turkish baths (*hammam*), which was host to an observing station on its roof and a flour mill in its yard. As the siege began shortly before Christmas, the festival was celebrated with an excellent dinner. In his book *In Kut and Captivity*, Major E. W. C. Sandes describes how they ate a kind of plum pudding, had asparagus among other things, and washed the whole meal down with Scotch whisky. For tea they enjoyed real plum cake from a tin with tea that had both milk and sugar. There was a strong belief in the early days in a rapid end to the siege, but the luxuries fizzled out as quickly as the optimism.

The first attempt to relieve Kut began on 4 January. General Younghusband arrived aboard the *Julnar* and successive strikes at the enemy over the next three weeks were a nightmare for the British troops. They fought through pelting rain, frequently advancing across flat land that afforded no cover whatsoever. The river was rising fast, becoming a 'swift turbid stream 400 yards wide'. The river banks were now a sea of mud in which guns, men and vehicles stuck fast. They camped in the bitter cold on ground that was sodden with rain. To make matters worse, the Turks now had three or four extra divisions, fresh from their success at Gallipoli. Their lines of entrenchment had been completed and strengthened under German supervision in the person of Marshal von der Goltz, a brilliant military strategist who advised, trained, organized and inspired the Turkish commanders.

One assault that failed saw the infantry struggling on through deep mud and pouring rain under heavy and accurate Turkish fire. In one regiment the only officer to come out alive and unharmed was a young subaltern. This was the final assault of the first attempt made on 21 January. After intense fighting all day through mud and rain, the troops were exhausted. It continued to rain through the night making the ground a quagmire and so there was no attempt to resume fighting. Instead, a truce was arranged to bury the dead and collect the wounded. According to *The Times History of the War*, 'vehicles and stretcher-bearers could scarcely move in the deep mud and some of those too much hurt to walk had remained through the night where they fell.'

The gallantry and courage of the men could not be doubted. Edmund Candler likened it to the Charge of the Light Brigade. Whole regiments were decimated. The Black Watch went into battle with 120 men; 50 survived. One major commanding a battalion, after being shot in the side was heard to shout to his troops in Hindustani, 'Forward, brave fellows! Go ahead. I am down. But today the regiment will win honour. Let none hold back.' It was a twentieth-century battle fought with eighteenth-century medical arrangements and equipment. It was fought on foot, by cavalry and by camelry.

Although the attempt to relieve the garrison had ended in failure with one man in every three killed or wounded, some progress had been made. The Turks had been driven out of two of their entrenched positions. The British were now seven miles nearer Kut-al-Amara, yet more than 8600 men had been killed or injured. The wounded found no comfort, only chaos. One ambulance to a thousand casualties could not hope to transport them all. The hospital consisted of two tents with three doctors and a hospital assistant. The stretchers too ran short; there was one to every fifty casualties. Men with broken limbs and worse were jolted over caked mud and furrowed ground in carts pulled by mules or oxen. In addition, as the wounded lay helpless on the ground waiting for the transport trucks, they were prey to marauding Marsh Arabs who stripped them of their clothes and valuables, often bayoneting or mutilating them in the process.

Back in Kut, on 22 January General Townshend decided that by reducing the men's rations to half he could hold out for an extra 27 days. On 25 January he announced that he had found a hidden store of food. These new stores belonged to the local population in the town. When the siege began they had been given the choice of staying in their homes or leaving the besieged town. Perhaps it was as a result of their confidence in the British army that they decided to stay, but they hid their stores. With these, and by killing the horses and mules for meat, Townshend could hold out for 84 days. The river was an important source of water although fetching it had become a hazardous task. At dusk the Arab women of the town would venture out with jars or skins, taking fright at the bullets, which often cracked into the walls as they were passing. Nearly every night a bullet would hit a woman or child by the riverside.

By now the siege had lasted for seven weeks. Rations were eked out by hunting the starlings that gathered on the trees in the evening. They were tasty when roasted but had to be decapitated and cooked quickly because they did not improve with keeping. Oxen, horses, mules and camels also fell victim to the butcher's knife, though many of the men held out for a long time against eating horse flesh. E.W.C. Sandes describes a great delicacy they enjoyed, mule's tongue in aspic, followed by a pudding concocted from *atta* (coarse flour) dates, date juice, ginger and a little fat. He pronounced it not very sweet, but quite eatable. Tobacco was also in short supply and, at a time when men considered it as essential as food for their well-being, it was much sought after. Supplies did get in thanks to night-time smuggling expeditions by local Arabs, but they were extortionately expensive.

The men had beaten off all attacks despite constant bombardment. The trenches and shelters were flooded, it was bitterly cold and fuel had run short. Every door or window frame in the town was used for fuel. Medical services were failing to keep up with demand, as there were so many sick and injured men. Many had also been killed. The Turks had five-centimetre guns able to fire rapidly and accurately over a distance of 7500 yards, which they used to devastating effect. The guns available to the troops in the garrison were old five-inch ones unable to fire more than 6000 yards with any accuracy.

In the light of the new supply situation in the garrison, General Aylmer postponed any further advance. At this stage the number of men lost in the relieving force was equal to more than half the number under siege. Maps were faulty and there was no information available on the enemy's position in relation to the wadi and Tigris. February was spent reorganizing, retraining and waiting for reinforcements. Time was not, however, on their side. In mid-March, when the snows melt in the northern highlands of the Zagros mountains, the flood season begins. With the Tigris in full flood, the Turks could easily cut the embankments or bunds containing it, thus inundating the whole area and making an advance impossible. So the second attempt to relieve the garrison had to be carried out before 15 March.

By this time the War Office had taken over the management of the Mesopotamian campaign from the Indian government. The War Office approved a plan by General Aylmer to attack with every man and gun he had. Reinforcements were route marched in or brought upriver by steamer while training and reorganization were carried on at the front. Frequent reconnaissance of both banks was carried out by land and air.

The Turks also reinforced and built two new lines of defence. Their defences covered both banks but the main ones were on the northern bank. Their lines consisted of terrain honeycombed with trenches and pits for machine guns. To attack these over flat bare ground bordered on the suicidal, so General Aylmer decided to carry out a turning movement. This was not possible on the north bank because of the marshes surrounding the Turkish positions but the south was still passable. The assault was to be against the Es Sinn line, the nearest of the Turkish positions to Kut.

In the first week of March the weather took a turn for the worse. Heavy rain once again turned the ground into a quagmire impassable for transport animals or guns. By 7 March the rain had stopped and the ground dried out sufficiently for an attack. General Younghusband, assisted by naval gunboats, held the enemy to his line north of the river. The remainder of the force under Generals Keary and Kemball were to advance by night across the 14 miles of bare ground to reach the Turkish lines on the south bank by morning. The plan was for Kemball's column to attack from the south at daybreak while Keary's column was to attack from the east.

Guided only by the stars, 20,000 men with transport, ambulances and guns marched steadily through the darkness. The only noise was the creak of a wheel or the clink of a stirrup. The column was two miles long and 600 yards wide. Keary's men succeeded in arriving as planned, taking the Turks by surprise. However, Kemball's column was an hour late and the attack did not happen for a further three hours. This delay allowed the enemy time to prepare for battle and the relief force was defeated once again. After a day of heavy fighting the water supply was running short and the troops were exhausted. The enemy position had not changed. General Aylmer was forced to withdraw.

There was naturally bitter disappointment in Kut at the failure of the second attempt to relieve them. February had come and gone and floods would soon increase the difficulty of further attacks. The situation had deteriorated badly in the garrison. Enemy bombing raids from the air caused much destruction and the shelling was also heavier than before. There were sharp frosts but fuel was running out. The lack of any vegetables meant that many began to suffer from scurvy. Attempts to grow some greens resulted in a few radishes becoming available and a substitute for spinach was found in the shape of a local dandelion leaf, but it was all too little too late. The reduced rations the men were on were barely enough to keep body and soul together. Some of those besieged had been in the siege at Ladysmith during the Boer War 16 years earlier and declared this to be far worse. They did get more news than those at Ladysmith. Letters, newspapers and telegrams were dropped by air but they often fell in the river or in the Turkish trenches.

Supplies of food were dropped by air, but these were limited as the primitive aircraft could only carry small quantities and were unable to drop them with any accuracy. Some fishing was also possible though dangerous, but still not enough to feed the thousands of people imprisoned in the town.

After the failure of 8 March, Major-General Sir George Gorringe replaced General Aylmer whom the War Office had suspended. Gorringe had a great deal of experience of fighting in Mesopotamia. New troops, including the thirteenth division, were brought in from Basra. Another attack was to take place as soon as possible, not least because General Townshend's 84 days would end in mid-April. Minor skirmishes occurred on the south bank during which some prisoners were taken and some trenches captured. However, rain stopped play and on 15 March, as expected, a heavy snow flood drove the British troops back.

Because of the flooding there was only one possible method of attack and that was unlikely to succeed. The plan was to take the river route and force the Turks out of their entrenchments on the north bank. Preparations for the attack included raising embankments to prevent flooding, while the seventh division, under heavy fire and in flooded territory, dug trenches taking the British line to within 150 yards of the Turks.

The strategy was similar to that of the previous attempt in that the third division went forward on the south bank to cooperate with the main thrust of the attack by the thirteenth division under General Maude. He was the general who later signed the proclamation published in the *Basra Times*. Three of the Turkish positions fell but there were at least three more. The last being at Es Sinn line was heavily defended and the river was still rising. The attack had to be carried out before the water got any higher, which would allow the Turks to open the embankments and flood the whole area north and south of the river. General Gorringe decided to try a night attack that same night with the element of surprise on his side.

Sir Percy Lake, commander-in-chief of the British forces in

Mesopotamia from January to August 1916 described what happened.

> After nightfall a heavy bombardment was directed on the Falahiyah position from 7.15 p.m. to 7.30 p.m., after which the 13th division assaulted and captured a series of deep trenches in several lines. The position was stubbornly held by about three battalions of Turks, but by 9.30 p.m. it was completely in our hands and consolidated.

Having taken the fourth Turkish position the British were now only 20 miles from Kut. The fifth position at Sanna'iyat was three miles ahead. The seventh division now took over from the exhausted thirteenth division to attack at dawn. The troops again marched at night but trenches crisscrossed the ground, making the going very difficult in the dark. Dawn found them still almost two miles from the Turkish entrenchments at Sanna'iyat. This meant advancing under fire with no cover. The terrain was as flat as a billiard table. The order was given to 'advance where the bullets are thickest'. Despite the impossibility of the situation the advance went ahead born of the determination to save Kut. Inevitably, the assault failed. By the time the first line had advanced within 300 yards of the Turkish trenches they had suffered over 500 casualties.

Severe disappointment set in at the failure of this attack. But the British were no less determined; Kut had to be saved. The river had continued to rise all the while, reaching its highest point of the year on 6 April. As a result there was extensive flooding worsened by a change in wind direction. It was now blowing from the north pushing the waters of the marshes southwards across the river onto the British positions. A delay in starting another attack could not be avoided as it was imperative to protect the positions from flooding as well as keeping open a route for their advance.

Eventually, by 8 and 9 April the ground was thought to be dry enough for a further attempt. It fell to the thirteenth division to lead the assault. The Turks counterattacked with far greater numbers and drove the troops back.

There were now only nine days left of General Townshend's 84. The garrison was on extremely tight rations. The men were allowed 7oz of meal and some horsemeat each day. This last, the Indian troops refused to eat for religious reasons, despite having a dispensation from their spiritual leaders to do so. The grain store was completely empty and the stock of meal was diminishing fast, so the ration was cut to 5 oz of meal. Unless the relief force broke through the Turkish lines very soon they would have to surrender or die of starvation. Every animal in the garrison was eventually slaughtered. The last to go was a mule that had served in three Indian campaigns on the frontier and wore the ribbons awarded for these around its neck. The butchers refused to kill it and sent it back twice, but starvation overcame finer feelings.

Fighting their way out was not a viable option for several reasons. They were heavily outnumbered and even supposing that they could get out and break through the surrounding Turkish entrenchments and fight on another 20 miles with no transport and very little ammunition, it would mean leaving sick and wounded men and stores behind in the hands of the Turks. So another attempt at rescue had to be made.

The next attempt to relieve the garrison was led by the seventh division from the trenches in front of the Turkish position at Sanna'iyat. The thirteenth division was kept in reserve while the third division under General Keary moved forward south of the river to set up communications. The plan was to capture the Turkish entrenchments at Beit Aiessa first. This position gave the Turks control of the embankments and the ability to flood the area by cutting them. A flood would prevent any further progress. The advance began on 12 April. For four days the troops struggled forward on meagre rations. Fighting all the way, they captured some entrenchments. On the night of 16 April they were ready for the assault. After advancing under cover of heavy fire they reached the Turkish trenches early on 17 April. When the artillery had ceased firing the men leapt into the trenches and bayoneted the Turkish troops. Beit Aiessa was taken. There were almost 300 dead Turks in the trenches and 180 prisoners were taken.

The second phase of the assault took place the following day. This was the advance to Sinn Aftar close to where General Aylmer had attacked in January. The thirteenth division was detailed to replace the third after dark in readiness for the strike. However, before nightfall the Turkish artillery began to bombard Beit Aiessa. They established a barrage to the rear of the entrenchments. The division was forced back and lost control of the embankments. Fighting continued throughout the night. After the initial retreat the division held its ground and at dawn the Turks withdrew. They lost almost 5000 men. The Turks were once more in control of the flood defences and the attack on Sinn Aftar had failed despite further skirmishes and the consolidation of some advance positions.

General Townshend's 84 days were now up. The garrison was on the verge of starvation. A desperate attempt was made to storm the position on the north bank that they had already failed to take twice. The seventh division received orders to attack on 20 April. Once again the weather turned nasty. The wind went round to the north so that marsh water flooded the trenches and ground. This is how one man who was there described the scene.

> Yesterday afternoon we had a waterspout, a hailstorm and a hurricane. The spray was leaping four feet high in the Tigris on our left, and on our right the Suwaikieh marsh threatened to come in and join the river and flood our camp. At about sunset it broke into our forward trenches and the Turkish position facing them, a wave of water coming over the bund like a wall, swamping kit, rations

> and entrenching tools. Some of the brigade on our right had to swim.

By the following day there was some dry ground but it was a narrow strip about 300 yards wide. There had also been some bombardment of the enemy so the assault was renewed. But it was hopeless. The Turkish position, surrounded by marsh and water on two sides and with only a narrow area for an advance to take place, was virtually impregnable. There was room for only one brigade. The men moved forward to attack the entrenchments under cover of artillery fire and machine guns from both banks. The Turks were able to concentrate their shells and send in masses of troops to repel the attack. The assault was quickly defeated with the loss of 1300 men.

During the last week of the siege the death toll in the garrison was 8 British and 21 Indians per day. When the end finally came the starving survivors were too weak to carry their own kit. Some Arabs in the town, driven by hunger, escaped by swimming down the river in the night, but many were shot by the Turks. Yet, the men and the townspeople still hoped, certain that the army would win through; so many times they had watched the assaults taking place with high hopes only to have them dashed.

Despite all these repeated attempts to save Kut, and the incredible determination of the British forces, the Turkish resistance had not been overcome; the weather as much as the enemy had defeated the Tigris Corps. In the wet and mud, rifle breeches jammed so soldiers were left tearing at them with their teeth, panting, sobbing and choking with tears in their eyes through the sheer exasperation of being unable to return the enemy's fire. Another problem for the British troops was the poor organization, equipment and provisions that supported them. They lacked heavy guns. There were not enough river steamers to ensure food supplies and in the early part of the struggle for Kut the medical arrangements were lamentable. The force in Mesopotamia was larger than had been envisaged and so the sheer weight of numbers overwhelmed the staff and facilities available.

A commission set up to enquire into the medical arrangements found that there were only two motor ambulances and some ox-drawn carts. There were no hospital ships. Two steamers, the *Blosse Lynch* and *Mosul* were pressed into service at the last minute and there was no time for them to be fitted out properly. The commission summed up the situation like this:

> The number of wounded at Ctesiphon was 3852 and the accommodation, such as it was, which these two steamers afforded was insufficient for a fraction of that number. … Wounds which required dressing and redressing were not attended to, and the condition of many of the patients who travelled by these steamers was, when they reached Basra deplorable. There the wounds of many were found to be in a septic condition and in urgent need of redressing. In some cases bed sores had developed, more than one patient arrived soaked in faeces, and urine, in a few cases wounds were found to contain maggots.

Major Carter was a medical officer who disclosed the failure of medical provision for the troops in Mesopotamia. He described his first sight of one of the convoys bringing the wounded into Basra from the defeat at Ctesiphon. His description was typical of medical provision throughout the campaign to relieve Kut.

> The stench when she was close was quite definite, and I found that what I mistook for ropes were stalactites of dried human faeces. … Then we found a mass of men huddled up anyhow – some with blankets and some without. They were lying in a pool of dysentery about 30 feet square.

The ship described was the *Mejidieh* on which my grandfather and Captain Cowley had served in the early part of the war. It was a steel paddle steamer built in 1882 by Rennie's of Greenwich, the same company where William had trained. It was 210 feet in length with a four-cylinder 150-horsepower engine. After the commission's report, medical provision was improved.

The commission came into being as a result of the action taken by Admiral Wemyss and his intelligence officer, Aubrey Herbert. Admiral Wemyss had come from the rout at Gallipoli to become commander in chief of navy operations in Mesopotamia. He and Aubrey Herbert were horrified at the conditions the wounded were forced to suffer. Wemyss sent a telegram to the secretary of state for India but then discovered it had gone directly to India first, for censoring. The two men were sure that the Indian authorities would suppress the truth so they decided that Herbert should take a ship to India where without landing he would immediately board the next steamer bound for England to tell the story. This led to a debate in the House of Commons and the setting up of the commission and its report. For his part, Wemyss took the story in person to the viceroy at Simla. After this, affairs were managed much better.

Following the failure of all attempts to relieve Kut, another commission was set up to look into the reasons. This commission found that those responsible for the organization of the campaign made significant errors and lacked the will to assist the troops on the ground. It condemned the advance on Baghdad as a blunder due to over optimism on the part of Sir John Nixon who was the overall military commander. General Townshend had already lost 4500 men before he was besieged. In the garrison a further 3800 died during the siege. Besides 9000 men taken prisoner, 23,000 were killed or wounded in the rescue attempts, nearly twice the number they were attempting to rescue. There was a failure to look after the needs of the troops. The Indian army was said to be unable to cope with the management of the war. This was due partly to the fact that serious spending cuts had reduced its capabilities; it was barely able to keep order internally and carry out frontier expeditions, let alone run a campaign overseas. In addition, many of its fighting men were engaged in other theatres of the war. As well as Sir John Nixon, the blame lay at the feet of the British government in India in the persons, among others, of the viceroy Lord Hardinge and the commander-in-chief Sir Beauchamp Duff. The Cabinet war committee also had its share of blame.

Sir George Buchanan noted the chaos that reigned in Basra where stores, equipment, ammunition and weapons arrived faster than they could be sent upriver to the fighting units. Storage space was limited and things were piled high in a higgledy-piggledy mess. Ships were lined up along the Shatt al-Arab waiting to come in and unload their vital cargoes in the dock.

While the different attempts were being made to relieve Kut in 1916 the navy and air services did all they could to try to delay the surrender of the garrison. The Royal Flying Corps and Royal Naval Air Service had dropped fishing nets, medicines and as many supplies as they could carry, although this was necessarily a very small quantity. The enemy had faster aircraft with more fighting power so it was an operation fraught with danger and there were some losses.

When all attempts to relieve Kut had failed, the navy determined to send a ship with a cargo of food in an attempt to run the blockade. This would give more time to the army to launch further assaults. The ship had to steam up 20 miles of meandering river against a strong flood with enemy forces on either side. Speed and secrecy were of the essence. One fast running steamer might just get through at night. The ship was going to carry enough supplies to feed the garrison for three weeks. The ship chosen was the *Julnar.*

5

In the Garrison

Ah with the Grape my fading life provide,
And wash my Body whence the life has died,
And in a Winding-sheet of Vine-leaf wrapt,
So bury me by some sweet Garden-side
(*Rubáiyát of Omar Khayyám*, verse 67)

It was night time in Kut. All in the garrison were sleeping but Robert could not. His eyes, grey as the cloudy Hampshire skies, were drooping with tiredness but his mind would not settle. Thoughts whirled round and round like autumn leaves. Yet it had been a good day for Robert. In the morning he had found a piece of string that he could tie round his waist to keep his shorts up. He thought about how upset his mother would be if she could see him now. She had always been concerned that he was too thin. 'Eat up, boy; you're just a streak of nothing. We got to put some flesh on those bones.'

And he had tucked into her good wholesome farmhouse cooking. As he lay on his bed he licked his lips at the thought of her game pies made from pheasant or rabbit shot on the farm – piles of home-grown fluffy potatoes, oozing golden butter from their own cows, blackberry and apple crumble with rich vanilla-fragrant custard. He moaned with pleasure at the thought, and the straw he was lying on rustled as he wriggled. All her hard work had come to nothing; even he could see that he was a walking skeleton now. Funny thing was it did not seem odd here where no one had enough to eat. Fishing brought in very little food for such a large number of men and was dangerous, for Turkish snipers were able to pick off the unwary who wandered by the river. Rats were there for the taking but not much to keep body and soul together. He thought back to what had made it a good day only to find that it all had to do with food.

The sergeant in charge of their mess woke them as usual at first light. Breakfast had been ordinary the usual single piece of flat dry bread and some water with a bit of tea in it, but then he had found his string belt to make up for that. They had worked all morning as usual. They did their regular cleaning of the mess, raking over the straw for bedding, emptying the foul-smelling buckets that served as latrines, fetching fresh water and washing laundry. Then they had to break down, clean and oil their rifles and any other guns so as to be always ready for battle. After that, his party had been detailed to break up more door and window frames for firewood. It had been so cold that wood was now very hard to come by. Even if they could have got out of the town without being shot by the Turks there was nothing but swamp for miles. Lunch was a surprise. Someone had the bright idea of shooting some of the starling-like birds that were all over the place. If you had not had much meat for a while they tasted quite good – not much on them, mind. There were no vegetables left, of course, so there was only rice and flat bread with it. Some of the men tried out a plant that grew like a weed all round the town. It was dark green, so they thought it might be like spinach. It was not. It tasted very bitter but it did not make them ill. Then in the afternoon the sergeant called them all together.

'Now then, Basra Mess. We've all been pretty hungry. Some men are very ill, but General Townshend has found some new supplies. Seems the Arabs here have been holding out on us, so tonight's going to be a bit of a feast, celebration like. After that we are back on the same old rations. This new food store just means we can hold out longer. Give the Tigris Corps more chance to reach us and defeat the beastly Turks.'

The people of Kut had thrown in their lot with the British. Townshend had been all for throwing them out into the desert. He made no secret of it. He did not want the extra mouths to feed. But Sir Percy Cox had pointed out that the people would die in the desert, especially the women and children, so Townshend had to back down. The townspeople were given the choice, stay in the besieged town or take their chances with the Turks. Townshend took 20 prominent citizens hostage to ensure the good behaviour of the other Arabs. A war raged through their country that was not of their making and was not their fight. Robert often saw them in the streets. They were suffering from hunger too. The girls' eyes looked out beseechingly from above their yashmaks. Many of them had been killed as they went to the river to fetch water. Some of Robert's companions in the mess bought tobacco and tea from the men. These men ran appalling risks getting the stuff and were often killed as they sneaked out of Kut in the dead of night. They charged exorbitantly high prices but the soldiers needed their tobacco. A pound of Arab tobacco cost 48 rupees.

There was little love lost between the local Arabs and most British troops, and very little trust. The Arabs saw the British as another invader, no different from their current imperial rulers, the Turks. The British saw little sign of the noble Arab that T. E. Lawrence described working with his liberators. They referred to the Arabs as 'Budoos' calling them a 'subhuman sort of Caliban'.

The town was small, not much more than a village by Hampshire standards. The houses were low mud buildings with flat roofs; from a distance they looked like humps in the land. They huddled together giving narrow shady streets. In the searing desert heat of summer the coolness was a boon. In the cold winter the houses sheltered you from the biting winds. To Robert they were mysterious places he knew he would never enter; he would never know what kind of life these people led. Only the mosque stood out with its tall minaret. On the southern side there was a wool press and liquorice factory.

Indian field ambulance cart.

The market puzzled him. There seemed to be so little there, even at the beginning of the siege. Dates and flat bread seemed to be the staple diet. Goats and sheep bleated their way round the town. Robert had seen these being slaughtered so meat was important too. When they had first arrived in Kut the army had bought the animals and grain from the townspeople so as to control the food supply and ensure fair distribution. Every so often a group of townspeople would make their escape under cover of darkness, either swimming down the river or hanging onto goatskins. Turkish snipers killed many of them, others were taken as informants.

Robert had not minded being besieged to begin with. It was better than fighting and being in the trenches. They had fought their way up the Tigris – 400 miles in all. They ate and slept in the trenches in the heat of the day and the cold of the night, in rain, shine and bitter wind. Robert had felt claustrophobic not being able to see where he was. He was used to open spaces as he followed the horses pulling the plough or brought the cattle in for milking. The trenches were unbearably hot with flies descending in great clouds so that everyone's eyes and lips and every other bit of bare flesh was swarming with them The distress of it often drove men out into the line of fire just to get some respite.

Then they had got to that place with a big arch. There was nothing there, just the arch. What did they want to fight over it for? It was beyond Robert to fathom it out. He just knew he had to obey orders even if it meant dying for this old arch. The Turks seemed to want it as badly as the British. The firing was fierce all day. Shells burst all round him. He saw many brave friends lying lifeless in the mud. It was the bayonets that really troubled him. He went over the top with the best of them whooping and hollering to keep up courage. He got close to a young Turkish soldier, a boy his own age. Robert hesitated but the other man came at him with teeth bared and bayonet pointed straight at Robert's stomach. In a swift reflex action he sidestepped the charge and caught the Turk in the chest with his own bayonet. Robert felt sick when he remembered the gurgling sound the wounded man made as he fell. And so much blood frothing and bubbling out. 'That's the ticket,' yelled one of the old hands from Robert's division. In the end the order had been given to retreat and here they were back in Kut, which they had taken before.

At first everyone was very confident of a swift rescue. General Townshend had announced that a relief force, the Tigris Corps, was on its way. They had eaten a little more sparingly than usual but there had still been enough food served to keep everyone comfortable. Robert thought back to Christmas, it was celebrated with an excellent dinner once they had repulsed yet another attack by the Turks. It was just after the beginning of the siege. A month later their rations had been halved.

Here in Kut, they had rooms. They had to lie on the bare ground but at least there was a roof and walls to keep out the

A gun in the mud.

weather, and straw to keep warm in. The straw reminded Robert of the big barns at home where he had played as a boy. Later he had had his first kiss in that straw. Lucy Melhuish. What a looker. He wondered where she was now. He had not had a letter for months and did not know if his own letters had got to her. They had only been stepping out together for a short time when he was called up but he knew already he was in deep. He loved the sweet smell of her warm neck as he nuzzled it and the soft feel of her long black hair. One summer's evening holding hands he said to her 'You are my Lucy in silver, the silver light of moon.'

'Oh, Robbie, don't. You make me feel so … I don't know. Shy like and hot.' 'Hot like when we kiss?' asked Robert. But she only looked down and hid her eyes from him.

Robert wriggled and rustled about in his straw bed again. 'Shut up. Some of us want to get some shut eye,' a rough voice brought him back to the present. He lay still and the next thing he knew was that it was morning and the sergeant was shouting at them all to stand by their beds. He looked round at the room. The floor was of beaten earth. The walls were of mud or earth and so was the ceiling. The smell was awful. There were ten men sleeping in a tiny space in the clothes they had worn all day on straw that they used over and over again. At least the clothes protected you from the mosquitoes.

'Right, Basra Mess. We're on burial duty today. Get yourselves up to the grounds with your spades at the double,' announced the sergeant. The men all groaned as he left the building. Each mess in turn had to take on this duty and they all hated it. So many men were suffering from diseases caused by malnutrition – starvation, dysentery, scurvy, dehydration. And they were dying like flies. Every morning there was a fresh group of fifteen or so corpses. Today there were eight Englishmen and ten Indians to bury. Basra Mess spent most of the morning digging the graves and placing the bodies in them. Then the padre came and said a few words, the leaders of the Hindus and the Muslims also prayed and that was it.

When they had finished most of the men went off for a smoke but Robert did not smoke. He walked down to the stables where the animals were kept. He often went there; it made him feel in touch with home. He had always loved working with the animals. The horses and oxen here were feeling the siege as much as the men. They too were on half rations. The mules and camels seemed to cope better. They were hardier animals. Robert went up to his favourite horse, Esmerelda, talking to her and stroking her long chestnut neck. She put her nose into his hand, its velvety softness snuffling gently. 'I'm sorry. I've no food for you, old girl. Not even a single lump of sugar.' He scooped a handful of bran out of the feed bin and gave her that. Esmeralda belonged to Lieutenant McNeal who was also in the Royal Field Artillery, but was the envy of the whole garrison. She was a magnificent chestnut charger with the heart of a lion. Robert talked to each of the horses in turn and the mules. Simla was everyone's favourite mule. He was named after the Indian government's summer residence and had served the regiment well through three frontier campaigns. The medal ribbons round his neck testified to his stout courage. The oxen and the camels did not appeal to him so much. The camels especially seemed impossibly haughty and remote but Robert knew they could be vicious. He had seen them spitting and biting.

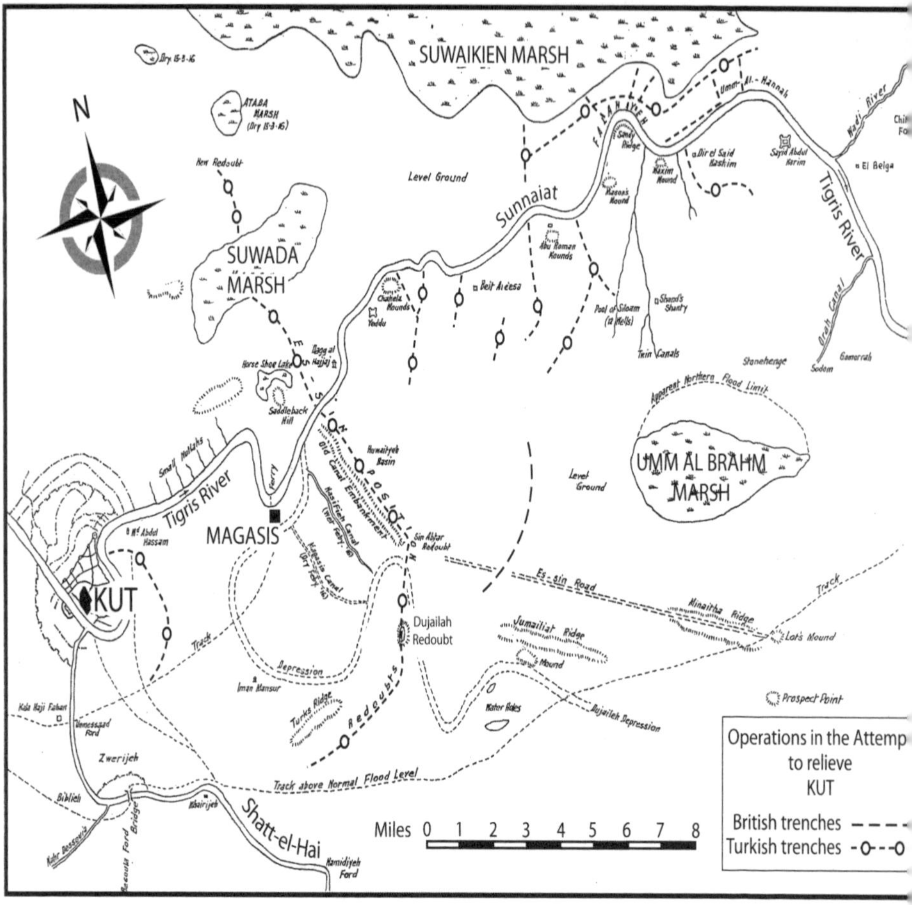

British and Turkish trenches.

The coolie who looked after the animals was there too. Robert thought he was Hindustani but he was not sure. They always greeted each other but conversation was difficult as the boy did not speak much English and Robert had not a word of the other's language. Robert talked and the coolie seemed to listen attentively, even sympathetically, uttering only an occasional 'Achay, Sahib.' Just then Lieutenant McNeal came in. 'Hello, you admiring my Esmerelda as usual. The boy here told me you'd taken a shine to her.' Robert stood to attention. 'Yessir, she is a beautiful horse, Sir.' McNeal had saved some of his meagre sugar ration and now fed it to Esmeralda, stroking her strong neck and talking to her in a low voice. Robert and he talked for a time about horses they had known. After a while Robert thought he had better rejoin his mess. The pain in his belly told him it was lunch time, after that they would be expected to work at cleaning the living quarters and servicing their guns.

The following day Robert's mess was on firing duty. Every day they tried to keep the Turks occupied to assist the Tigris Corps, which was fighting towards them. They kept up an aggressive presence both to frighten the enemy and keep up morale. Robert privately thought it was a pity they did not have as much food as they had ammunition but he went out there shooting alongside his companions. Even he could see that their guns were no match for the Turks who seemed to have the latest long range artillery. And the reconnaissance parties brought back no information.

They could not be sure exactly where the Turkish positions were. So they were firing at random. This time they were positioned just by the liquorice factory crossing over to it in the gunboat the *Sumana*. They all had to be as keen as mustard as General Townshend came down to see what the troops were doing. At his heels was his faithful fox terrier Spot, veteran of many of Townshend's campaigns. The general carried his usual volume on Napoleon's campaigns with him. He was rarely seen without it. The other men said that Napoleon was his hero and that he tried to run his campaigns along the same lines. They also said that he was a 'pompous old git who liked the sound of his own voice'. At home Townshend was a hero written up in all the newspapers but not in the eyes of the men. They wondered why he was not doing more to help the Tigris Corps instead of sitting tight and screaming 'get me out of here'.

While Spot ran in and out among the guns and the soldiers, he spoke to the men, 'Well done, Men, You're doing a fine job. We have to keep the Turks busy. Holding Kut is a positive contribution to the war effort. It makes a Turkish advance to command the rivers impossible. Maintaining the territory we have already won at the expense of much blood. Duty to empire, beloved king and country! Keeps 'em from making mischief elsewhere too!

Make this defence a glorious one! We've got to give the Tigris Corps time to reach us. I remember when I was besieged at Chitral,' but Robert and many others had stopped listening by now. Spot's antics chasing one of the local cats was far more interesting.

An aeroplane flew overhead, one of the air corps' regular attempts to get food and mail to the garrison. This time it was successful. Watching the nets full of supplies crash land Robert hoped there would be some letters among the boxes. He wished the planes could carry more, they could only carry 3000 pounds in weight, but the general and his staff had worked out that 5000 pounds each day was needed to feed the garrison. Much of what was dropped missed the mark and fell in the river where it was spoiled or it landed on the Turkish side. He knew it was difficult to make their drops accurately as they were under constant fire when they came over the town both from the ground and from Turkish planes. As soon as he was off duty Robert rushed to the post room to see if there was a letter for him.

As he walked away with his letter in his hand Robert felt guilty at the stab of disappointment he felt when he saw that it was from his father not Lucy. Still it was good to have news from home.

Dear Robert,

How are you? I trust this letter finds you well. Here on the farm your mother and I are very busy. All the young men have been taken to war. There is no one to do the work only us and some old timers that we have got in from retirement. I miss working with you, Son.

Your mother and I are very glad that you weren't sent to France. It seems the soldiers are dying in their thousands. A hell hole by all accounts.

That Bubbles of yours is doing well. He has turned out to be a good dog. He is a grand ratter but he does pine for you. He always sits by your chair and sleeps outside your bedroom. The horses miss you too. You always had a way with them. Have you got horses with you in Messpots?

We saw your friend Lucy Melhuish at church last Sunday. She's a lovely girl. Told us she is going to do some nursing. She is training at the hospital then she is going to the Western Front. She asked to be remembered to you and says she has written but has heard nothing. We told her we have not either.

Write soon, Son. We want to hear your news and know that you are well.

All love

Mum and Dad.

Robert was sorry to hear that none of his letters had got through but the mention of Lucy more than made up for it, especially to be told that she had written even if he never received it. He read and reread his letter several times that day and the next. He fretted at the thought of his Lucy being in the 'hell hole'. He thought about the last time they had seen each other. He walked her home after an evening's stroll by the river. As she turned to go into her house she suddenly looked back at him, 'You will come home Robert Gage, won't you? Be sure and come home to me.' Then she was gone.

A startling announcement wiped his personal worries from his mind. At supper that evening they had what amounted to a feast by Kut standards. By now they were only allowed seven ounces of meal or flour per person per day and very little meat. At this meal they had plenty of meat. This was followed by a pudding with dates and ginger. Robert had enjoyed it, so had most of the others; it was tasty compared with what they had been on. Then the sergeant told them,

'It's been decided. There is hardly any grain left and very little meal. The only meat we have is on the hoof. We have to start eating the animals we have with us if we are going to last. That dish tonight? That was ox. As fine a snack as I have ever had, bit chewy but wholesome.'

Robert was confident that they would be out of Kut before they ran out of oxen. He didn't think beyond filling his belly and ox was not so very different from beef. When they finished the oxen with no sign of rescue and started on the camels a shadow of doubt began to cross his mind. The camel meat was horrible. It had to be chewed for hours but it kept the men going – just. Then, as Robert feared, they ran out of camels. Only the horses and mules remained.

The Sergeant announced in the mess, 'I hope you all enjoyed tonight's tea – mule tongue in aspic. We've run out of camels.' He was interrupted by a shout from Robert.

'No. No. They can't do that.' There was a general rumble of horrified agreement.

'Bombardier 855315, attention.' Robert leaped to his feet.

'Now then, Gage, orders is orders. And who's going to stop them? You and who's army?' asked the Sergeant.

'I don't know. But I'm not eating that stuff.'

'You just did, laddie, and when your meal ration is cut to five ounces like they're planning from tomorrow you'll be glad of it.'

As soon as he could, Robert rushed to the stable to check that Esmerelda was still there. She whinnied in greeting as he went in. He leaned his forehead against her neck and was deeply sorry that he had a full stomach when he saw that the stall next to Simla's was empty. The coolie came up to Robert. For once language was not a problem. He put his hand on Robert's shoulder in a gesture of understanding.

Over the following days the butchers slaughtered every remaining animal, even Esmerelda. Robert never had the chance to say goodbye. He took a forlorn walk down to the stables where he met Lieutenant McNeal. 'My poor Esmeralda! She died in harness all right.' Robert could not speak.

Robert was thinner than ever and very weak. His bones stuck out so much that it now hurt him to lie on the straw. The others in his mess had taken to calling him 'Stick' though none of them had an ounce of flesh on their bodies either. Every one was desperately emaciated. Men often fainted on sentry duty now and increasing numbers of the Indian troops were shot for desertion as they tried to run away. Robert, along with some of the Indians, never let a piece of horse meat or mule flesh pass his lips. His eyes were huge and dark, sunk deep into their sockets.

Soon only Simla remained. Every time he was brought forward the men and the butchers objected that they couldn't do it. He was the regimental mascot for God's sake. He had been with them through thick and thin. But he was all that stood between them and starvation. Survival ruled the day and Simla made the ultimate sacrifice. Still Robert did not eat meat and with only five ounces of bread and four ounces of barley meal each day he soon became ill.

The day that the good news was announced, they carried Robert to the infirmary.

'Don't worry, mate,' they said to him. 'We just heard, the navy's sending us a ship full of provisions, medicines and all. We're going to be all right.'

GARRISON OF KUT: PERSONNEL AND RATION DETAILS

HEADQUARTERS
MAJOR-GEN. C. V. TOWNSHEND, GOC

16th Infantry Brigade, MAJ.-GEN. DELAMAIN	2nd Dorsets 66th Punjabis 104th Rifles 117th Mahrattas
17th Infantry Brigade, GEN. HOGHTON	Oxford and Bucks LI 22nd Punjabis 103rd Infantry 119th Infantry

18th Infantry Brigade, GEN. HAMILTON	2nd Norfolks 120th Infantry 110th Infantry 7th Rajputs
30th Infantry Brigade, MAJ.-GEN. MELLIS	2 Coys. Royal West Kents 3 Coys. 4th Hants TF 2/7th Ghurka Rifles 24th Punjabis 67th Punjabis 76th Punjabis

DIVISIONAL TROOPS

17th Coy., S. & M.
34th (Poona) Signalling Co.
Sirmoor Sappers (Imperial Service).
1 Squadron 7th Hariana Lancers.
48th Pioneers.
63rd, 76th, 82nd Batteries, RFA 18 guns, 18 pdr.
104th Battery, RGA 2 4" guns.
84th Battery, RGA 4 5" guns.
Volunteer Battery. 4 15 pdr. guns.
"S" Battery, RHA, left behind 2 14 pdr. guns.

Naval Detachment. 4 4.7" pdr. guns.

HMS *Samarra*: 2 3 pdr. guns; 1 13 pdr. gun.
Machine Gun Battery (6 guns).
Supply and Transport, including Jeypore Transport Train, Wireless, Royal Flying Corps, Depot and other details.

MEDICAL SERVICE

One British General Hospital.
One Indian General Hospital.
3 Field Ambulances.

Strength of garrison at beginning of siege		*Strength on surrender*
British officers	301	277
British rank and file	2851	2592

Indian officers	225	204
Indian rank and file	8230	6988
Indian followers	3530	3248
Total	15137	13309

Losses: Killed and died of wounds, 1025
Died of disease, and missing, 803
Arab population of Kut (?) 3700
Animals (horses and mules) before killing for food, 3000

COMPARISON OF RATIONS ISSUED IN KUT AT THE MIDDLE OF APRIL, 1916, WITH FULL SERVICE RATIONS

BRITISH

Normal Field Service	*In Kut*
Bread, 1¼ lb	4 oz (from 17 April)
Fresh meat, 1¼ lb	1¼–1½ (horse and mule)
Potatoes and vegetables, ½ lb	Nil (except ság)
Bacon, 3 oz (or butter 1½ oz twice a week)	Nil
Tea, 5/8 oz	Nil
Sugar, 3 oz	Nil
Salt, ½ oz	Nil
Jam, 4 oz	Nil
Cheese, 3 oz	Nil
Ginger, —	1/3 oz

INDIAN

Normal Field Service	*In Kut*
Atta (wheat meal), 1½ lb	4 oz (barley meal)
Ghi, 2 oz	½ oz
Dal, 4 oz	Nil
Meat, 4 oz	9 oz (horse)
Gur, 1 oz	Nil
Potatoes, 2 oz	Nil
Tea, 1/3 oz	Nil
Ginger, 1/3 oz	
Chillies, 1/6 oz	
Turmeric, 1/6 oz	1/8 oz
Garlic, 1/6 oz	
Salt, ½ oz	

6

Running the Blockade

One Moment in Annihilation's Waste,
One Moment, of the Well of Life to taste –
The stars are setting and the Caravan
Starts for the Dawn of Nothing –
Oh, make haste!

(*Rubáiyát of Omar Khayyám*, verse 38)

Piercing blue eyes glinted shrewdly at the horizon from a face leathered brown by sun, wind and desert sands and topped by smooth, sleek, jet black hair. His magnificent moustache was always immaculately curled and combed. Cowley handled both his ship and his men with the same confident air of command. He was a legend in the Euphrates and Tigris Steamship Company. It was said that he shot the last lion in Mesopotamia. The king of beasts had prowled throughout the region in previous centuries. With the acquisition of firearms the Arabs protected themselves from them so enthusiastically that lions became increasingly rare. The last lion to hunt along the banks of the Tigris and Euphrates rivers fell to Captain Cowley.

Cowley spoke Arabic like a native and fluent Turkish, a fact that earned him the respect of the local people. Some said he was an Arab. Any questions about his origins were always met with the enigmatic reply, 'Where I am now is where I come from. I know no other home.' Certainly, he never went back to England on leave as others did. Some said he dared not, for he was a

Lieutenant Commander C. H. Cowley.

wanted man there, but they could not say what his crime might have been. His name was whispered to be linked to quelling riots and capturing bandits or river pirates, but no one knew for sure.

That first trip together on the *Medjedieh* in Persia, William had been the newcomer. He was soon in awe of this man about whom everyone talked, to whom everyone deferred. When the crew did not understand his shaky Arabic, it was Cowley who mediated. William had a particularly difficult day with one agra-wallah. He had come upon him by chance searching through the sarangs' jackets, slipping his booty into his own pocket. 'Hey, you can't do that. Put it back this instant,' called William. The man refused at first but William insisted, 'You'll lose a day's pay for insubordination. Imshi, Imshi, go away.' At this the man grew angry, shouting, the veins in his forehead bulging. The other agra-wallahs and one of the sarangs held him back but he had a murderous glint in his eye.

That evening, with work done and the ship tied up alongside, William went for a stroll to stretch his legs in the cool of the evening. Leaning against a tree, listening to the clattering of the palm leaves, the whirring of crickets, the croaking frogs busy in the reeds and the occasional plop of a fish, he looked up at a sky studded with stars. He took out a slim silver box. He had bought it in Basra, one side was etched with a river scene not unlike the one he was idly gazing at now. There was a palm tree by a river, a late lazy dhow gliding by and a townscape of domes and temples beyond. On the back was an image of the Arch of Ctesiphon, the place that had seen so many empires and mighty rulers fall. He turned it over in his hand a few times then opened it and took out one of his flat Turkish cigarettes. He tapped the end of it against the Arch of Ctesiphon and then struck a match, filling the air with the spicy scent of tobacco as he inhaled deeply. Silent and swift, a shape appeared out of the shadows, with a razor sharp curved dagger (*khandjar*) in hand, but before he could get close to William another figure moved behind him. Cowley was recognizable only by the glow and aroma of the pipe always clenched between his teeth. A burst of gunfire roared past William's assailant who took to his heels through the night.

Preparations for this special mission on which they were now engaged had been continuing for several days. It was good that it was the old team working together with Cowley on the bridge and Reed in the engine room. When they had first sailed together four years earlier on the paddle steamer *Medjedieh*, Cowley had been the captain. On this venture they had put a naval officer, a lieutenant, in command, but the crew knew who the real leader was: Cowley knew that river better than he knew his own home, for he had spent more time there. Now they were back together on the *Julnar*. William was as usual in charge of the engines, a hot and sweaty job in a climate where the heat shimmered and hummed round your head. His face was permanently ruddy from the combined effects of sun and engines. The old *Medjedieh* seemed so outdated now compared with this ship. They had done the Turks a lot of damage between them on the *Medjedieh*.

When war broke out, the *Julnar* and several others, *Blosse Lynch*, *Miner*, *Shaitan*, *Salimi*, *Malamir*, *Louis Pelly* as well as the *Medjedieh* were pressed into service as hospital ships and troop carriers. He remembered how on one occasion there was heavy firing all day but with Cowley in command they continued to work delivering troops, ammunition and horses to wherever they were most needed. They went in under heavy fire and frequently fired back using the two big 18-pound guns mounted on the foredeck. It was a bitterly cold winter's day. As the evening sun sank into the sands stretching away on either side of the river they anchored near Basra. The canna-wallah had made their tiffin. Working all day at their stations, they had built up a thirst so they had a few pegs of whisky first. Then Cowley and William and the other officers sat down to their meal of the usual flat chapatti bread, rice and chicken. What William would have given for some steak and kidney pudding! Their mood was expanding with their waistlines when, with a flash, a shell from the Turkish guns crashed onto the table. William shot out of his seat as flames licked towards the deckhead. William doused the flames with water from the jug and turned to see if his captain and other officers were all right. Cowley had not moved and was just enjoying his last mouthful of food. Taking his cue from his captain William got his breath under control and sat down. 'Damned nuisance,' he said replacing his napkin on his lap and picking up his knife and fork again.

As neither of them was part of the official fighting force, the Turks had accused them of piracy. He laughed when he remembered that after the accusations they had taken to flying the Jolly Roger.

After several months leave in 1915 William had come back to join the *Julnar* in November that year. He had been aboard the *Julnar* for the first time in 1911, then again when travelling to the Godar Bridge to make repairs. Since its refit two years earlier it was state of the art, with its oil-fired boiler powering the triple expansion steam reciprocating engines. William had also had the job of towing it upriver to Mohammerah with the *Mejidieh* at the outbreak of war, so it was as if the two ships, like Cowley and him, were old friends.

Things had become serious; an assassination attempt had been made against Cowley and they began to feel threatened. He remembered taking General Younghusband upriver from Ali Gerby to Kut. After General Townshend's brief success at Ctesiphon, he seemed to have made a pretty mess of things. He and his troops had been driven back to Kut and were holed up there. Younghusband was part of the relieving force but in four months of fighting they had been unable to take Kut back. The *Julnar*, their little ship, now offered the last hope of saving the garrison at Kut. After transporting Younghusband upriver, the ship had been commissioned to ferry the wounded back to Basra.

William could still smell the stench of death and rotting flesh. The crew had stood by helpless with no equipment, not even blankets, to care for the poor devils.

It was while the ship was on transport duty that orders came to go to Amara and William learnt from Vice-Admiral Wemyss when he was on board that he intended to run the *Julnar* upriver to Kut with food for the besieged garrison.

Wemyss had recently arrived in Mesopotamia as Commander in Chief, East Indies after the horrors of Gallipoli. Now he was faced with managing another defeat. By his own assessment the chance of success for the enterprise that the army proposed was one in a hundred. William promptly volunteered for the job, whereupon Cowley offered to go too.

'Good man,' Wemyss had said. 'It'll take some persuading at HQ. They want navy men only. I'll do what I can.'

Later he had told them that they had been accepted by HQ as the best men for the job, although his intelligence officer, a fluent Turkish speaker, was refused.

'I told them with you two on board it increased our chances … you both know the river and the ship better than any of our chaps. Reed you will have to become a sub-lieutenant RNR.' Cowley already had RNR rank as a lieutenant-commander.

William was glad that they were now involved in a real job. They all knew it was hopeless, but the attempt had to be made. There were thousands of men trapped in Kut dying of starvation. Everyone knew that Kut had to be taken, that was why the army had fought so hard these four months. The military said it was the gateway to Baghdad. When they had asked for volunteers to run the blockade they had stipulated unmarried men only, for, as they put it, 'we are not in the business of deliberately making widows'.

Then they had removed all the native crews, with which he and Cowley were used to working, replacing them with British able-bodied seamen and they had given them Lieutenant Firman as captain over Cowley.

Lieutenant H. O. B. Firman.

He came with a reputation for courage and, like them, had volunteered for the duty. He had been in the navy for 14 years, including serving on HMS *Glory* in China. He already knew the Persian Gulf as he had expedition medals from both there and Somaliland. William was confident that Cowley knew every curve, bend, current and sandbank of the river. And Cowley knew William was the best engineer on the river. Speed was going to be essential and he knew how to get maximum power out of the *Julnar.* It was as familiar to him as the lines on his own hand.

Secrecy was essential, but William could not help feeling that they were going to have to manage without it. The little port of Amara where they had moored to complete preparations was full of spies, of men who would stand peering quietly from behind a palm tree then melt into the desert when you approached. It takes time and manpower to load 270 tons of supplies and there was precious little of either. Then there were the workmen detailed to prepare the ship for battle. The noise of their hammering travelled for miles across the flat, quiet landscape as they stripped the mahogany panelling from the inside of the *Julnar,* cut away the mast and top deck stanchions, and armour plated the bridge and engine rooms. William and Cowley fretted as they watched the engineer lieutenant Commander Cooke and Captain Burmester supervise the work the Royal Navy staff carried out, for they felt keenly the intrusion in their ship. Every morning bright-eyed children and curious adults would gather to watch bales of flour (*atta*) being placed between the armour and the ship's side to protect against bullets and shells, and bales of dried grass (*bhoosa*) loaded onto the deck as further protection against rifle fire.

Down in the engine room William supervised the cleaning of the tanks and boiler tubes. At least here he was still in charge. First the boilers had to be put out and allowed to cool down, and then every tube raked with a large cleaning brush. Finally, before the tubes were pressure tested each one was tested by rolling a ball bearing down it to detect any blockage. He took on a full load of fuel. He and Cowley checked the ship's telegraph, its bell ringing clearly to alert the engine room to orders from the bridge – full astern, slow and full steam ahead. They steamed up and down testing every faculty of the ship on which the lives of so many depended – steering gear, lights, and boiler.

Six days after their arrival in Amara, Cowley asked, 'Well, Reed, what do you think, are we ready? We must leave soon or the poor devils in the garrison will die of starvation before we get there. Any day now the river will start to dry up … the snow water has stopped coming down the mountains to feed it. We need to go while it's still in flood.'

'Right, I've checked everything and all the boiler tubes twice. She's running sweet as a nut, top hole.'

'That's it then. I'll tell Firman.'

'He seems to know his stuff this Firman,' commented William.

'Yes, well, He's got a name for himself, did some sterling work on the *Greenfly*. Gave the Turks a thing or two to think about,' replied Cowley.

The following day they left for Arab Village. William walked through his engine room with its gleaming brass pipework. At its heart were the magnificent brass pressure gauges. He took out his handkerchief to rub an imaginary smudge off them. The pistons pounded up and down with a satisfactory hiss. Every joint, shiny with grease, moved smoothly. 'Yep, she was in fine fettle this grand lady,' thought William. As they arrived alongside, he gave a few instructions to the stokers and then made his way up to the bridge.

'Oh, hello there, Reed,' said Lieutenant Firman. 'I was just telling Cowley here – I've been looking at the weather – fine of course at this time of year. And from the old almanac, it seems that tomorrow the moon won't be up until 1.52 a.m. so we can guarantee total darkness for our little venture. We'll stop here, then make a dash for it tomorrow at 6.45 p.m. It should be getting dark by then. Also it gives the military time to get distraction tactics organized. Your engine room ready for action?'

'Yes Sir, grand.'

'Good man, I know I can rely on you to get the most out of her. And Cowley … I'm confident you know this river better than anyone else. I'll be relying on you to keep a look out and navigate us through the deep channels. Keep us off the putty, old man.'

'Right ho, time for tiffin, I think. Are you two coming to the mess for a peg or two of whisky?' asked Cowley.

And with that they all went down and tried to relax for the evening.

The next day seemed interminable. The ship's chronometer, a timepiece by which you could set your heart, crawled slowly through the day. They could not leave until sunset. Everything was ready, they could only wait. William continued his check of the boiler and engine rooms. The ship was so low in the water it was remarkable that it was still afloat. At last the sun sank slowly away and it was time to go. Admiral Wemyss, his intelligence officer Aubrey Herbert and their staff came down to see the brave crew off and handed out a Gieves waistcoat to every man. They wished them a hushed farewell – there was no cheering – and the *Julnar* quietly slipped its ropes and set off in the twilight. The sandgrouse calling overhead, the sigh of the desert wind, the faint sound of the river and of the bagpipes of the nearby Black Watch floated across the evening air. Bathed in the glory of evening light, a filigree of masts and rigging against the sunset, the *Julnar* sailed off into the river.

As Firman had predicted, it was a night with no moon. Under cover of the gathering darkness the ship made its way upriver but could only reach a maximum speed of six knots. The river was in flood, which gave them plenty of draught but meant that the current was flowing against them. The armour plating and all the supplies also weighed them down. The ship passed quietly under the pontoon bridge at Falahiyah, but 15 minutes later the night sky was ablaze with bursts of light from hundreds of flares let off by the Turks. Soft popping sounds putt-putted across the river.

The sudden incandescence dazzled the eyes of the men on the *Julnar*. It was as if the Turks were sending a message – we know you are there, we are coming to get you.

The flares died away into the darkness and the *Julnar* continued quietly and peacefully on its way for another hour or so. The crew spoke only in whispers; noise carries so clearly across the water. The chug-chug of an engine is anonymous whereas speech is not. As it reached the enemy trenches at Sanna'iyat, *Julnar* was caught in a blast of gunfire as the Turks opened up on the ship with their rifles. It was soon riddled with bullet holes. The bullets penetrated the engine room and rained down among the engines. There came a loud shout from Petty Officer Cook, one of the stokers. William rushed to him at once. He had fallen on the deck and blood was oozing from a wound on his arm. 'Let me have a look at that,' he said and gave orders for Stoker Fox to fetch bandages. By now Cook was sitting up and the colour had returned to his face as they both realized that it was just a graze. William ordered him to be bandaged up and he went back to his post. All the while the bullets kept coming, pinging off the metal surfaces and ricocheting around the compartment or cutting big chips out of the metal work. Then Blanchard went down. His leg was very painful but again it was just a graze.

Once they had passed Sanna'iyat the firing became less persistent until there was just an occasional rattle of sniper fire. At Sinn Bank, where there was a heavy concentration of Turkish troops, they once again came under attack. This time it was from both rifles and artillery; guns and canon blazed. The rattle of rapid fire seemed never ending. With their ears ringing and hearts thumping, the men continued upstream as best they could.

Suddenly there was a big explosion right over the engine room. 'My God, that was close,' yelled William, as he realized that a piece of shell had landed in the settling debris. The explosion's shock wave had blown out the boiler. William ran to stop the oil flow before the fuel vaporized and the boiler exploded. 'Come on, men, get these oil burners started again or we won't be going anywhere … can't wait for the boiler to cool … got to risk it.' The stokers sweated for the next 20 minutes to relight the boiler. The ship kept going under its own momentum.

With the boiler working again the ship continued to make way towards Kut. The Turks had further attacks planned for them. As the *Julnar* approached Maqasis Fort, only about four miles from Kut, it was bombarded with massive and very accurate artillery fire. The armour plating proved useless. It was breached time and time again. Then a shell hit the bridge where Cowley, Firman and Seaman Williams were standing at their posts. Cowley was looking ahead, peering through the darkness, to see the way forward, guiding the ship through the narrow, navigable channel and round the bends of the river. The explosion threw all of them off their feet. As he picked himself up Cowley saw Firman lying in a pool of blood. He called to the seaman to fetch some first aid and went over to Firman, but it was too late. He had taken a direct hit. Cowley had some slight scratches on his hands and a stray bullet had grazed his back. Seaman Williams was cut about the face where splinters of flying wood chipped out by the shell had hit. Between them they kept the ship steering. 'You all right?' Cowley asked Seaman Williams. 'I am fine, thank you, Sir. Just got a bit bruised … you know … when I fell like. Oh and a couple of scratches. That was a bad one.'

'Yes, especially for Firman I'm afraid.'

The next shell hit the ship astern causing little damage. Then Cowley noticed the flames. 'Water,' he yelled, 'bring water and put out those God damned atta bags.' Petty Officer Rowbotham heard him shout. He could see the lethal rain of bullets peppering the upper deck but reckoned that he could make it. He ran out from under cover with buckets of water. He kept down as low as he could to avoid being hit. He hurled the water onto the fire. It hissed and sizzled into extinction. He had only just got his breath back when the atta was hit again. This time he was watching for it and did not need to be told. He rushed out with his bucket and doused the flames once more.

As they came up exactly level with the mud fort of Maqasis, still under heavy fire the ship shuddered violently to a halt. Cowley on the bridge nearly lost his footing again. William in his engine room also had trouble staying upright. He could hear the sound of metal scraping against the steel plates of the ship's hull. The shout went up all over the ship. 'What the hell's happening?' Several crew members ran to look over the side. The ship had stopped in mid-channel after striking a wire cable under the water. The current was strong on this sharp bend and with no headway on, the *Julnar*'s stern swung round so that it grounded in the soft mud that silted up on either side of the deep channels.

Cowley barked out his orders. 'Get down to the engine room. Tell them to put full steam on. We have to drive ourselves out of this.' William and his team in the engine room wound up the boilers to maximum pressure in response to the ringing telegraph. The propellers churned, mud and water flew up in all directions. Crew members standing on deck were saturated. Up on the bridge Cowley gave the order to Seaman Williams, 'Hard a-port. Hard a-starboard,' as they tried to zigzag their way out of their predicament. It was to no avail, the *Julnar* was stuck fast. It was midnight, more than five hours after they had set off with such hope. Cowley decided there was no way out and went to light a white signalling lamp. The Turkish bullets continued to rain down on the ship, one of them putting out the white lamp. Cowley then lit a red lamp.

On seeing the red lamp, the Turks ceased fire. Cowley put the telegraph to 'full steam ahead' then immediately to 'finish with engines'. The message rang down in the engine room and William turned the wheel to close the valve and cut off the flow of oil to the boiler. The engine, the heart of the ship, hissed slowly to a stop as its pistons pumped up and down – slow, slower, stop. At that moment Seaman Williams arrived down in the engine room: 'You're wanted on the bridge, Sir.' William went up with a slow, heavy tread. The first thing he saw was Firman's body. Then he noticed there were Turkish officers and men surrounding Cowley. 'Oh, my God, I had no idea.' 'Yes,' replied Cowley, 'crying shame. I've decided … we must surrender, Reed, old chap. We seem to be stuck fast … we can't possibly match their fire. So, to avoid any more deaths we have to give in.' He hit the helm with the flat of his hand as the Turks led him away. William was ordered to follow.

The Turks were soon swarming all over the ship. They called her 'the gift', telling Cowley that they had known for days that they were coming. They took most of the supplies for themselves but did allow some to go to the garrison. Meanwhile, they rounded up the full ship's company and took them across the river on a raft to a camp on the opposite bank. Here they were all allocated tents and those who were wounded were treated with iodine. Cowley and William were told to share a tent. By now it was three o'clock in the morning and both men fell into an exhausted sleep despite the hardness of the ground.

They were awoken by shouts. 'What are they saying?' William asked Cowley. 'They want us to go to another camp. We've got to get up.' The two men struggled out of their tent and joined the others for a small, bitter, black coffee and a lump of hard bread. When this was finished the Turks indicated, by pushing the men with their rifle butts, that they wanted them to start walking. Cowley told them that they didn't need to use such rough methods, for he spoke Turkish and could interpret. They did not seem to take any notice.

On seeing the *Julnar* captured, the garrison also surrendered. Their last hope was gone, dashed before their very eyes. That morning under the fluttering white flag, the men from Kut were detailed to join the captive crew. Cowley, William and the others were marched five miles to another camp, together with men from the garrison. They were in a terrible emaciated condition, hardly able to stand never mind walk five miles. As they left, William turned to take a last look at the *Julnar.* The Turks had taken it over and were already hoisting their flag. Listing forlornly to starboard, propellers damaged and funnel and upper deck scarred with bullet holes, the *Julnar* was a sad sight. With his vision blurred and unable to see the ground properly, William stubbed his toe on a rock. The sun was climbing higher and the temperature was rising. Many of the men from the garrison were unable to keep up; they were beaten with rifle butts. There was no water to drink.

At last they arrived at the new camp where Cowley and William were once more placed in the same tent. They sat cross-legged on the ground not knowing what to do or what was expected of them.

'Been a hell of a do, old man. I didn't keep her off the putty. Pity we didn't make it.'

'You can't blame yourself. Wonder when they put that wire there. Shame about Firman though.'

The two men sat in silence a while. Then William went over to Cowley, patted him on the shoulder, 'Smoke?' Cowley took a cigarette from the proffered silver case.

'I shouldn't let the Turks see that if I were you. They'll have that off you.'

'I'll hide it somewhere,' replied William as they both inhaled deeply and relaxed a little as the nicotine slipped into their bloodstream.

'I don't hold out much for my chances,' said Cowley. 'Always knew they'd get me somehow in the end.'

'You'll be fine, old chap.'

An hour went by and suddenly a soldier appeared at their tent flap. 'You, come with me,' he barked pointing at Cowley. Cowley got up and followed him, leaving William alone wondering what they wanted. When Cowley returned he leapt up, 'What happened, what did they want?' He looked anxiously at his friend whose face was white underneath its tan. 'The staff officer had me in for questioning. You know, what are we doing? What are the British plans? Oh, and they asked me where I come from. They're probably going to kill me.' He sat down worn out.

'They can't do that,' interrupted William. 'You're a British naval officer – they gave you RNR rank. There'd be repercussions. Didn't you tell them?'

'I didn't tell them anything, I don't know anything for heaven's sake. They don't like the fact that I speak Turkish, it makes them uncomfortable. It's the past catching up.'

'I suppose your mother's Armenian and they don't like the Armenians. They massacred a million of them.'

'And she lives in Baghdad, definitely not British. But it's all those skirmishes on the *Mejidieh*. Remember? It seems we annoyed the hell out of them.'

'Yes. I remember. We even flew the old skull and crossbones.'

'I've lived and worked with the Turks all my life but they're out of their depth at the moment.' He paused a while, then grinned, 'How about that time we had a shell land in the mess when we were eating our canna? You were quick off the mark then. Yes, they've taken Kut but at such a price; there's a long way to go to take control of the whole country. They're just stooges of the Germans. They were told they were fighting a jihad against the infidel Christians; their brothers the Arabs would fight alongside them. Poor dupes, they didn't take account of Arab resentment against 400 years of Turkish imperialism. Now their "brothers" are stabbing them in the back, the whole war is …' His words tailed off as a soldier appeared at our tent flap again. 'Stand up. Outside.' As they obeyed he stood aside and a staff officer stepped forward. 'We cannot allow two officers to be in one tent. You, Reed, will come with me.'

William was led to a tent a few yards away and told to stay there. He could not account for this sudden urgency to separate him from Cowley. They had no escape plan up their sleeves; both of them were unarmed and helpless. What could be in their captors' minds? It seemed to him that he sat there for hours on his own but it was in fact only a half hour. The same soldier came and told him he was to go with the other prisoners to Baghdad. They were setting off immediately. When William went outside it became obvious that Cowley was not going with them.

'May I go and say goodbye to Cowley?' he asked. 'No. Not permitted. We are waiting for horse. Lieutenant Cowley will ride.'

As William left he could see Cowley walking up and down in front of his tent. William stopped to wave to him but was urged on by a rifle butt between his shoulder blades. And so began a long, long journey.

7

Julnar of the Sea

Awake! for Morning in the Bowl of Night
Has flung the Stone that puts the stars to Flight:
And Lo! the Hunter of the East has caught
The Sultan's Turret in a Noose of Light.
(*Rubáiyát of Omar Khayyám*, verse 1)

A great sultan was so grieved at finding his wives were being unfaithful to him that he lost all trust in women. He had all his wives and their paramours executed but then had the problem of wanting a wife but not wanting to be betrayed again. His solution was to choose wives from among the women of his city and to execute them after the wedding night. One day his eye fell upon Scheherazade, the beautiful daughter of one of his vizirs. Her family were desolated and wept bitter tears but could not deny their sultan. She reassured them telling them that she had a plan to outwit the sultan. This made them even more afraid that she would do something that would bring shame on her family, but they had to go through with the wedding.

Now Scheherazade was not only beautiful but also very clever with a lively imagination. In her father's household she had often entertained the other women by telling them stories. It was this talent that was to become her weapon against the sultan. On their wedding night after all passion was spent Scheherazade began to tell a story. She wove her web of magic and fantasy to fascinate the sultan until the end of the night. But she did not finish the story. The sultan was then so keen to know the rest that he kept her alive for another night. And so she survived to see 1001 dawns. After this time the sultan had half forgotten his grievances against women and trusted her.

Scheherazade began this story on her 738th night of survival. She finished the story at dawn on the 756th day, starting a new one immediately that would keep her alive until the next day at least.

Once there was a great king whose land by the sea was called Ajam-land. He lived in a fine palace of towers and minarets at a place known as Khorosan. His throne was of beaten gold to show that he was truly the most magnificent and powerful ruler in the region. The floors of his palace were of marble so highly polished that they gleamed like the waters of a lake. His bed was made of ivory all set about with precious stones and in his gardens great fountains sparkled in the sunlight as peacocks fanned out their proud tail feathers. He had a hundred concubines and wives, all of great beauty, yet not one had blessed him with a child.

One day one of his mamelukes brought a wily merchant of the town to him with a slave girl for sale. King Shahriman sat on his throne of beaten gold and ordered the merchant to take off the woman's veil so that he might see if he spoke the truth when he praised her beauty. The merchant took the first veil off her head, revealing a thick and glossy black coiffure. The next veil he removed was from her face. King Shahriman gasped, for never had he seen such loveliness. Her eyes were great dark limpid pools as deep as the sea. Her skin was like the smoothest ivory, more precious than the ivory of his bed. Her pale pink lips curved with the promise of heavenly pleasures. The next veil fell from her shoulders so that King Shahriman could see her slender waist and full hips. Then the wily merchant released a pin from her hair so that it fell, tumbling down her back. She reached up her hands instinctively to catch it and the king could just make out the perfect rounds of her breasts move under the last and thinnest of veils, a whisper of gold silk. Then she stood quietly before the king, her midnight tresses reaching to her ankles that were circled with coral and pearls.

The merchant extolled her beauty as she stood waiting in all patience. Then the king said, 'She is indeed the loveliest creature I have ever seen. I am half in love with her already but how much is the price of such beauty?'

'And it please your Majesty, I paid 2000 dinars for her from another merchant since when I have travelled with her these three years and have spent a further 3000 gold pieces but such beauty is beyond price and only the very noblest of men should possess it. So I now offer her as a gift from me to you.'

King Shahriman thanked the merchant and asked 'Is she pure and untouched by man?' To which the merchant replied, 'She is as pure as the day she was born and knows not any man.' All the while the girl stood in silence.

The king told his mamelukes to take the slave girl to the harem where the tire women would care for her. He was so delighted with the gift that in return he made the merchant a gift of 10,000 ducats and a handsome robe of rich cloth. The slave girl was placed in a room with windows overlooking the sea, which whispered and foamed ceaselessly below and as far as the eye could see. That evening the king had her brought to his bed-chamber where he lay on his bed of ivory set about with precious stones. She seemed to glide across the watery silkiness of the marble floor as she approached. But still she said not a word. 'She has not been taught to be mannerly,' the king thought as he stood up to meet her. 'Yet she is fair.' He took her hand and drew her to him. He held her close pressing his lips to hers, which were sweeter than the morning dew. Then he drew her to his bed where he lay with her and found her, as the merchant had promised, to be a true virgin.

At this he rejoiced and asked her name but still she would not speak. Then he clapped his hands and ordered all manner of exquisite wines and dishes to be brought. With his own hands he served her wine in a silver goblet and fed her the juiciest figs with honey. Still she did not speak but each time his anger flared he looked upon her body and its beauty enthralled him once more. 'Truly,' he thought, 'this merchant was wise to have seen the value of his merchandise and to preserve its purity.' Then he forsook all his other concubines and wives staying always with her whose face was as lovely as the moon and sun.

He tried all kinds of music and entertainment to make her smile and speak. The best musicians in the land came to perform their most joyful pieces. The best actors in the country presented their funniest plays. The best athletes competed in the most exciting contests. Still she did not speak, though he constantly vowed his love to her; and still he did not know her name. Time passed and he said to her one day, 'you whose beauty has captivated me so much yet who will not speak, I pray that Allah (may his name be praised) grant me the gift of a child from you since I have forsaken all other women for love of you, give me a sign that you love me in return.'

At this she smiled, lifting her eyes to meet his for the first time. 'Your prayer has been answered, my lord, for I am already with child.' King Shahriman was overjoyed: her first words to him carried news of the thing he most wanted in the world. When he told her this she said, 'Had I not been with child I would not have spoken.' Tears of pure happiness welled in his eyes as he went and sat upon his throne of beaten gold. He called his vizir to him and by way of thanking Allah ordered him to distribute 100,000 dinars to the poor and needy of the city. There was much feasting and celebrating throughout Khorasan.

The king went to find his beloved and came upon her in her room where she sat by the open casement staring out across the sea with rivers of sorrow in her eyes. 'My precious one, all this time you have kept silent but I have loved you all the same. Tell me the cause of your unhappiness at this moment when we should be most joyful.'

'Know then that I have been the most wretched of beings,' she replied.

'How can you say so when I have lavished so much finery and love on you?'

'I must tell you that I am Julnar the seaborn. My father was of the kings of the main. He died leaving us his kingdom. Before we could become settled we were usurped by one of the other kings. I have a brother Salih and a mother who is also a woman of the sea. I quarrelled with my brother and swore that henceforth I would make my life in the kingdom of men. So I left our kingdom under the sea and came to the shore where an old man took me to his home. He tried to ravish me but I would have none of him and after I had hit him desire turned to hatred and he sold me to the merchant who brought me to you: you who are good and true and have preferred me above all his other women. If it had not been so I would have thrown myself from this window into the sea. But now that I am with child by you I cannot go back to that watery region. My family would treat me ill even if I told them how you have bought me for a high price in gold and set me above all other women. Yet I am sad. I long for my mother and even for my brother, the pious one with whom I quarrelled. Now that my time of delivery is near I need my mother by my side. The women of the land know nothing of the manner of delivery of the women of the sea and know nothing of our customs. If my family come here and see how it is with us they will be reconciled with me.'

'How can the people of the sea walk under the water without being wet?' asked King Shahriman.

'We walk with our heads high and our eyes open just as the people of the land do, under the seal of Solomon. And we look up and see the moon, stars and sun set in the firmament above as you do. I will tell my people how high you have placed me, how good and kind you are and they will be happy.' Then the king answered, 'Bring them here with my blessing.'

At this Julnar took some twigs of fragrant herbs and set them alight. She told the king to hide himself so that she could speak to her people before they saw him. Then she threw more wonderful herbs and spices on the fire and spoke some secret incantations. As the sea frothed with high-leaping waves that rushed at the land, a young man arose out of it and walked ashore, surrounded by all kinds of wonderful creatures from the deep. He was tall and strong with a face as handsome as Julnar's was beautiful. Behind him there followed an older woman, still beautiful though her hair was speckled with grey. She was attended by five maidens, her brother's daughters, and each one resembled Julnar so that where she had the moon and sun in her face they were like the twinkling stars in the night sky.

On seeing Julnar they embraced her and wept tears of joy. 'How could you leave us with no word of where you were for four long years? We have been out of our minds with worry. Not a morsel of food not a sip of drink has passed our lips with any pleasure, so frightened have we been for you.' Then she told them of how she had come out of the sea into the land of men who walk the earth only to be taken captive by an old man who would have ravished her but that she hit him and defended herself. She told them how in anger he had sold her to a wily merchant who had then sold her to the king called Shahriman for a high price in gold. She told how good the king was and how true, how much he loved her, showering her with rich clothes and jewellery and treating her with great honour, how he had forsaken all other women to be only with her.

'Allah be praised that he has reunited us,' said her brother Salih. 'Now you must rise up and come back with us to our country beneath the sea.' On hearing this, the king, hiding in the closet, was near to fainting with fear that he would lose his beautiful and beloved Julnar. But she answered, 'Oh my brother you must know that the mortal who has bought me is the king of this country. He is wise and good as well as powerful and wealthy. He has treated me fair and would die for love of me if I were to leave him. I think too that I should die without him for I love him as truly as he loves me. And moreover, I am with child by him. Praise be to Allah who has made me the daughter of the kings of the sea and given me for husband the mightiest of kings of the land. I pray now that I shall bear him a son who shall inherit all this great sovereignty.'

When her mother and brother and cousins heard this they were chilled to the bone saying, 'You know how much we love you and how dear you are to each and every one of us. Come now; leave this land of earth and mortals. Return to our watery kingdom beneath the waves and we shall live in all ease and harmony.' But she would not. 'I cannot go with you and leave my sovereign lord who has done me so much honour and I am in all ease and harmony here.'

When he heard Julnar speak this way the king was overjoyed and his love for her increased a hundredfold. Meanwhile, Julnar clapped her hands and ordered her women to bring out all kinds of fruit and sweetmeats and delicate little dishes for her family to feast on. As they were enjoying the delicious spread they said to Julnar that they were still strangers to her king and would like to meet him so that they could share bread and salt with him. They became angry, breathing fire from their mouths and terrifying the king out of his wits. Julnar soothed them and went to the closet. She opened the door and brought the king into the room. 'Oh, my lord, did you see and hear how I praised you to my kinsfolk and swore that I would stand by you even though they want me to return with them to their watery kingdom?'

'I most certainly did,' replied Shahriman. 'And I love you all the more for that.'

'I could not do otherwise after all the love and kindness you have shown me. And now for courtesy you must come and meet them. They too now love you by reason of the great praises I have sung you and the honour and love you have given me.'

Then the king went to greet Julnar's mother, brother and five cousins and he sat and ate with them. They stayed 30 days in all but at the end of that time sought out the king and queen to tell them that they must go home.

Some time later Julnar came to her time for delivery. She bore a son so beautiful that it was as though the moon shone in his face. The king and queen held a great festival in the city and the feasting and jollity went on for seven days and seven nights. On the seventh day Julnar's mother Farashah came from the sea bringing Salih and the five cousins whose beauty twinkled like the stars in the night sky. Only when they came did the king and queen decide on a name for the baby, wanting his kinsfolk from under the sea to help in naming him. Thus then the son of Julnar the seaborn and of King Shahriman became known as Badr Basim. Salih was so delighted with his newborn nephew that he took him in his arms. He walked through the palace, past the throne of beaten gold, through the gardens where the fountains sparkled and peacocks strutted and on down to the shore. Then he walked through the foaming waves and on into the deep, carrying the baby with him all the while.

Then the king became very afraid. He began to weep and wail at the loss of his first born, his only son. Julnar reassured him saying, 'You know that Salih, my brother loves me. And he knows that I love my son. He will not let any harm come to him. He will bring him back safe to my arms. Inshallah – god willing' And so it was. After an hour Salih reappeared from the salt waves still carrying the infant Badr Basim who was gurgling and waving his tiny fists. The child's face shone with the beauty of the moon and Salih went to the king and said to him, 'You were afraid that your son might drown were you not?' The king nodded his head. Then Salih replied, 'I took him down to our watery kingdom where we placed a special powder on his eyelids and we spoke over him the words from the seal of Solomon as we do for all newborn babes in our world. This powder and these words will protect him from drowning or coming to any harm in the watery regions of the world. For, as you walk on land, so we walk in the water.' Then he took a casket out of his pocket and gave it to the king. 'King of the age this is a gift from us to you, a symbol of the love that unites us all as one. These jewels are plentiful in our watery kingdom. Enjoy them' When the king saw the jewels he was delighted. Just one of them was worth the value of his realm, so he thanked Salih with all his heart.

The people from the sea stayed 40 days and 40 nights with King Shahriman and Queen Julnar. At the end of that time they went to the king to take their leave. 'We were born to live in the kingdom beneath the waves. We miss our watery regions and the salt sea. Though we love you both and hate to leave you we must return from whence we came.' So the king and queen wept with her kinsfolk at parting but they promised to return for a visit every few days. They went down to the shoreline where the merman and merwomen walked through the foaming waves and on into the deep.

Badr Basim grew up surrounded by the love of his family. His uncle and his grandmother from the watery kingdom beneath the sea visited as promised. He became the most handsome youth in the kingdom and all praised his sparkling eyes and fine figure. He grew in knowledge too, learning writing, the Koran, history, syntax, lexicography, archery, spearplay and horsemanship as well as all other things suitable to a king. When Badr Basim was 16 years of age the king called his grand vizir and his emirs and the chief officers of state to him and made them swear an oath that Badr Basim would become king after Shahriman. This they were happy to do since King Shahriman had been a good sovereign who did everything for the benefit of his people.

The following day King Shahriman went out into the city on horseback with all his emirs and grandees and his son Badr Basim. As they came back towards the palace Shahriman dismounted and so did all the grandees and emirs. Between them they carried the saddle cloth of honour to Badr Basim and held it in front of him as he rode back into the palace. Here they seated him on the throne of kingship, the throne of beaten gold and all bowed before him. Then from his throne of beaten gold Badr Basim began to mete out justice as he had seen his father do. The unjust were punished and the good men rewarded. He continued this way until noon. Then he went to see his mother, Julnar the seaborn wearing the crown on his head. She kissed him for sheer joy. He rested with her until mid-afternoon when he rode out once again with his father and all the men of the court to the maidan where they played at arms until evening. He returned preceded by all his retinue. Thus was the pattern of his days was set and he was revered above all kings for his glory and valour and his just dealings with his subjects.

Soon after this, the old king was taken ill. The fluttering of his once stout heart warned him that he did not have long to live. Julnar and Badr Basim were at his bedside night and day. Then he called his vizir, his emirs and all the grandees of the kingdom to him. He made them swear another oath of allegiance to Badr Basim to secure his succession to the throne. Then at peace with the world he said his farewells to Badr Basim and at the end kissed Julnar for the last time.

Julnar wept bitter tears with her son Badr Basim and there was great sorrowing and mourning throughout the city for the whole month. At the end of this time her brother Salih came out of the sea to comfort her. He said to her, 'Although you have lost the finest king that ever lived in the world of men who walk the earth, you have his son. This handsome youth has the heart of a lion, and the wisdom of Solomon in meting out justice. He will be a worthy successor to his father and will bring honour to the throne of beaten gold. Your place is beside him now.'

The vizir and the grandees went to Badr Basim and said to him that the period of mourning must now end. They told him that it would be effeminate for him to continue to grieve any longer. Then they took him to the *hammam*. When he came out of the baths refreshed they handed him new rich robes of cloth of gold all embroidered with precious jewels and placed on his head a golden crown. King Badr Basim then went and sat on the throne of beaten gold and spent the remainder of the day dealing with the affairs of the people in all the fairness and justice that he had learnt from his father. And so his life continued for more than a year.

Salih came to visit his sister where she was eating and resting with Badr Basim. Julnar invited him to join them and after a while he noticed that Badr Basim was sleeping. He seized his chance to speak to Julnar of him saying, 'Your son has now come of age to be married and I being afraid that some accident happen and he should die and leave no son would like to marry him to one of the princesses of the sea who would match him in wealth and beauty.'

'Name them for me and I will think on it.' So Salih named more than a hundred maidens from the watery kingdom beneath the waves. Soon he stopped and, noticing his sister's look, said 'Julnar, I have named more than a hundred maidens, all of whom you know. I can see that not one of them meets with your approval. There is one more I can mention but I am afraid Badr Basim may hear us, is he really asleep?'

Julnar checked on her son but the young king seemed to be deep asleep. So she told her brother to continue. 'Know then that there is one other who is worthy of him but I am afraid that he may fall in love just on hearing her name. She is the mermaid of mermaids and surpasses all others in her beauty and grace.' All this time, Badr Basim was only feigning sleep and heard every word his uncle spoke. 'Love at first sight is a dangerous thing and may lead your son into danger. This mermaid is the Princess Jauharah, daughter of the King Samandal. She walks with the grace of a gazelle and her face is all perfect radiance.' Julnar replied, 'Only she is worthy of my son.' 'But you must wait, my sister. Her father is of a violent temper. I will approach him first to ask for the Princess's hand.'

Hearing these words Badr Basim did indeed fall half in love with the Princess Jauharah. He began to dream of her and his heart became enflamed with passion for her. He was drowning in a sea that had no bottom and no shore. He could not keep his feelings to himself and soon his uncle became aware that he was burning for this girl he had never seen. Salih then wanted to take Badr Basim to Julnar and ask her permission to allow him to go with Salih to the realm of King Samandal, but Badr Basim would not. 'If I ask my mother she will forbid it for fear of mortal danger that would leave the state without a king. No, take me with you, I implore you and we will tell her later.' Salih took from his finger a seal ring engraved with the names of Allah the Most High, and gave it to him, saying, 'Put this on your finger, and you will be safe from drowning and the perils of sea beasts and great fishes.' So King Badr Basim took the ring and set it on his finger. Then they dived into the deep. First they went to Salih's mother.

The old woman was happy to see her grandson who was grown to be so fine a young man but when Salih told her why he had come a troubled look came over her face. She told them that many suitors had approached King Samandal asking for the hand of his daughter. He had turned them all down even the mightiest monarchs of the main. Salih defended Badr Basim saying that his father had been the noblest king of all the Persians and that his son now ruled in that mighty kingdom and sat on the throne of beaten gold. So the old woman sighed and told them to go and do as they wished for she could see by his sighs and the deep longing in his eyes that Badr Basim had been plunged into an ocean of love.

Salih took many precious jewels, rubies the size of birds' eggs, diamonds that sparkled like water in sunshine, emeralds as green as the seaweed, corals for love and pearls for purity. These he placed in a leather pouch and took them with him to the court of King Samandal. He entered the room where the king of the age was seated on his throne. The king asked him his business and Salih told him, 'Not for myself but for my sister's son have I come. He is already deep in love just on hearing her description and would have the hand of your lovely daughter the Princess

Jauharah in marriage.' He kissed the ground in front of the king and held out to him the precious jewels.

The king rose up and roared in his anger, 'Who is this son of Julnar the seaborn who dares to aspire to marry my daughter? He cannot be worthy; I have already turned away the mightiest monarchs of the main. Who is your sister? Who are you that you should think yourselves worthy?' To this Salih replied without fear. Sire, I am Salih and my sister is Julnar the seaborn; we are the son and daughter of the king of the main. Her son is Badr Basim son of King Shahriman who was ruler of all the Persians, a mighty empire among the people who walk the earth. As your daughter is the most precious jewel of your kingdom so too is King Badr Basim in his.' But Samandal was not to be persuaded. He roared again. 'We will have none of you that come creeping with jewels to buy my consent.' Then to his men at arms, 'Take this gallows bird out of my sight.' The men drew their swords chasing Salih out of the palace where he came upon others of his kinsmen. These then fought with Samandal's men and chased them back to the palace where they captured the king.

When Princess Jauharah heard that her father had been taken prisoner and all their guards were gone she became afraid and fled from the palace taking refuge high in a tree. Badr Basim sought her out and came upon her in her hiding place. She saw that he was as radiant as the new day and heard his words of love that he declared to her. 'I am King Badr Basim, king of all the Persians and I am half mad for love of you. You have captivated me with your dark eyes.' So she beguiled him with sweet words of love in return and came down from her tree. Then she began to kiss and fondle him so that he was consumed by passion for her. And then, suddenly, she spat in his face saying, 'Quit this form of man that you have. From now on you will take the form of a handsome bird with a white robe and red beak and legs.' Then she called her slave girl to her and told her to take him to the thirsty island and leave him there to die of thirst. But the girl did not think that one of such beauty deserved to die so she left him on another island that he might live.

All the while, Julnar was alone in the kingdom by the sea. She sighed as she looked at the throne of beaten gold that now stood empty. She wept when she saw the peacocks strutting in the gardens for their beauty reminded her of her son's proud beauty. She wondered and wondered where he was and longed for him. And all the while she worked to keep the kingdom going. As time passed she went down into the watery kingdom to speak to her mother and to enquire also after her brother whom she had not seen for many moons.

Her mother told her what had happened at the court of King Samandal and that Salih now sat on his throne. She said that Badr Basim had fled and was lost. Then Julnar wept and mourned for her son but said to her mother, 'I cannot leave the kingdom for fear that chaos will descend. I must go back and rule in my son's place. You must look for him for me and send word.' Her mother agreed and with that Julnar returned to her kingdom with a heavy heart and in black depression.

All this time, Badr Basim was living on the green island where the slave girl had left him in the form of a bird. A fowler found him and, on seeing the handsome white bird with red legs and beak, resolved to catch him and sell him for a high price. He took the bird to the king who bought him and then held a banquet to see what the bird would eat. When he, his eunuchs and serving women saw the bird eat all the rich meats, fruit and sweetmeats, they were amazed and the king called his wife to see the marvellous new creature he had bought. On seeing the bird, the king's wife immediately drew her veil across her face. The king was astonished saying, 'Why do you veil your face when there is no one here except the women and eunuchs who wait on us?' She replied, 'O King, this bird is no bird, but a man like you.' He rejoined, 'You lie, this is too much of a jest. How could he be other than a bird?' And she said, 'O King, by Allah, I do not jest with you nor do I tell you anything but the truth; this bird is

King Badr Basim, son of King Shahriman, lord of the land of the Persians, and his mother is Julnar the seaborn.'

The king was astonished and wanted to know how Badr Basim had come to be a bird. His wife told him the story of King Samandal and Princess Jauharah. The king then told his wife to return Badr Basim to his natural shape as he had been cruelly treated. This she did speaking words over him, as she was a great sorceress, so that in place of a white bird the king saw a youth so handsome that the moon seemed to shine in his face. Badr Basim gave thanks saying, 'There is no god but the God and Mohammed is the Apostle of God! Glory be to the Creator of all creatures and Provider of their provision, and Ruler of their destiny!' Then he kissed the king's hand and wished him long life, and the king kissed his head demanding to know every detail of his story. When Badr Basim had finished he asked the king for a fine ship to sail back to his own kingdom by the sea. This the king gladly gave and Badr Basim set sail with a fair wind that continued for ten days. On the eleventh day the wind whipped the ocean into frenzy and, with a mighty roar, it rose up against Badr Basim's ship; he was left clinging to a plank from the ship and all his sailors drowned. Clinging to the plank he was washed this way and that at the whim of the sea and near dying of hunger and thirst until he was thrown up by the waves onto a foreign shore. He walked into a city where he saw nothing but mules, horses and asses. There seemed to be no people.

He wandered for hours until he eventually came upon an old man who took him to his home and gave him food and drink. The old man told him that he had come to a city of magicians that a mighty sorceress, a real she devil, ruled. The mules, horses and asses had all once been sons of Adam. The witch took the young men and kept them with her enjoying their favours for 40 days and nights. When she tired of them she turned them into the animals now roaming the streets.

Badr Basim stayed with the old man until he regained his strength. Then one day the witch came for him and took him away, promising the old man that she would not hurt him. She placed him on her finest horse with a golden bridle and saddle all set with jewels. She took him to her palace where he was given the finest robes and jewels to wear and fed the finest sweetmeats and wine. Badr Basim was pleased with his feast and saw that her realm was greater than his own and that she was even more beautiful than Princess Jauharah, so he resolved to stay with her. Then the witch, Queen Lab, dismissed all her slaves. She poured some more wine and lay back on the bed drawing Badr Basim down beside her. They lay together in all the joy of life until morning.

The feasting and pleasure continued for 40 days and 40 nights. Then one morning Badr Basim woke to find that Queen Lab was not lying next to him in their bed. He found her in the garden where she had turned herself into a white hen to enjoy the favours of a large black bird. Badr Basim went quietly back to the bedchamber and lay down on the bed to await her return, pretending he had been there all along. Later he asked the old man the meaning of this. He told the prince that the birds on the trees were also once young men the queen had loved and that the black bird was once one of her mamelukes whom she had adored until he dared to look at another woman with desire. Then the old man promised to help protect him from her.

Badr Basim went back to the palace. The following night Queen Lab told him that she knew he had seen her as a white bird and spoke of her great love for the mameluke who was now a black bird. Then she told Badr Basim how much she loved him and fed him wine with her own hands and made love to him most passionately. When she thought he was asleep she rose from the bed, took something red out of a red bag and put it in the middle of the room where it turned into a rushing stream. Then she took some barley and watered it with water from the stream so that it turned into ears of wheat that she ground into flour. She put this to one side and returned to bed until morning, unaware that Badr Basim had seen everything.

Badr Basim went to the faithful old man and told him what he had seen. The old man warned him that the witch meant him harm and would cast a spell on him.

> After giving you all these good things to eat and drink she will offer you this parched dry grain. Take what she gives you and pretend to eat it but eat this grain I give you instead. She will throw water over you and call out 'Quit this form of man'. But you will be protected because you have not really eaten her grain. She will pretend she was joking and make believe she loves you and is still dying of passion for you. You must do likewise and persuade her to eat the grain and throw water in her face telling her to quit her human form. When all is done come back to me, and I will help you.

All happened just as the old man said it would. Badr Basim succeeded in turning Queen Lab into a she-mule. He went to see the old man where the Queen clip-clopped after him. The old man told Badr Basim that he must hurry away from the city and take the mule with him and not give her up to anyone. So they said their goodbyes and Badr Basim set off with the mule. As they travelled on their way they met an old woman. She began to weep saying that the mule reminded her of a pretty she mule her son had owned that was now dead, that she missed her so much and was now prepared to pay a goodly sum for this pretty little mule. Badr Basim declared that he could not sell the mule for less than 1000 ducats, thinking that the old woman would never have that much money. But the old woman produced a sackful of gold coins for him. When he tried to back out of his bargain her companion told him that they were in a city where the penalty for lying was death. So Badr Basim handed over the mule.

The old woman sprinkled water over the mule, which turned it back to its former shape and Queen Lab was reunited with her mother, the old woman. Badr Basim tried to escape, but the old woman gave a loud whistle, which a genie or *ifrit* answered, a veritable mountain of a creature that blocked the path. With her daughter the old woman mounted its back and, taking Badr Basim with them, the *ifrit* flew for an hour or more until they were back in Queen Lab's palace. Here, the witch queen turned Badr Basim into a foul bird and clapped him in a cage. There he festered for many days and nights until a woman servant, on hearing that the queen was planning to kill him, took pity on him. She went to the old man in the city, King Badr Basim's faithful friend, and told him of the queen's plans. The old man then whistled up an *ifrit* of his own and told him to carry the girl to Queen Julnar of the sea.

When they reached the kingdom by the sea where Julnar the seaborn sat on the throne of beaten gold, the girl knelt down and reverently kissed the ground before telling the queen what had happened to her son. Julnar was overjoyed to have news of him but alarmed at his plight. She treated the girl as an honoured guest and called her mother Farashah and her brother Salih to rejoice with her that Badr Basim had been found. Between them they gathered all the tribes of the jinn and all the troops of the main. They flew across land and sea to the country of Queen Lab, which they attacked with great ferocity.

They sacked the town in the beat of a bird's wing, killing all the unbelievers. When the battle was over, Julnar immediately asked for her son to be brought to her. A slave girl brought the wretched looking bird to her saying, 'This is your son.' And Julnar looked upon the bird in great sorrow but taking some water sprinkled it over him saying, 'Quit this form and take the shape you once were.' Suddenly, there before her stood her son, so beautiful that it was as though the moon shone in his face. They greeted each other with weeping, kissing and smiling. Then Farashah, his grandmother, and his uncle Salih also greeted him joyously. All the townsfolk began beating their drums and held a high festival that lasted three days. Julnar rewarded the faithful old man by marrying him to the young slave who had brought news of Badr Basim to her and making him king in place of the witch.

But King Badr Basim still sighed, longing for greater happiness. He told Julnar that he still wished to marry but could find no bride. She sent her people out to look for a suitable princess for him, but he told her that none would do save Jauharah, daughter of King Samandal, for she truly was a jewel. So Julnar had King Samandal brought to her and sent for Badr Basim also. He then asked the king again for his daughter's hand in marriage. This time the king spoke humbly saying, 'She is your handmaid.' And he sent for the princess. When she arrived he said to her, 'Know that I have given your hand to this sovereign king, Badr Basim, son of Queen Julnar born of the sea. He is the best, most exalted and noblest lord and only he is fit for you and only you for him.' She answered, 'I would not cause you pain, my father, and I accept this man you have chosen for me.' They called the grand vizir and witnesses, and the marriage took place then and there.

The citizens of the town beat the drums of rejoicing, gifts were bestowed on the poor and needy, robes of honour given to the grandees and lords of the realm and the feasting went on for ten days. Princess Jauharah was paraded in a different bride dress for each day. King Badr Basim gave his father-in-law an honourable robe and sent him back to his own country to rule in peace. From then on they all lived a happy luxurious life with much feasting until they were visited by the Destroyer of Delights and the Sunderer of Societies, but that tale is for another night. Look, the sun is already waking in the bowl of night.

In 1909 a small oil-fired steamship was ready to go down the slipway on its maiden voyage at Margil. The parts had been made at Rennie's shipyard in Greenwich and sent out to Margil for assembly. Oil was the new technology and this was a modern ship. Mrs. F. W. Perry, wife of the manager of the Euphrates and Tigris Steam Navigation Company, was invited to perform the honours at the launch. As she hurled the bottle of champagne at the ship's bow she pronounced in a clear voice, 'I name this ship *Julnar*. God bless her and all who sail in her.' Amid polite clapping the *Julnar* slowly slid down the slips and into the river. Lynch Brothers were its owners and it was destined to work the Shatt al-Arab and the two great rivers of Mesopotamia. Its name was considered appropriate to its proposed location. Little did anyone at the launch realize what role it would play in international events.

8

Home Fires

Ah Love! could thou and I with Fate conspire
To grasp this sorry Scheme of Things entire,
Would not we shatter it to bits – and then
Re-mould it nearer to the Heart's Desire!
(*Rubáiyát of Omar Khayyám*, verse 73)

'Edie, what are you doing? Have you finished those dishes yet?' Edie sighed. 'Not quite,' she replied. She had been standing at the kitchen sink staring out of the window. Her eyes followed the neat rope-edged path down the middle of the garden to the end. Against the wall on one side leant the privy, opposite was the garden shed. Both were places whose gloomy spidery interiors she hated. She plunged her hands into the already cold water with its slick of congealing grease. Life went on, an endless round of meals and washing up, cleaning and scrubbing. It was months now since she had heard about Johnny but somehow it still felt as sharp as if it were yesterday. Not an hour went by when she did not think of him.

She had received no official letter. She was neither a wife nor even a fiancée. His parents had been unable to face her. It fell to his sister to give her the news. She remembered the moment. She had put her hands straight out in front of her to fend off the truth. Dorothy had taken hold of them and pulled Edie to her, putting her arms around her as they both wept. A shudder ran through her. Mustard gas, trench foot, the cold and mud; those terrible trenches and her Johnny – there was no hero's death for him. A severe cold had turned to pneumonia and he had died alone in some faraway field hospital. A death uncelebrated, unnoticed, one among thousands. She knew other women were working in the munitions factory or driving trucks down in the docks, but somehow she could not bring herself to do these things. They loomed large and frightening in her mind. She preferred to stay at home wrapping the familiar emptiness around herself.

Just then her mother bustled in, breaking her train of thought. 'I'll sweep the step then, or we'll never get the jobs done,' Mary fretted, taking out the broom. Ever since Edie's brother William had gone to war mother had worked harder than ever around the house. Fighting the dirt fended off worry. It was as if being a model housewife would earn the safe return of her son.

Father was away working. Like many others, he had to work extra hard to make up for those who had gone to fight. So it was just the two of them at home now. Sometimes they were silent for hours at a time. Edie's thoughts were with Johnny while her mother's were in Mesopotamia with William, her son. The remorseless ticking of the clock counted the hours, minutes and seconds of these absences. Only the evenings at the Red Cross, rolling bandages or packing parcels for the prisoners of war relieved the monotonous rhythm of the days.

Mary went out to sweep the already immaculate front step and garden path. The brass trim that edged the hall floor tiles shone brightly in the spring sunshine. Their home was a Victorian town house in a row with a little square of garden in front and an oblong at the back. With her mother's exhortation to respectability ringing in her ears, 'if each before his own door swept, the village would be clean', she even opened the little front gate and swept the pavement in front of their house. As she went back in she looked up at what had been her home for 30 years, where she had brought up four children. The laburnum tree she had planted when they first moved there was now a mature tree heavy with blossom. Who would have thought she would have had four children, she who at one time had despaired of ever marrying? 'You must try to make more of yourself,' her mother had kept saying, pinching Mary's cheeks to put roses in them before taking her to yet another social event where she might meet a suitable young man. In the end, at 27, she had married a near neighbour, a ship's engineer who was often away, but she did not mind being on her own.

Now with her elder daughter, Kit, married and the first baby, Eileen, already lisping a few words, it should have been a happy golden time. A grandchild – imagine that. Instead, William, her husband was away more than ever to make up for all the young men being at the front. Her youngest son, her baby, named William after his father, was God knows where fighting the heathen Turks. There was only Edie at home, fretting over her young man. Edie reminded her of herself at the same age – not obviously a beauty but with her quiet thoughtful expression, she had a gentle appeal. Her deep blue eyes were now smudged with grief and she often stood as she had this morning staring blankly. And she was eating next to nothing. Mary sighed and went back into the house, shutting the door behind her.

She went to look for Edie who was heating up the irons on the range – the little one for her lace blouse and the big one to tackle the sheets. The small iron heated up first. She did not need it to be too hot. As her mother came in she spat on it to test the temperature and held it close to her face to be extra sure. She was very fond of that lace blouse and did not want to burn it. She was not looking forward to doing the sheets. The big iron was so heavy and you had to keep reheating it. She knew it would take her most of the morning.

Seeing the irons heating reminded Mary that they must get some more coal as they needed it even in the summer to keep the range burning brightly for cooking and hot water. Just then, they heard the clack of the letterbox as the postman pushed the mail through. There had been no letter from William for quite some time. The lack of news made her fear the worst. The newspapers had recently reported a siege and a great defeat and surrender in Kut on the Tigris. 'That's where William is', she said to Edie. 'Do you think he was involved? My God, I hope not, but he could be. He could be.'

Every day she rushed to pick up the post, both dreading and looking forward to what she might find. Today it was Edie who went to collect it. There were only three letters. Not one of them had her son William's familiar writing on it. The first one they opened was from William, her husband, who was working in Liverpool. They had recognized the handwriting immediately and were anxious to read his news. It told of his imminent return for a few days' leave. The second was from Mary's elder sister who now lived in Sussex and was her usual gossipy missive, boasting of the achievements of her children and grandchildren, full of domestic detail. The third one was typed and looked as though it might be a bill. When she opened it, the official looking heading at the top instantly filled Mary with alarm. It was from the Admiralty, dated 2 May 1916. Mary could not bring herself to read it. With a low moan, she sat down on the kitchen chair and held the letter out to Edie.

> Madam,
>
> I am commanded by my Lords Commissioners of the Admiralty to inform you that your son, Engineer Sub-Lieutenant Louis Reed, RNR has been missing since the night of the 24th April, but that there is every reason to hope that he is a prisoner in the hands of the Turks in Mesopotamia.
>
> Any further information received will be immediately communicated to you.
>
> I am, Madam,
>
> Your obedient Servant,
>
> Charles Walker
>
> For Secretary.

William Louis Reed's parents with Jack.

Edie read the letter quickly to herself. Then, with a sharp intake of breath, aloud to her mother, 'Oh, Ma,' she said, putting her arms round her mother's shoulders. 'He'll be fine. You'll see. He's a survivor, our William.' Inside her head, 'Not again, Oh God, please not again,' went round and round until she felt dizzy.

'Missing, missing, what does that mean? They hope he's in the hands of the Turks. Do they have any idea what that means? Those cruel Turks! Anything could happen to him. They could starve him, beat him or worse,' Mary sobbed. Edie could see that her mother was becoming hysterical. She knelt down in front of her on the cold kitchen flagstones and rubbed her hands, trying to find soothing words to reassure her. 'I'll make us a cup of tea,' she said eventually when her mother became a little calmer. She stood up with some difficulty. She was so thin now. The stone floor had been painful and her knees had gone stiff.

As she expected, the tea, strong with plenty of sugar, revived her mother's spirits and she began to go back to the everyday practical problems of ordering coal and doing the cleaning. She kept returning to the subject of William throughout the day and the succeeding days. 'It's so terrible not knowing, though.' Or again, 'If only we knew for sure.' One of them would start a sentence and then it would trail away to nothing 'Do you think…?' or 'I don't know how he's going to…'

For Edie it was like reliving her own nightmare. She and William were very close. He, though younger, had always looked after her. She missed his cheerful teasing, his reassuring presence and his sense of humour whenever he was away; now she might never see him again. She remembered all those happy evenings before the war, evenings spent with friends in the neighbourhood playing '31s' or 'Chase the Ace', evenings that had glowed with warmth and laughter. For the next three weeks the two women carried out their household tasks and social commitments mechanically, going through the motions, but their minds were far away in the deserts of Mesopotamia. At church on Sundays they prayed their most fervent prayers.

Their mood went up and down with the headline of the moment. 'Prisoners were being taken to Anatolia.' Was William one of them? Where was that? How would the men get there?

'Exchange of wounded prisoners from Kut.' Was William among the wounded? His name did not appear on any of the published lists. This hope for his return died when they read on 11 May that the 'last wounded from Kut' had been exchanged. There had been no sign of their William. The full story of what had happened at Kut emerged little by little, a comment here and an article there.

Sir John Nixon, the general commanding the Indian Expeditionary Force, wrote a dispatch that included the following tribute:

> The officers and crews of the Tigris Steamers belonging to Messrs Lynch Brothers and of the other river craft have always displayed gallantry of a high order in bringing their ships on, often under heavy fire, and it is not much to say that without this assistance, and the indefatigable manner in which they have worked, that the movement of troops and supplies would not have been possible.

Mary and Edie both felt proud to read that, knowing that William was working on the Lynch Brothers boats. On 15 May, an article in *The Times* by Edmund Candler, correspondent in Mesopotamia, mentioned the *Julnar* and its attempt to relieve the garrison. Both women remembered William writing to them about this ship that he had worked on so many times. Had he been on board on the night of 24 April?

Eventually, on 24 May, another letter arrived in a familiar typed envelope. Recognizing it, Mary shouted for Edie who came running. Then she ripped the letter open with shaking hands and read aloud to Edie.

> Madam,
>
> In continuation of Admiralty Letter CW of the 2nd instant, reporting your son, Engineer Sub Lieutenant Louis reed, RNR, as missing on the 24th ultimo, during the operations in Mesopotamia, I am commanded by My Lords

Commissioners of the Admiralty to acquaint you that the information has now been received from Turkish sources which shows that Engineer Sub Lieutenant Reed was not among those killed or wounded and that the captured are all doing well.

Any further information received will be immediately communicated to you.

I am, Madam,

Your obedient Servant,

Charles Walker

For secretary.

'He's alive, Edie, he's alive.' She devoured the letter once more, but a bleakness came over her. 'If you read it carefully, they still don't really know what has happened to him. This only tells us that his body has not been found.'

In her turn Edie read the letter over and over again. She was forced to agree with her mother. The wording was optimistic but when you thought carefully about it there was simply no evidence of him being among the dead, no proof, no body or identification. Among all those other dead he could have been easily overlooked. It did not state that he was among the captured. That was merely assumed. Then there was the time lapse. It takes days for information to filter through from these faraway places; anything could have happened since then. All through that summer they waited, corroded with anxiety, for news. They took out the two letters and read them over and over again trying to extract every nugget of hope yet fearful of disappointment.

It was after this that the first details of the *Julnar*'s involvement became known through an article entitled 'Hero of the Kut Relief Ship'. It was a tribute to a man named Lieutenant Firman who had been the commander of the vessel. Humphrey Osbaldston Brooke Firman, only son of Mr Henry Brooke Firman, from Gateforth Hall, Selby in Yorkshire was 30 years of age when he died. His name meant nothing to Mary and Edie.

He was not someone William had ever mentioned in his letters. It was only the name of the boat that drew their attention, though they felt sad for his family in the usual detached way that people do for strangers.

They read every newspaper they could get hold of. 'Kut Prisoners Excellent Treatment in Asia Minor'. The Turks were looking after our boys well and taking good care of the wounded. Mary and Edith's spirits soared. 'Prisoners from Kut' had them in the depth of depression for days as they read that the Turks did not know exactly how many men they were holding and there were details of the privations that men and officers were suffering. The Turks had refused access by Red Cross teams to the Kut prisoners. William's name still did not appear on any official lists of prisoners. An article headed 'Parcels to Mesopotamia' gave the standard way of sending parcels to loved ones and listed the items that would be appreciated. 'If only we had somewhere to send a parcel to,' sighed Edie. She cut it out and kept it anyway in case they might have the chance to send their William parcels.

As the news spread that William was missing in action, neighbours came to offer their sympathy. 'Well, it must be so difficult for you and Edie with her troubles already' or 'Of course, those Turks aren't at all civilized. Been reading 'bout them in the papers. Don't bear thinking about … but I'm sure your William'll be all right.' Edie and Mary found themselves involved in long conversations with the various tradesmen, purveyors of milk, meat, bread – and gossip. News carried on a roundsman's bicycle, or clopping along the street rattling alongside the chattering milk bottles behind the dairy's old work horse.

Once Mary would have scorned standing on her doorstep wasting time conversing with such people. Her dealings with them had been entirely business-like, which was proper for a respectable woman. They seemed to know so much more about the war, its progress and the enemy than she did. If the two women had been avid readers of newspapers before, they now became obsessive. They greedily consumed every snippet of information they could find about the war in Mesopotamia. It seemed their only hope of learning anything new.

Summer turned to autumn, fires were lit; the rooms in the house with their brown paintwork and flower crowded walls were at once cosy and oppressive. Mid-October brought the first real cold weather of the year and little Eileen's second birthday. The family drew together to celebrate the event, an excuse to put their worries behind them for a while. Mary was proud of the fine spread that Kit had put on for her family and friends. Eileen clapped her hands with delight when she saw the ruby coloured jelly wobbling on its plate, and she got the pink sugar icing from her cake all over her dress, but no one minded. Smiles and laughter, those precious commodities, were extravagantly spent that day.

At about the same time a long report appeared in *The Times*, a dispatch from Sir Percy Lake KCB that gave details of the *Julnar*'s part in the siege and surrender at Kut. 'That's William's ship again,' cried Mary in excitement. The report did not name him but it did name Lieutenant Firman and Captain Cowley. 'But that's William's friend. They've sailed together so often. I'll bet William was with him. It says here he was killed, with that man Firman that we read about before. That's terrible. But where, oh where is William? Why doesn't someone tell us what's happening?'

November opened with no further news. Finally, two weeks later the waiting and the doubt were over. A third letter from the Admiralty arrived. Mother and daughter opened it together, sitting at the kitchen table. It was dated 14 November.

> Madam,
>
> I am commanded by my Lords Commissioners of the Admiralty to acquaint you that the following information has been received through the War Office respecting the Officer named.
>
> Name: William L. Reed
>
> Rank: Engineer Sub-Lieutenant RNR

Now a Prisoner of War in Turkey at 'Afion Kara Hissar.'

I am, Madam,

Your obedient Servant

Charles Walker

For Secretary

Edie and Mary looked at each other, breathing sighs of relief wreathed in smiles because now they knew. Their William was alive.

'There, you see, I told you he'd be fine,' declared Edie. 'You can stop worrying now.'

But Mary's mind had already clouded over again. 'Yes, he's alive but what kind of treatment is he getting?'

Now they read every article about prisoners of war, and about Turkey. What they read filled them with gloom. At least they had an address and could write and send William parcels in the hope that something might get through. Edie dug out the article that gave instructions on sending parcels to Mesopotamia. All parcels less than 11 lb in weight had to be sent to the Indian Expeditionary Force 'D', c/o India Office, London SW. Anything larger had to go to an address in Devonport. Mary and Edie packed the parcels at their local Red Cross centre with renewed vigour, thinking that it was possible that one of them would find its way to William. The section they were in was packing the 'First Capture' parcels. They folded cardigan jackets, socks and towels, neatly placing them in the boxes with handkerchiefs, Vaseline, brush and comb, toothbrush and powder, shaving brush, safety razor and soap, as well as a tin-opener and spoon and fork. On top they carefully placed a housewife containing sewing materials.

It was early December before they finally heard from William himself. He wrote telling them that they should address all their letters and parcels to him as Prisoner of War No. 1612 Afion Kara Hissar, Turkey. They rushed to send him a parcel as quickly as possible. Everyone knew how much the men in the prison camps depended on them.

'Prisoners of the Turks' in *The Times* at the end of December alarmed them with its details of the terrible ordeals some prisoners suffered, the boredom and cold they endured in the high mountains of Anatolia and of how the parcels did not get through. Their mood veered up and down as they read every scrap of news, listened to every bit of gossip. And they lived for the clack of the letterbox for the next two years.

9

The Journey North

And that inverted Bowl we call The Sky,
Whereunder crawling coop't we live and die,
Lift not thy hands to *It* For help – for It
Rolls impotently on as Thou or I.

(*Rubáiyát of Omar Khayyám*, verse 52)

After the end of the siege and the dramatic final attempt to get food through to the garrison, the Turks took thousands of the troops as prisoners. Among them were some of the crew of the *Julnar* including my grandfather William Louis Reed. A few hundred desperately sick or wounded British and Indian men were exchanged for some Turkish prisoners, but most became prisoners of war. The Arab citizens of Kut were executed. This was Lieutenant McNeal's description of the end of the siege:

> Great excitement prevailed in Kut when it was heard that the relieving force would attempt to send the steamboat *Julnar* through with rations. It was decided that if the boat got through undisabled it was to come up to Kut itself and be unloaded, but that if it was hit it was to be beached at the fort. The artillery made special preparations to cover its arrival, and everyone was on edge with expectation. Shortly after midnight heavy rifle fire was heard down river, and we knew that the attempt had begun. For fifteen

> minutes the firing was very rapid; then it died down, and our spirits with it. Another burst of firing came, and our spirits rose accordingly; but this also died away into silence, and we knew that the attempt had failed.

Aubrey Herbert and T. E. Lawrence were sent to negotiate freedom for the prisoners, but even the offer of £2,000,000 did not sway the Turks. The two negotiators were blindfolded for their journey to the area but were otherwise well treated. They were horrified by the scenes of devastation at Kut and by the swarms of flies that blackened everything and coated every morsel of food before they could get it to their mouths. To write their reports in their tents at night they had to take it in turns to hold a paraffin lamp to repel the insects while the other got on with his work.

The Turks were angry that Townshend had destroyed all his guns when he surrendered, so Herbert and Lawrence were only able to gain the smallest of concessions. Agreements were reached on the evacuation of sick and wounded. General Lake had to promise to transport these by river. At this point he also reminded Halil, the Turkish negotiator, of his promise to feed, transport to Baghdad and pay the Kut garrison. He had promised good treatment for all prisoners.

When the armistice was concluded it was found that 2680 British NCOs and privates had been taken captive at Kut. Of these 1306 died and 449 were unaccounted for. Of the 10,486 Indians taken, 1290 perished and 1773 remained untraced. Most of the prisoners died crossing the cruel desert as they travelled up through northern Iraq to prison camps in Turkey and Syria. The men were for the most part separated from their officers and their Turkish guards beat, brutalized and frequently buggered them. Those too weak to march were left to die by the roadside where Arab tribesmen often beat them and stripped them of their clothing. Many suffered from dysentery and starvation and had no medical care. The callousness and brutality of this neglect and abuse was a cruel ending for such brave men.

My grandfather's second diary described his experiences after he was captured. The first part that described the journey to his prisoner of war camp was written as a normal diary. The second part dealt with his two year incarceration in Afion Kara Hissar prison camp and is written in the form of letters to friends and family that he has copied out.

THE LAST HOPE

24 April 1916

Sailed from Wadi in HMS *Julnar* to try to run the blockade through to the Kut Garrison who were starving.

25 April 1916

12.30 a.m. Captured at about three miles from Kut, not giving in until we were riddled with bullets and Lieutenant Firman killed by a shell that hit the bridge and exploded.

26 April 1916

Left at 2 a.m. by the steamer Kahlifah which was captured by the Turks from us at the outbreak of war of which I was engineer in peace times, so will leave you to guess how degraded I felt.

28 April 1916

Arrived at Baghdad after a very painful journey, whilst in Baghdad met a lot of old friends who were afraid to speak to me, heard at Baghdad of Captain Cowley's death. I had left him behind at the camp we were captured at, he was only very slightly wounded.

The journey to Baghdad was on foot across miles of empty desert in searing heat. Having suffered through all the floods and bitter cold of the winter fighting for Kut, the troops from the garrison and the men from the *Julnar* now had to endure temperatures that soared to 40° and more, and they lacked water. Men who were already weakened and made ill by starvation over the months of the siege now had to march on a diet of one small chapatti per day and had very little access to water. Many of them were without shoes because their boots fell apart as they travelled or they were stolen by marauding Arabs in the areas through which they walked. Prisoners who failed to keep up were shouted at and beaten with rifle butts, whips or sticks by their Turkish guards even when obviously too weak or ill for such a march. If they fell by the wayside unable to keep going they were left behind to die in the desert.

6 May 1916

General Townshend arrived at Baghdad, great jollifications by the Turks as Kut surrendered on the 29th April.

8 May 1916

Left Baghdad for Summara 6 p.m. arrived 11.30.

11 May 1916

Left on our terrible journey, same day arrived Dhore slept in filthy stable & latrines.

On this day Major E. W. C. Sandes was a prisoner on board the *Burnanieh*. They overtook the *Julnar*. He wrote,

> She had aboard her several of the British Officers left behind on duty in Kut in connection with medical work and also our general hospital staff and some of our sick and wounded from Kut. She was steaming slowly, and her funnel and hull were like sieves from bullet holes; all her stern cabins had been removed, presumably to give her more space for stores when she made her disastrous dash for Kut. On her bridge was an inscription in Turkish reading 'She came by herself'.

My grandfather would have been devastated to see that but

Reed outside the prison hospital. Reed is on the right.

luckily he had been taken upriver three days before Sandes. On board the *Julnar* was Flight Sergeant P. W. Long of the RAF who had also been taken prisoner at Kut. His book *Other Ranks of Kut* shows how the men were treated and describes in detail their experiences. The *Julnar* took the injured and sick prisoners as far as Baghdad. 'When the full complement of sick were aboard, the shot-riddled *Julnar* got underway and began to puff and clank its way upstream.' He then describes how another boat of prisoners overtook them, 'we exchanged cheers as lustily as we could'. This was probably the *Burnanieh* with E. W. C. Sandes on board. Like my grandfather, from here the prisoners all had to walk at least as far as Ras-al-Ain, which was where the railway terminus was.

12 May 1916

Left Dhore for Tekrit arrived same day.

Tekrit is the town now infamous for being the home of Saddam Hussein and is the site of the pile of skulls left by Tamerlaine and his Mongol hordes.

15 May 1916

Met General Townshend, Captain Moreland and Colonel Parr going through the desert, had a long conversation with them, he gave me some money, day after day going through terrible hardships vicinity of Arab camps during these marches we had almost nothing to eat and the men were footsore having no boots.

Townshend describes this meeting in his book *My Campaign in Mesopotamia*:

> We overtook a party of about forty ragged and weary British and Indian prisoners, who had been taken from Gorringe's force and included the survivors of the *Julnar*. They were under Sub-Lieutenant Reid [*sic*], RNR, who told us they had to pay for donkey hire, and that one of their number was ill. Before we moved off I made Isakh Bey give Reid fifteen liras for expenses of this nature, and deliver a severe lecture to the Turkish Officer in charge of the prisoners. This was all I could do.

William was probably better off than many of the others. On board ship he was comparatively well fed. Supplies were more plentiful than those available to the fighting troops and certainly to those in the besieged garrison. The men were not only a prey to hunger and thirst but also to Arab looters who stole their boots. Most of them had no shelter day or night as they had no tents. The rations the Turks handed out consisted of an army biscuit that, according to E. W. C. Sandes, resembled a slab of rock about five inches in diameter and nearly an inch thick. 'It was made of the very roughest flour with bits of husk and earth in it.' The prisoners were supposed to be supplied with small amounts of money to buy food and fuel but it was woefully inadequate and often failed to materialize, so that they were reduced to begging, bartering or selling the very few possessions they had. When a choice has to be made between keeping your boots and being able to buy food there is not much contest even when you are faced with a march of several hundred miles.

22 May 1916

Arrived at Mosul where we were put into a disused mosque which was in a dirty disgusting condition.

23 May 1916

5 p.m. left Mosul throughout each day suffering terrible hardships, our great trouble was miles and miles of desert and no water or food; food did not matter so much as lack of water. Pte Ponting & Pte Gardiner joined our party, they had been left behind sick at Mosul by a previous party.

The guards beat any prisoners who lagged behind on the march with rifle butts or sticks to urge them on. Those who collapsed were abandoned. With Ponting and Gardner was Robert Gage, who had recovered sufficiently in the infirmary to be excluded from the sick and wounded permitted to return to Basra.

27 May 1916

Pte Ponting died in the desert of thirst 39 miles march in the boiling sun without water many men very ill after journey lips baked and badly cracked

Typhus, dysentery, enteritis and cholerine were rife. Hunger and thirst had weakened the men who could not keep themselves clean and suffered from exposure to either excessive heat or excessive cold at night.

30 May 1916

Arrived Sabeen camped in dirty ruined mosque. Sent Veal to hospital, looked very much like a case of typhus.

I think this place is in fact called Nisibin as there is no mention of Sabeen on maps or in other books but they all refer to a place called Nisibin at about this stage of the journey.

5 June 1916

Arrived at Ras-al-Ain this being the railhead again left one fellow in hospital here he also looks like a case of typhus.

Thousands of prisoners from the allied forces were put to work on extending the railway beyond Ras-al-Ain to Baghdad in much the same way as the Japanese forced their prisoners of war to work on the Burma railway in the Second World War. Among them were Armenians who had come through the 1915 massacre they suffered at the hands of the Turks. They were now refugees and worked on the railway alongside the prisoners. Men, women and children worked for their rations. Children were given half the meagre amount of food that adults received. Many died as a result of appalling conditions, lack of sanitation, poor diet and disastrously unsafe working practices.

P. W. Long, in *Other Ranks of Kut*, described one particularly horrifying incident. At the labour camp they had built bridging over the various streams to enable them to cross without getting wet. A Kurdish woman had taken to the habit of stowing her bundle and cloak under one end of one of these bridges while she was at work. Herr Vinger, the German in charge of the camp, came across on his horse, but by this time, because they were short of lumber, the workers had taken the top layer of boards off the bridge and it was no longer strong enough to take the weight. As he had reached the opposite bank, the structure gave way and his horse's hooves smashed through the board just where the Kurdish woman had stowed her belongings. The horse plunged about and, kicking itself free, cantered up the bank. The woman rushed up and pulled her bundle out. Unwrapping, it she revealed that it contained a baby of a few months old. 'Its head had been crushed like an egg by the hoofs of the plunging horse.' The journey from Kut to Ras-al-Ain was 600 miles.

7 June 1916

Left by train for Halep (Aleppo).

One irony of this journey is that it is the same route as the Orient Express, Constantinople to Baghdad, made famous for its luxury and romance by none other than Agatha Christie. It was a route she later travelled often.

Here the men, not the officers, were packed into goods vans where they were locked in for hours on end. Many were so ill they could not stand and others were suffering from galloping dysentery. The stench in the vans can only be imagined not to mention the horror of men, squashed in with some who were already dead, falling on top of each other at every jolt of the train. As an officer, William was treated with more consideration.

8 June 1916

Arrived at Halep. I left the men and was put in a hotel where I met Capt Stilwell and Lt Brown.

It seemed that William had taken responsibility for his party of men but as an officer he was sent by a different route from them. It seems strange to think of a prisoner being put up in a hotel but this was the general custom at the time.

9 June 1916

Was taken to hospital here (Aleppo) with typhus, was very bad indeed nearly pegged out was unconscious for seven days. On my coming to again, was shifted into another ward where I met Major Fortner & Lt Chitty. Must say we were very well treated here.

Other writers and witnesses speak of the dreadful conditions in Turkish hospitals. They say that they were filthy and men were not properly cared for. Some were even injected with a fluid that hastened their deaths. Again this could be a class difference. The

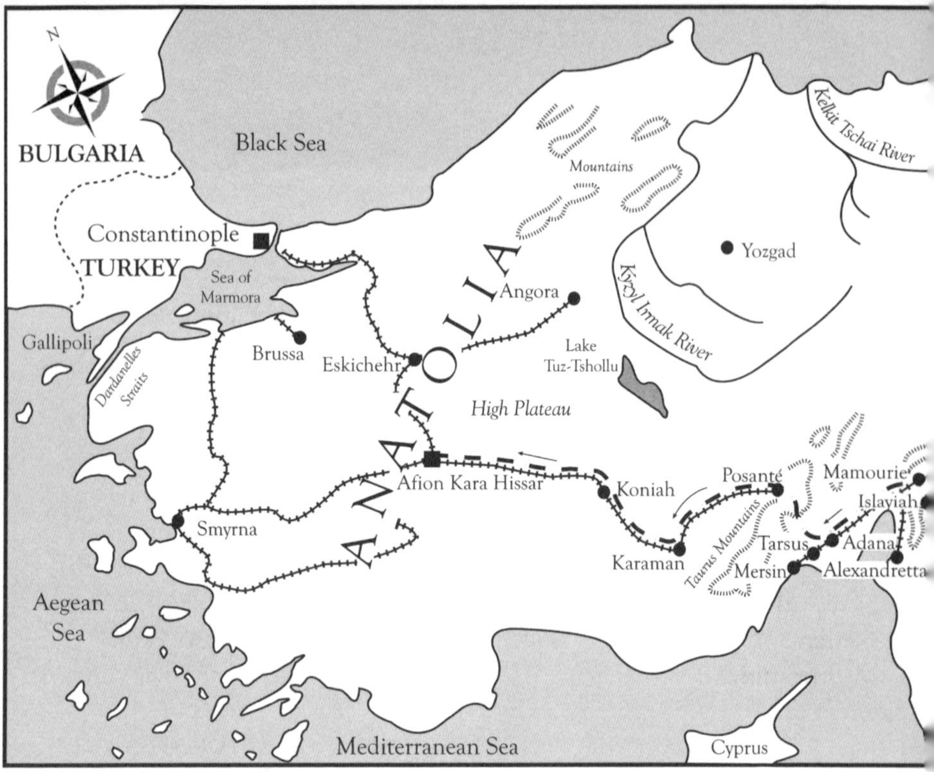

Turks perhaps felt that there were more likely to be repercussions if officers complained of ill treatment.

14 September 1916

Left hospital with Chitty and put in a very dirty hotel bed full of bugs.

16 September 1916

Left the hotel, started by train for Islayiah arrived same day, left again for Marmorah by motor lorry arrived 7.20 p.m.

17 September 1916

Left Marmorah by train arrived at Tarsus 2.30 p.m. had a very good dinner here at quite a decent hotel.

Tarsus is the main town in the Tarsus mountains and is famous as St Paul's home town. He had been a lawyer called Saul of

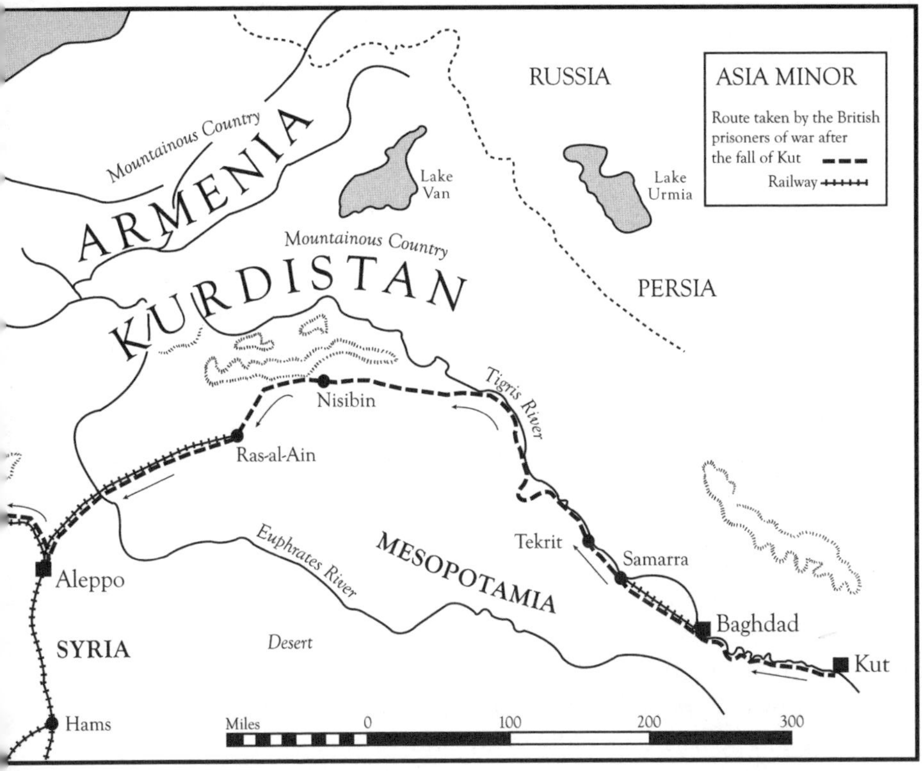

Journey of prisoners west from Kut to Afion Kara Hissar (ending on facing page).

Tarsus before converting to Christianity on his way to Damascus in Syria. Around Tarsus they would have travelled through beautiful pine forests and valleys where swift-flowing mountain streams fed the rivers. There were great peaks of rocks and high cliffs. They followed the route taken by Alexander the Great along a narrow, steep pathway known as Alexander the Great's Gate. An inscription in stone commemorates his army's march.

18 September 1916

Left Tarsus by motor lorry for Posanté had to pass over the Tarsus mountains arrived at 4 p.m. Left again at 5.30 p.m. by train for Koniah.

19 September 1916

Arrived at Konia went up town and had a good look round and lunch. Left again same afternoon for Afion Kara Hissar.

20 September 1916

Arrived Afion Kara Hissar 6.30 a.m. prisoner of war camp met Furneaux here.

Descriptions of the terrible conditions that prisoners endured were not freely published. The official line was that the Turks were essentially civilized, this despite the massacres they had perpetrated in Bulgaria and against the Armenians. They were thought to have been drawn into the war by the wiles of the Germans and that they were to be respected as a worthy opponent. Hatred was reserved for the 'Hun'. However, Enver Pasha's promise to the prisoners, that they were to be treated as 'honoured guests of Turkey' quickly turned out to be like the mirages of the desert. In his book *The Road to Endor* E. H. Jones, himself a prisoner from Kut, describes how they had been driven across the deserts like stolen cattle, 'herded at their journey's end in foul cellars and filthy mud huts, left unclothed, unfed and unwarmed. ... Seven out of every ten prisoners from Kut died at the hands of their hosts.'

The majority of the prisoners taken at Kut were Indian troops, but 2555 European soldiers were also imprisoned. By the beginning of 1917, 483 of them had died. Officers were given care, but not the other ranks. The worst aspect of the camps was the lack of medical care. William's arrival was the start of a very long two years.

At the camp, William heard that Robert Gage was already imprisoned there, but that he was bedridden with an unnamed illness. He died two days after William's arrival at the age of 24. Like thousands of others, he was buried in an unmarked grave.

10

Afion Kara Hissar

For in and out, above, about, below,
'Tis nothing but a Magic Shadow-show,
Play'd in a Box whose Candle is the Sun,
Round which we Phantom Figures come and go.
(*Rubáiyát of Omar Khayyám*, verse 46)

William arrived at Afion Kara Hissar on 20 September 1916, yet there is no entry in his prison diary until December. The name Afion Kara Hissar means the Black Fortress of Opium. The most prominent feature of the town is a huge rock with the remains of an ancient castle or fort perched on top of it. The rock is in the centre of the historic town, which is the capital of its province. The history of the town can be traced back 3000 years when the Hittites, Phrygians, Lydians and Persians occupied it. The Romans then conquered it and they in turn were ousted by the Byzantines. In 1071 a Seljuk victory brought it under Turkish rule where it has remained ever since.

Its main industries were agriculture, carpet weaving and growing opium for use in medicines. The cows in the area were fed on the leaves and stems left over from the opium plants, so were probably the happiest cows in the world. As a result of their lovely tranquil existence, they produced the finest, richest clotted cream in the world. It is known as 'kaymak' and can still be bought in Afion.

Afion Kara Hissar today.

The prisoners were kept in separate houses around the town. Rations consisted of one loaf of bread and a pot of kurrawana, a watery stew made mostly of tomatoes, aubergines and olive oil. Sometimes it contained broad beans in the pod and sometimes grape cuttings. To a modern gourmet it could be appealing but not to someone reared on roast beef and Yorkshire pudding.

The camp commandant Masloum Bey was renowned for his brutality and sexual assaults on some of the young prisoners. Officers were kept apart from the men and so were unable to help them. He became so notorious for his cruelty that the Turks were shamed into removing him from his post in the summer of 1917 when he was court-martialled.

Officers in the camp had servants or batmen appointed to them and P. W. Long served in this capacity. Officers had a life of luxury compared with other ranks. Afion Kara Hissar was the place at which all parcels for prisoners of war in Turkey were received. From there they were then sent to the various prison or labour camps where the recipients were held. The commandant and his 'thieving staff' helped themselves.

Those that were sent on were often plundered by the commandant and guards at their destination, but some made it through to the prisoners. Parcels sent to men who were known to have died were shared out among the prisoners at Afion. Those sent to men whose address was uncertain were retained there pending confirmation of their whereabouts. Money was also sent by various war fund organizations and regimental support funds. The greater part of what was sent never reached its hopeful recipients.

When news of the treatment to which prisoners were being subjected began to filter through, public concern led to the formation of various prisoner of war societies. Some were based on regiments, others on counties. These societies made it their business to send parcels of food and other necessities to prisoners. A central prisoners of war help committee was established in London to coordinate the different groups and work closely with the Red Cross in Switzerland. The system was haphazard, which meant that while some prisoners received lots of parcels others got nothing. Private parcels were badly packed and wrongly addressed; some contained perishables that contaminated everything in the consignment. Parcels were also censored. Enclosing a forbidden item such as a newspaper article could delay the delivery of a whole batch of parcels. So, from 1 December 1916 until the end of the war, the Central Prisoners of War Committee (CPoWC) under the chairmanship of Sir Starr Jameson made sure that every prisoner received supplies of food and clothing. It was forbidden to send private parcels except to officers, but independent groups such as the various prisoner of war societies were encouraged. The CPoWC issued special labels and instructions on the correct way to pack parcels. Pledges were also made to the enemy countries that these parcels would not contain any banned material. When people protested at the ban on private parcels they were allowed to send them from selected stores.

A report by the Red Cross in Geneva dated 28/29 November 1916 states that Afion Kara Hissar had been used as a prison camp from the start of hostilities. Situated at the foot of a 200-metre high rock, the town is 1008 metres above sea level. French and English officers were imprisoned there, as well as English, French, Hindu and Russian soldiers. There were 2300 in all under the command of Major Masloum Bey. A representative from the United States embassy inspected the camp in the spring of 1915.

There were 67 English and 9 French officers served by 29 English, 2 Hindu and one French soldier. There were military doctors among them, but they were not permitted to work in the hospital. The officers were held in seven different houses. Four were constructed in a block and overlooked a courtyard. They were on the outskirts of the town. The three others were in the town centre, all in the same street. The men housed on the edge of town were better off because they received more sunlight. The town centre houses were dark and dingy. The soldiers who served the officers prepared the food. Officers had the right to take walks

Officials of Afion Kara Hissar.

in groups twice a week, but found this barely adequate. William Louis Reed was imprisoned in one of these seven houses.

Of the soldiers imprisoned at Afion, 482 were English, 223 Hindu, 26 Russian and 6 French and they were far worse off than the officers. Their lodgings were an old Armenian church and its outbuildings and a Muslim school. With its stone walls and bare wooden floor the church was not comfortable, yet that was where the weak, sick and convalescent were housed. There was no heating and the beds consisted of planks with a straw mattress on top. There were few blankets. The healthy prisoners were lodged in the school. It had whitewashed walls, no heating and missing window panes. There were rats and other infestations in both the church and school. Both places were dirty and the lavatories, the Turkish kind you have to crouch over, were filthy and stinking.

These men were confined to the courtyard of their building and rarely had a chance to walk outside. They cooked their own food, usually burghul with vegetable soup and meat. The food was fine but the portions were not generous. The healthy men were expected to work long hours building a school half an hour's walk away. They worked from five in the morning until five in the evening with a one-hour break. They were supposed to be paid a piastre a day but many complained they never received it. Money was often deducted from their pay to repair damaged tools. William's diary contains a list of the pay he received from the Turkish government and from the US embassy, which was sending money to prisoners of war. Clothes were provided but not uniforms. Complaints were also made about the mail. Soldiers were only permitted to write four postcards of four lines per month while incoming post was extremely erratic.

There were serious complaints made about some of the guards who mistreated the men. This corroborates the descriptions in other books about the prisoner of war camp. It seems that men were bastinadoed, that is beaten on the soles of their feet, and the camp commandant had a fondness for young men, which he exercised freely. My grandfather mentions none of these things. It may be that he did not want to alarm his family, but it is probably due more to the censorship of letters and the fact that the officers were treated so much better than the men.

It seems strange that with the freedom to move around the town, not many tried to escape. However, it was a very remote place surrounded by difficult terrain. In addition to that there was the very real fear that the Turkish guards would take it out on the prisoners left behind. When William arrived in the camp many of the men captured at Gallipoli were already there, including Able Seaman Albert Knaggs. He had served on an Australian submarine, AE2, from the first year of the war until a German torpedo boat sank his submarine on 30 April 1915. He describes being eaten alive by bugs and lice and marched though the streets of Constantinople (now Istanbul) wearing Turkish soldier suits and red fezzes. Their officers rode in carriages. The men's heads were shaved and many were kept in chains. There was only a bare floor to sleep on and filthy food to eat.

After a couple of days they were sent to Afion where it was impossible to sleep because it was bitterly cold at night. Men kept warm by walking up and down all night. At Afion they were packed into rooms too small for their number and again there were no beds. Sanitary arrangements were also inadequate and the prisoners were allowed only two hours exercise each day for the first couple of months.

Prisoners were expected to work and Albert's group had the task of breaking stones and road-making. They worked from 6.30 a.m. to 5.30 p.m. Albert and others left Afion to work in the countryside where they lived in tents; when they returned to Afion they found they had been given beds of hay in relatively spacious accommodation that had been washed and disinfected. Shortly after this the American ambassador visited the camp. He distributed some supplies to the men held there and told the Turkish officers that the place was unfit for human habitation. On 5 October 39 British prisoners were sent to another camp at Angora. The train was due to leave at 2 p.m. but was delayed for four hours. The 39 men were shut in a horse van with not even enough room to sit down from 2 p.m. until 10 p.m. the following night when they arrived at their destination. Conditions were similar in the new camp to those they had already encountered.

On 9 June 1916 Albert noted in his diary that General Townshend and 8000 prisoners from Baghdad were on their way to Afion Kara Hissar. At that time Albert was in Bozanli where he eventually died from acute dysentery on 22 October 1916, just two months before the start of William's diary. This second diary is in the form of letters home that he copied up and that were consequently subject to the fierce eye of the censor. It feels as though these letters are not the first he sent as he makes no mention of his journey or arrival at Afion.

17 December 1916

Dear Ma,

All's well very pleased to say that I have received several letters lately, some two months ago I sent home for twenty pounds through the American Embassy, Constantinople on my bank and as yet have not received it, you might enquire about this for me and if they have not paid it to stop payment.

Dear Betty,

All's well, thanks very much for your letter. I can assure you that you have not offended me in any way, we are only allowed to write a PC a week and two letters a month so you will understand why it is that I cannot write you more often. Dear Betty should very much like to know your feelings regards myself. I noticed that when I was home on leave after I had asked you to let me have as much of your time as you could, instead of seeing more of you I saw much less in fact not at all for several weekends as I often wonder. We are now allowed to play football twice a week you can just guess how tired I was after the first game. You might ask my people to write to my old firm and let them know where I am and also to thank them for what they are doing for me. Also ask Edie to enquire about some money I sent home for: about two months ago I sent home through the American Embassy Constantinople for twenty pounds on my bank since which I have heard nothing further, if it as not been paid tell her to tell my bank to stop payment.

Don't forget to answer my question, we have known each other for a long time now should like to know your thoughts. We have been very lucky lately about a fortnight ago we all had a complete outfit of warm clothing boots overcoats etc. sent us by the American Embassy, but still am looking forward to receiving your socks thanks very much parcels take a long time to reach here. You might also ask Edie to write to General C. Townshend prisoner of war Constantinople Turkey and thank him for the assistance he gave me when I met him in the desert give him my full name and address. Well Betty Xmas will soon be on us again we are getting ready for a big feast. You might ask my Dad if he brought home my gear with him, ask them to write about my pay.

31 December 1916

Dear Betty,

Thanks for your letter also card from Flo. We had a grand time on Christmas day the Commandant sent us a basket of mistletoe which made me think of you. You might tell my people to send the PC with my request up to the Admiralty. Have just returned from the Turkish bath, we are allowed to go once a week. No news of parcels so far they take a long time.

Dear Edie,

We had a very good time Xmas Day we had the French prisoners over to lunch with us the commandant sent us up a large basket of mistletoe so we decorated the place up a bit so far have heard nothing about the parcels but of course they take a long time to reach here the chocolate, cocoa & cigarettes will be quite a treat when they do arrive, I have just come back from the Turkish Bath where we are allowed to go once a week they are very fine indeed. Glad to hear that you wrote to Mr Catherick also the result very good of them. About three months ago I sent home through the American Embassy Constantinople for twenty pounds on my bank since which I have heard nothing further if it has not been paid tell my bank to stop payment as I have no need for it now. You might send me out a statement of my accounts in Bank also Post Office. You might also send up the postcard with my written request on it. How is Dad, is he home yet did he bring my gear home with him tell him to write me as I am longing to hear from him. The people who get the most letters through are those that have their envelopes printed so you might try this, if not print the address in ink. We are now allowed to play football twice a week, and feel much better for it. You might send me Aunt Millie's address as I should like to write to her give her my kind regards and thank her for the chocolate. Trust Syd, Gertie, Kit, Bert and Eileen are all keeping very fit give my kindest regards to Cook and Tommy Pierce.

Well Edie old girl must draw to a close trusting you Ma, Dad and all at home are in the best of health and spirits.

I remain

Your loving brother

Will

P.S. Send my kindest regards to Miss Redding.

17 January 1917

Dear Syd & Gertie,

You might tell my Ma to get the address printed on the envelopes she send me failing this print the address in ink. Mrs Reeks will very likely call on Ma. Ask Dad to send me out some Fan Fan cigars. Betty Redding has been very decent in sending me letters every week, send my postcard up to the Admiralty about pay. Please send me a photo of Eileen. I am now growing a beard. Love to Miss Jennings also Wilkinsons.

21 January 1917

My Dearest Ma,

All's well. Some months ago I sent home for twenty pounds on my bank. If not cashed pleased stop payment, send the PC with my written request on it, Write and thank the old firm for what they are doing for me. Much love to yourself and all at home.

28 January 1917

Dear Betty,

All's well, thanks very much for letters have also just received one from Ray & Flo, thank them very much indeed for me as we simply long for letters here. We are still allowed to play football twice a week, yesterday we went for a long country walk wish you had been with us. You might tell my Ma to send me out some tea tabloids, coffee, cocoa, biscuits, potted meats, cigars, toilet soap, jams etc. tell them not to think that I am asking for a lot, but this is simply a list to guide them as to what is the best to send. How are you getting on at home I often think of you and wonder what you are doing, how did the concert go off guess you had a jolly time what would you give for a stroll across the Hilly Fields this evening. You might tell them at home to get the address printed on the envelopes they send me, failing this print the address in ink as the people that get the most letters through have the address printed, but must say as regards your letters have been very lucky they seem to be coming through very well. We have a very decent time here, we have a very good commandant which means a lot, we live three in a room, their are twelve of us in our house, and we have privates for servants we get a game of bridge every night, and we have a fine library of about two hundred books which various officers have had sent them: so what with one thing and another we do fairly well. Well Betty really don't think I have any fresh news for this mail. Kindest regards to your Ma, Ray & Flo.

My dearest Ma,

All's well, please send me out some Tea Tabloids, coffee & cocoa, jams etc. We are still allowed to play football twice a week & yesterday we went for a nice long walk. I am very pleased to say that I am very fit. Much love to yourself, Edie & all at home.

4 February 1917

Dear Sirs,

Have just heard from my people that you are still paying me for which I thank you all very much indeed. I had Typhus & was in Aleppo Hospital three months, but am very pleased to say that I am quite fit again now,

Trusting you are all well.

11 February 1917

Dear Aunt Millie,

Have just heard from home that you have put some sweets for which I thank you very much indeed, am pleased to say that we are very well treated here. Give my kindest regards to Arthur, Percy & Uncle Ted.

Dear Mrs Firman

I have just received a postcard from you dated July 23rd & one from the Central Prisoners of War Committee dated Nov 8th, enquiring about your son. I am very sorry indeed to have to inform you that he was killed about a quarter of an hour before we surrendered, by a shell that hit the bridge and exploded, am very pleased to say that he suffered no pain as death took place instantly, I am the only officer left. Do you know if any awards were given, everybody here seems certain that your son should at least get the DSO, a good man to enquire from is Rear Admiral Wemyss as he saw us about half an hour before we started. Am very pleased to say that we are fairly well treated here and that letters are now getting through quickly. My home address is 58 Ashmead Road St Johns London SE.

I remain

Yours truly W. Louis Reed.

Dear Edie,

All's well. I have just received several back postcards from you Miss Redding, also need a photo of Miss Jennings last mail when are you going to send me your photo you must put it in a letter don't make a larger parcel out of it. Just lately I have received two sums of money one for about two pounds and the other about one. You might try and find out who sent these to me as I have no idea and should like to thank them, it was very thoughtful. Have you heard any more about my pay if not you might ask Dad to go up and enquire about it for me. Last week I had a letter from Mrs Firman, mother of the officer that was killed on our affair. You might write and tell her that her son was killed by a shell hitting the bridge which exploded tell her that I am very pleased to say that he suffered no pain as death took place instantly. Give her my full postal address. Her address is Gateforth Lodge, New Malden, Surrey also tell Miss Redding to send me her photo I should also like one of Eileen. What a surprise I had this morning, received the first parcel from home, for which I thank you all very much indeed, the cigarettes were a treat; it contained 1 pair pants, 1 vest, 5 pair socks, cigarettes and sweets. Don't stop sending parcels as they get through alright only take some time.

Dear Ma,

Very many happy returns of March 1st. I was awfully glad to hear that Dad had arrived home safely is he doing anything yet. Why don't you write more than once a week you should repeat anything you want me to know as letters easily go astray. Write to W. Coxon c/o his firm give him my kind regards and tell them also W. Muse also to Miss E. Walker. Well really don't think I have any fresh news for this mail so trusting you, Dad & all at home are in the best of health.

Will

P.S. Kindest regards to Wilkinsons & Grace.

19 February 1917

Dear Mabel,

I have just received a postcard and letter from you, thanks very much indeed for the photo. We are allowed to play football twice a week and are fairly well treated here, let Gertie know that you've heard from me.

25 February 1917

My dearest Dad,

All's well, I was very pleased indeed to hear that you had arrived home again & that you are feeling very fit, have you heard any more about my pay. If not you might go up and enquire for me. Last week I received my first parcel from home for which I thank you all very much indeed, about two months ago I received two sums of money one for about one pound & the other for two. I have not got any idea who sent them, you might try to find out for me as it was very thoughtful of them. We have no work to do here & are allowed to play football twice a week, and a Turkish bath once.

You might send me out a box of cigars of a hundred not cheap ones, some of the very best. We can get plenty of cigarettes here but must say that some Abdullahs would be very nice for a change. What did you think of Jack when you arrived, as he turned out as good a dog as we thought he would, How is Edie looking and keeping sincerely hope very fit, I expect her Goss collection is a nice large one by now, tell her that she may treat herself to a china cabinet whenever she likes. Write more than once a week to me & if you have anything you want me to know repeat yourself as letters are liable to go astray. We feed ourselves very well here we are allowed seven Turkish pounds a month, & also receive three pounds from the Embassy, so as you can just imagine we do ourselves fairly well. I grew a beard, quite a decent one, but have taken it off again, so you might send me out two sticks of shaving soap. Tell Edie to send me out her photo, also one of Miss Redding & Eileen put them in an envelope separately. Well Dad really don't think I have any fresh news for this mail. Trusting you, Ma, Edie & all at home are in the best of health.

Sunday 25 February 1917

My dear Betty,

Thanks very much for letters, it is awfully good of you writing every week. I had my first parcel from home last week. Please send me out one of your photos put it in an envelope. Tell them at home if they have not heard any more about my pay to go up and enquire about it. Much love to yourself, Ma & all.

Sunday 5 March 1917

Dear Dad,

Glad to hear gear is home safely. Recvd letter from Kit & Gertie. Have you heard any more about my pay if not you might go up and enquire. Write me more than once a week repeat everything you want me to know, send me full statement of my accounts. Send me Photo of Eileen & Edie put them in an envelope. Much love to Yourself, Ma, Edie & all at home, tell them to write.

12 March 1917

Dear ma,

All's well, I received my first parcel from home about two weeks ago. I received a letter from Kit & one from Gertie thank them for me, please. Send me out two or three caps size 7 or 7⅛. Much love to yourself Dad, Edie & all at home. Write me more than once a week.

Dear Betty

Thanks very much for your letter dated 6/2/17. Very glad to hear that you enjoyed yourself at the Theatre don't go falling in love you know at any rate wait for me to arrive home so as I can be present. Don't forget and look quick and send me one of your photos put it in an envelope I should like one very much indeed. On the 17th Dec I wrote you a letter something like this from 1 to 2. You might ask my people to send me out two or three very good caps size 7 or 7⅛. I am very sorry to hear that Jack has taken such a dislike to you what sort of dog as he turned out does he look smart or common. So far have not received your socks but they will arrive alright later on, parcels are come through much better now. Tell my people to write more than once a week & anything they want me to know to repeat themselves as letters easily go astray. I was surprised to hear that Fred is married.

18 March 1917

Dear Dad,

All's well, still going strong please send me out 2 or 3 caps size 7 or 7⅛, I have not received any letters from home for about a month, have received several from Miss Redding & one from Miss Jennings have you heard anything about my pay yet, if not you might go up and enquire for me. How is Edie? I hear she has been feeling unwell trust alright now. Much love to yourself, Ma, Edie & all at home. Tell them to write Will.

Sunday 25 March 1917

Dear Syd & Gertie,

All's well, thanks very much for your letter of Jan 24th. Glad to hear that you got my letter about the dog licence. We have not received any mail for a fortnight. We went for a good country walk yesterday. The weather here is grand. Much love to you both & all at home.

My dearest Ma,

All's well, am very pleased indeed to say am keeping very fit, yesterday we went for a long country walk, the weather here now is grand, warm in the daytime & nice and cool in the evening. We have not had any mail for over a fortnight but hope to shortly, how is Arthur & Cook are they both still at home? I was glad to hear that my gear has arrived home safely, hope there was nothing stolen from it. Have you heard any more about my pay, if not you might get Dad to go up & enquire about it for me. I had a letter from Jennings some weeks ago she was then staying with Gertie, she told me that she had been down home playing '31' so I suppose you still play every Sat. night. Hope you are lucky sometimes. Miss Redding has been very good indeed whenever I get a mail I get one from her she must be writing every week she always raves about Eileen, and says what a dear little girl she is, according to Betty she must have lovely hair and nice little ways. I heard from her that Dad is sending me out the cigars I wrote for, I think the selection of sweets is top hole won't we have a bust if they arrive alright guess we shall make ourselves sick. We recvd quite a lot of cocoa from the American Embassy recently, I can assure you it was a treat after not having had any for a long time. You might ask Edie to write to Miss Janekian give her my love tell her shall be very pleased to hear from her whenever she has time, also write to W. Coxon c/o his firm, give him my kindest regards & let him know where I am, also to W. Muse. Some weeks ago I received my first parcel from home thanks very much indeed hope to receive some more shortly. Well Ma really don't think I have any fresh news. So trusting You, Dad & all at home are in the best of health. Send me Aunt Millie's address.

2 April 1917 Monday

Dear Dad,

I hear from Mrs Chitty that Cowley & Firman have been awarded the VC. You might write up & find out if any other awards were given. Thanks very much for letter with statement of my accounts. I am very fit, received letters from Syd, Redding & home Trust all at home are well.

Much love Will

Sunday 8 April 1917

My dear Edie,

All's well, am very pleased to say that I am keeping very fit indeed, yesterday we went for a nice long country walk picked a lot of violets on the way. I was very pleased indeed to receive Dad letter with a statement of my accounts, also to know that the money is now being paid into my bank alright let me know how much they pay in next quarter.

I hear from Mr Chitty that Cowley & Firman have been awarded the VC, you might write up & enquire if anybody else recvd any awards. Some week ago I recvd my first parcel from home. Have enquired about Lieut. Jones they tell me that he was in hospital the first week in August 1915 this is the information I got from Major Brett. Was very glad to hear that Tommy Pearce is keeping fit, hope you enjoyed yourselves at the theatre remember me to him when you next write. Guess old Grace nearly had a fit when she won three times running at '31's do you play every Saturday. Thanks very much for your letter wishing me many happy returns. How is Eileen getting on she must be quite a big girl by this time. I expect she chats away like anything now, pleased to hear she is great pals with Jack.

Thank Syd very much for his letter tell him I would write more often only we have a very small limit here how are his beans this year. I had a letter from Betty Redding dated Mar 12th telling me that she had called on you. We have two clergy men with us now, & today being Easter Sunday we had an early morning service & one in the evening I attended both. Well really don't think I have any fresh news for this week so trusting you, Ma, Dad & all at home are in the best of health & spirits. With much love to all.

Tuesday 9 April 1917

Dear Betty,

I hear that Cowley & Firman have been awarded the VC ask my people to enquire if any other awards were given. Pleased to say am very fit. We had a fine time on Easter Monday, went down & had lunch with the other camp. Much love to yourself & all at your home.

Sunday 15 April

I hear that Cowley & Firman have been awarded the VC you might write & find out if any other awards were given. Thanks very much for statement of accounts also pay let me know how much they pay in next time. Pleased to say am very fit,

Much love to yourself, Ma, Dad & all at home.

22 April 1917

Dear Mr Lee,

No doubt you will be very surprised at hearing from me, only thought that perhaps you would like a few lines to know how I am getting on. Some time ago I wrote to the firm thanking them for what they are doing for me, do you know if they received my postcard, if not you might let Mr Parry know that I am very thankful. We are fairly well treated here, are allowed to play football twice a week & a walk once, we are also allowed to write two letters a month & a postcard each week. Last year I was in hospital in Aleppo with Typhus but was very well treated & am pleased to say am fit now. I should be very pleased to hear from you, as to how you all are, write more than once as letters easily go astray. The weather here is top hole very warm in the day time but nice & cool mornings and evenings. Batty is not here he is at another camp. I heard a few weeks ago that he is keeping very fit. We have these two parsons here with us, so we can have a service every Sunday morning & evening, which is very nice. Kindest regards to yourself, Mr Parry & all at the office, Trust you are all keeping well.

My Dear Aunt Millie

I am very pleased to say that I am keeping very fit. We are allowed to play football twice a week & a stroll once. The weather here is top hole very warm in the daytime but nice & cool in the evenings. How are Arthur & Percy getting on. Kindest regards to yourself & Uncle, Ruby & all at home.

24 April 1917

One year since he was captured.

Sunday 29 April 1917

Dear Charlie,

I am very pleased to say am keeping very fit. We are very well treated here. Shall be very pleased to hear from you or any club members, also

Coxon, Muse & Dixon. Give my kindest regards to all the Woolston branch. Trust you, your sister & all are in the best of health.

Secretary Admiralty

Dear Sir,

I would be very much obliged if you would let me know how much my pay is & how much I am being stopped. I was captured on the 24th April 1916 whilst trying to get through to Kut-El-Mara was then in charge of HMS *Julnar*. Would also be very glad if you could let me know if any awards were given as the crew are also here prisoners with me.

6 May 1917

Dear Betty,

All's well. I am very pleased to hear that you call on my people now & again. I recvd my second parcel on Sunday boots, cocoa etc. Try & write more than once a week. We have 2 parsons with us now so we have a service every Sunday evening. Much love to yourself. Trust you & all at home are very fit.

Yours ever Billy.

Dear old Kit,

How goes it after all this time, am very pleased to say that I am keeping very fit indeed we have no work to do here we are allowed football twice a week & a walk once, we went for a nice long mountain climb last week. How is Eileen getting on expect she is quite a big girl. You might send me out one of her photos if you have already sent one send another in case the first has gone astray. I hear that Syd has now got an allotment & that he is very busy digging it up. Give him & Gertie my kindest regards & tell them that I shall be very pleased to hear from them whenever they have time, also tell them at home to write more than once a week. Recvd my 2nd parcel from home on Thurs, the boots fit a treat am wearing them now. Thank them all at home very much indeed. I hear from Betty Redding every week. Tell Edie to write to Annie Giles & give her my kindest regards & tell her I should be very glad to hear how she is getting on. Remember me kindly to old Bert tell him I wish him the very best of luck should be very glad to hear from him. I hear that Cowley & Firman have been awarded the VC you might ask them to write up & find out if any other awards were given. Also ask them to let me know how much is paid into my bank each quarter not including Lynch's. Tell them that Lt. C. Chitty is quite fit & sound what they saw in the paper must have been a mistake, you might let his people know this.

We have got two parsons with us now, so we have a service every Sunday evening which I attend regular. Well Kit really don't think I have any fresh news this mail. Much love to yourself, Bert & Eileen. Trusting all at home are in the best of health. Recvd parcel from Betty Redding. Remember me to Mr & Mrs Gillard.

Sunday 6 May 1917

Dear Betty

Thanks very much for calling on my people. I recvd my 2nd parcel from home Thurs, boots, cocoa etc. Also a parcel from you thanks very much indeed it is awfully good of you. Try & write more than once a week as I am always looking forward to your letters. Much love to yourself. Trust all at home are very fit.

Sunday 17 May 1917

Dear Edie Walker,

No doubt you will be very surprised at hearing from me. I am very pleased to say that I am keeping very fit & that we are well treated. Should be very pleased to hear from you write me a letter, more than one as letters easily go astray. Trusting You, Yours & your Ma are in the best of health & spirits.

20 May 1917

Dear Mrs Firman,

I have just recvd your letter of Jan 28th am awfully sorry that you have not heard from me, as I have written twice so my letters have gone astray. I am very sorry indeed to have to inform you that your son was killed about a quarter of an hour before we surrendered, by a shell that hit the bridge & exploded am very pleased indeed to say that he suffered no pain as death took place instantly. I was very pleased to hear the other week that both your son and Capt. Cowley had been awarded the VC do you know if any other awards were given. I am very sorry but cannot give you any account of the burial of your son, bar that they promised me that they would give him a decent funeral. Am very pleased to say that we are very well treated here & letters & parcels are now coming through fairly quickly. I should be very much obliged if you will thank Miss Thornton for the money I received from them about a fortnight ago. Shall be pleased to call on you when I return, shall then be able to explain things better.

With my kindest regards

My Dear Betty

All's well, last week I recvd two parcels one from home containing boots, cocoa etc & one from you socks & chocolate the socks are top hole really clever of you, thanks very much indeed mine had several holes in them have tried darning them but am not an expert. Have just this minute recvd another one from home a blue serge suit this makes four parcels I have recvd in all.

Dear Betty you ask me if I like you calling on my people of course I do you silly girl, it is awfully good of you, & I know that they appreciate it for they have said in their letters how good it was of you, do try & write me more than once a week letters easily go astray & I simply long for letters from you. We have two parsons with us now so we have a service every Sunday evening which I always attend, I think everybody ought to attend a place of worship at least once on Sundays. We have got quite a decent garden. Peas, Sweet Peas, Carrots, Melons etc. I am generally busy in the mornings digging, watering & weeding etc. Do send me out one of your photos if you have already sent me one send another in case the first has gone astray put them in separate envelopes to the letter you write me. You might ask them at home to let me know how much is paid into my bank each quarter not including Lynch's & thank them for the statement of my account which I received some time ago. How is Ray & Florrie getting on have either of them got off yet, you might kindly remember me to Fred when next you write and tell him that I wish him the best of luck. I have not received any letters for about a month but hope to shortly, you will understand why I ask you & my people to write more than once a week. Well Betty dear really don't think that I have any fresh news for this time, So trusting You, Your Ma, Ray & Florrie are in the best of health.

With much love Billy.

Dear Syd,

Am very pleased to say that I am keeping very fit. I reecvd my blue serge suit about a week ago. I hear that you are very busy on an allotment how do you like hard work. I have not recvd any letters for a month tell them to write more often.

Much love to Yourself, Gertie & all at home, best of luck.

27 May 1917

Dear Edie,

All's well, have recvd several letters from home & a photo of Betty very good indeed, you might write & thank her for me, when are you sending yours. Try & write more than once a week. Recvd my suit a week ago, went for a fine walk yesterday.

Much love to yourself, Ma, Dad & all at home.

Secretary Admiralty, 2 June 1917

Dear Sir,

I would be very much obliged if you will let me know how much my pay is being stopped. I hear from my people that I am being paid a certain sum which is fixed provisionally pending receipt of information from owners of the ship as to my rate of pay. I was captured on the 24th April 1916 whilst trying to get through to the Kut-El-Amara Garrison was then engineer in charge of the *Julnar*. I hear that the other officers were both awarded the VC would be very much obliged if you could tell me of any other awards.

My Dear Dad,

All's well, thanks very much for the statement of my accounts, I wish you would write up & draw their attention to the fact that my pay was fixed provisionally pending receipt of information from owners of the ship & ask them if they have done anything in this matter as I think the pay very small. I recvd several letters lately, a very nice one from Mrs. Firman & two photos from Betty, also a letter from Billy Coxon & parcels have been coming through quite well really. We have got a small garden here which keeps me very busy in the mornings our green peas are looking a treat full of bloom. We get plenty of cherries here very cheap. We have just recvd some light summer clothing from the Embassy so we will be nicely fixed up for the summer. Was very glad to hear that Edie has got such a nice big Goss china collection, tell her to buy a cabinet. I wish you would ask them to transfer all but forty pounds from my current account to deposit. Was very sorry to hear that Miss Yanakian had been very ill sincerely hope she is alright again by now. I never here from her. I was very glad to hear that you are allowed to send parcels again can assure you that they will be very acceptable. Do try to write me more than once a week as it is one of the things we look forward to most & as letters easily go astray you might try & write more often, get the others to write also I feel sure that Syd & Kit have plenty of time. In one of the parcels please send seeds & bulbs also tell Betty this. How is Syd getting on with his allotment I have got several good engineering books, so get plenty of reading, you might write & ask the ASE to send me out some books. I am very pleased to say that I am keeping very fit. We get three good walks a week & football once.

3 June 1917

My Dearest Betty

All's well. Thanks very much for the photos. I like the head and shoulders one best. Notice you are wearing the watch in the other. I had two frames made for them, they now hang over my bed. They look a treat. Much love to yourself. Kindest regards to your Ma.

Sunday 10 June 1917

Dear Mrs Thornton

Thanks very much indeed for the money you sent some time ago. I recvd it safely, it was really awfully good of you. Could you find out for me if any other awards were given besides the two VCs for Lieutenant Cowley & Lieutenant Firman. We are treated very well, letters & parcels arrive safely. Very pleased to hear from you. Kindest regards.

17 June 1917

My Dearest Ma,

All's well. Thank Dad very much for the statement of my accounts was very pleased indeed to hear that you had transferred some of the money to my deposit accounts. I wish you would write up and draw their attention to the fact that my pay was fixed provisionally pending receipt of information from owners of the ship & ask them if they have done anything in this matter as I think my pay very small. About a fortnight ago we recvd some light summer clothing from the Embassy so are nicely fixed up for the summer. Was very glad to hear that Edie has got such a nice Goss collection has she bought a china cabinet yet? You might tell her to write to Annie Giles & give her my kindest regards should be very pleased to hear from her, Was very sorry to hear that Miss Yanakian had been very ill. Sincerely hope that she is fit again by now. Do try to write me more than once a week as it is one of the things we look forward to most & as letters easily go astray you might try & write me more often. Get the others to write also. I feel certain that Syd, Kit, Gertie have plenty of time. I recvd one of my boxes of sweets about a fortnight ago they are really top hole, in every parcel you send me in future you might put in several packets of seeds also some bulbs mark them so as I shall know which is which. I have got quite a decent garden here my green peas tomatoes are growing a treat. I pass quite a lot of time away looking after them. You might write & ask the ASE to send me out some books on engineering. We can get plenty of fruit & vegetables here and fairly cheap. Well, Ma really don't think I have any fresh news for this mail. So trusting you, Dad, Edie & all at home are in the best of health and spirits.

My Dearest Betty,

Thanks very much indeed for the two photos they are top hole. I recvd one of my boxes of sweets last week. I have got quite a decent garden, pass a lot of time away in it. I am going to service this evening. Much love to yourself and all.

24 June 1917

Dear Uncle Ted,

All's well. I am very pleased to say that I am keeping very fit indeed, we are very well treated here, allowed to play cricket three times a week. Trust you, Aunt Millie, Ruby, Arthur & Percy are as well.

1 July 1917

My Dearest Betty,

All's well thank you very much indeed for the two photos I have had them both framed they are now hanging over my bed. I have not recvd any letters for about three weeks but hope to shortly I simply long for letters from you. Would it be asking too much of you to ask you to write more than once a week. You might also tell them at home as letters easily go astray. We have a fairly good time here now, get cricket about three times a week & parcels are now coming through better. I have recvd several from home and one from you, the socks I am wearing now. You might ask my people to write up and find out if they have done anything more about my pay, as they say it was fixed provisionally. There's good health am just about to drink a very nice glass of beer. My garden is looking top hole the sweet peas are in full bloom, you might ask them to send me in every parcel a packet of seeds, also some bulbs, mark them so as I shall know which is which. Copy of 1 to 2 in my letter of March 11th. I was very sorry indeed to hear that Fred has been ill, sincerely hope he is quite alright again now tell him that I should be very pleased to hear from him if he has time, also your Ma, Ray & Florrie, give my kindest regards to Ann. How is Eileen getting on have you seen her lately. I hear from them at home that you called on them thank you very much indeed. You might ask them to write to King, Cleverly & Barlow & tell them I shall be very pleased indeed to hear from them (at home) as to how they are all getting on let them know that Batty is keeping very fit, he is not here but I heard about him recently. Ask my Ma to send me out some shirts & tell her to put a tuck in the sleeves. Well Betty don't really think I have any fresh news with my fondest love to yourself & much love to your Ma, Ray & Florrie.

My Dearest Ma,

All's well I have not recvd any letters for three weeks. Please write up about my pay & point out that it was only fixed provisionally. Send me out some shirts. We are now allowed to play cricket three times a week. Much love to yourself, Dad & all at home, tell them to write often. Letter to the Admiralty exact copy of my letter of 2 June 1917.

15 July 1917

My dear Edie,

All's well thanks for the letters I recvd from you two from you, two from Dad, two from Betty thanks very much for the snapshot. It is quite good, a pity Jack moved he seems to have grown a fine dog try

& send me out some more photos. All I have now is two of Betty & the snapshot do try to write me more than once a week & get the others to write also. I was very surprised to hear that you were moving sincerely hope you will like it alright a nice change. Fancy old Kit moving too, it will be quite nice for Kit & Bert to be together again I guess Bert will make a great fuss of Eileen. I was glad to hear that Syd has got a soft job don't forget to remember me to him & tell that I wish him the very best of luck. Dear Edie I think I told you before have recvd several parcels the suit & boots fit a treat & have also recvd one of my boxes of sweets they are top hole, also recvd one parcel from Betty. I was taken in one of the groups here but don't know if it is the one you saw. We are still allowed to play cricket three times a week. You might write up and ask them if they have done anything further about my pay & point out that it was only fixed provisionally. If ever you write to Annie Giles you might remember me to her & tell her that I should be very pleased to hear how she is getting on. You might ask Ma to send me out some shirts with collars attached put a tuck in the sleeves. No I never hear from Miss Gill she wrote to me twice but I never answered them. Tell Dad to give my best regards to Mrs & Mr Jefferys. Well Edie old girl really don't think that I have any fresh news for this mail so trusting that you, Ma, Dad & all at home are in the best of health. Don't part with the dog.

22 July 1917

Dear Miss Thornton

Thanks very much indeed for the money you sent me some time ago, it was really awfully good of you. Could you find out for me if any other awards were given besides the VCs. We are treated fairly well here. Kindest regards.

28 July 1917

Dear Mr Juniper,

All's well. I have been here over a year am very pleased to say that we are fairly well treated here. Remember me to Tal & Nell tell them I should be very pleased to hear from them. Write more than once. Letters easily go astray.

Kindest regards to you and yours.

My Dearest Betty,

All's well. Thanks very much for your letter I am awfully sorry you have not recvd a long letter from me, as I have sent you several. Last week I had a snapshot sent me from home you might let them know that I recvd it alright and think it quite good. I was very surprised to hear that Kit was moving I guess Bert will make a rare fuss of Eileen. We are still allowed to play cricket three times a week last week we played thirty and over against under thirty the old birds won easily. I made seventeen not out. Was very surprised to hear from you that my Dad was at Birmingham sincerely hope that Ma & Edie will have a good time. How is Fred getting on is he home yet, trust he is quite fit again now. Tell Ray from me that she must not get too thin and fall down the drain until I get home, as should very much like to be there when it happens, might get a chance of seeing some sight. You might ask them at home to send me out some soft collars 16. Sincerely hope you will have a very good time on your holidays this year. Don't forget me when you are enjoying yourself & write & let me know everything that happens expect you will be swimming best part of the day how I wish I could be with you we would have great fun. Kindest regards to Ray, Florrie & Ma. Much love to yourself.

5 August 1917

My Dear Edie.

All's well. I was awfully sorry to hear of Arthur death, also to hear that you have been ill again sincerely hope you are quite well by this time. Yes I have recvd several parcels since I have been a prisoner. Much love to yourself, Ma, Dad & all at home.

6 August 1917

Dear Mr Parry.

I am very pleased to say that I am keeping as well as can be expected. Must again thank the firm very much indeed, for what they are doing for me I heard recently that Mr T & Mr & Mrs L, are well Sincerely hope all is well with you & yours.

My dearest Ma,

All's well, we have not recvd any letters for about a fortnight but hope to shortly. Sorry to hear that Edie has been ill. Sincerely hope that she is quite alright by this time. Also very sorry to hear of Arthur's death, you might remember me to Aunt Millie and Uncle Ted and tell them how sorry I was to hear of their great loss. Send me out tea in every parcel you send me as there is none to be obtained here. I hear that there are new orders about parcels something about the government sending us two a month you might find out the rights of this. My garden is going on top hole. We are still allowed to play cricket three times a week which helps to pass away the time nicely. Write to the old firm and thank them very much indeed for what they are doing for me also let them know that I am keeping very fit.

Sunday 8 August 1917

My dearest Betty.

All's well, ask my Ma if she has heard anything about the new scheme for sending parcels. Give Ray my kindest regards you might tell her from me I should like to know how 'Fairy Feet' is getting on has he joined up, if not why not. Fondest love to you & all at home.

12 August 1917

Dear Billy.

All's well. Thanks very much for your letter was very pleased indeed to hear that you are keeping fit. We are fairly well treated here allowed to play cricket three times a week. Don't forget to write me also Billy Muse. Kindest regards to you both.

Dear old Syd,

All's well. How goes it with you & yours after all this long time, am very pleased to say that I am keeping very fit, we are fairly well treated here are allowed to play cricket three times a week. I was awfully sorry to hear that Edie had been ill again sincerely hope she is quite alright by this time tell her from me that she must take great care of herself. Was very sorry to hear of Arthur's death I expect they were all very much grieved, remember me to Aunt Millie & Uncle Ted & tell how awfully sorry I was to hear of Arthur's death. You might ask Ma to send me out tea in every parcel she sends me as there is practically none to be obtained here. The suit you got for me from Tuffs arrived safely some time ago, it fits top hole & looks a treat. We have quite a nice little garden I spend a lot of time in it, my tomatoes are bearing quite a lot of fruit. How is Dad getting on is he still away from home, have you still got Billy. What sort of dog has Jack turned out, does he look worth the money we gave for him, if you like to buy a bitch of the same breed I will pay for it, would very likely get some fine puppies. Well Syd really don't think I have any fresh news for this time. Much love to yourself Gertie & all at home tell them to write often, have only heard from you twice since I have been a prisoner.

2 September 1917

My dear Ray

How goes it old girl, am very pleased to say that I am top hole. How is 'Fairy Feet' getting on, do you go mixed bathing together, why has he not joined up? Much love to yourself, Betty, Florrie and all at your home.

8 September 1917

My dearest Betty.

All's well, I received several letters from you last week & some from home, also one from Dad he seems to be enjoying himself very well. Was very pleased to hear that you recvd my long letter of May 20th I generally send once a month. You might ask my people to send me out two suits of pyjamas a packet of Gillette razor blades & plenty of tea. We have started amateur theatricals, I am taking the part of a lady we rehearse every morning. I make quite a good woman but haven't yet found out the way to Wareham. I notice that you are now writing more than once a week it is awfully good of you, You have no idea how we look forward to the Mail, it is our red letter day. We have not received any parcels for a long time now, but hope to get them all in a bunch shortly, they are very uncertain lately. You might send me out a book now and again I believe you can do it through W. H. Smiths Strand. The cheap editions 7d they come through very quickly, you asked me once if I had read *Milestones*, why not try & send it to me. I know you won't mind me asking you to do this, let my people know also as we pass a lot of time away reading. I envy you smoking cigarettes you bounder I would give a lot for a really decent one now. Well Betty don't think Have any fresh news for this week. Trust you Ray, Florrie, your Ma & all are well & in the best of spirits. Much love to yourself.

23 September 1917

Dear Mr Ford,

No doubt you will be very surprised at hearing from me, but I thought perhaps you would like to know how I am getting on. Very pleased indeed to say that I am keeping very fit, in the summer we were allowed to play cricket three times a week, but as it is much colder now we have started to play football, which helps to pass the time. How is Frank & Walter sincerely hope they are fit and well have either of them had to join up.

I had quite a decent garden here last summer grew a lot of tomatoes, it put me in remind of those you used to grow years ago (Golden Nuggets). Should very much like to hear from you write more than once as letters easily go astray, we have not had any letters now for about a month. How is Mrs Ford & the girls sincerely hope they are fit and well, also in the best of spirits. Well Mr Ford really don't think I have any more news for this mail so trusting you, Mrs Ford & all are well, with much love to all.

30 September 1917

My dearest Ma,

All's well. We have not received any letters or parcels for the last six weeks. Next Thursday & Wednesday we are playing a cricket match against the lower camp. How is Dad, sincerely hope he is better again. Much love to yourself, Dad, Edie and all at home.

7 October 1917

My darling Niece.

All's well. Many Happy Returns of your birthday [25 October]. We have started theatricals here we gave our first show last night it was a great success. I took the part of a woman. We have not received any letters.

Much love.

My dearest Betty.

All's well. We have not recvd any letters for over seven weeks. I think I told you that we have started amateur theatricals. We put our first show on last night, we have rigged up a proper stage, curtain, footlights etc, it was a great success. I took the part of a woman and

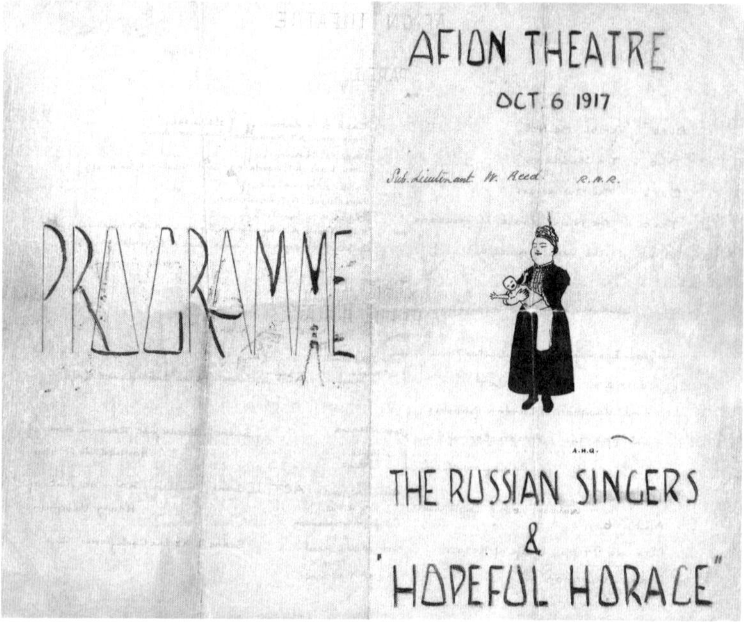

Cover of theatre programme.

fairly brought the house down when I appeared nursing a baby (little Willie) you should have seen me washing and doing the usual things I have most certainly found the way to Warham now.

Must not forget to wish Ray & you many happy returns of your birthday sincerely hope we shall spend the next together. You might also write to my Dad on his birthday Nov 9th & wish him the usual greetings for me.

The weather here is getting much colder we have finished cricket & expect to start football shortly. You might send me out a book now and again, you can send them through W. H. Smith, Strand by book post, they come through very quickly try & send me the book you spoke about, *Milestones*, also let my people know this. Please ask my Ma to send me out two suits of pyjamas, some Gillette razor blades & plenty of tea. Well Betty dear, really don't think I have any fresh news for this mail. Trust you, your Ma, Ray, Florrie and all are well. Much love to yourself.

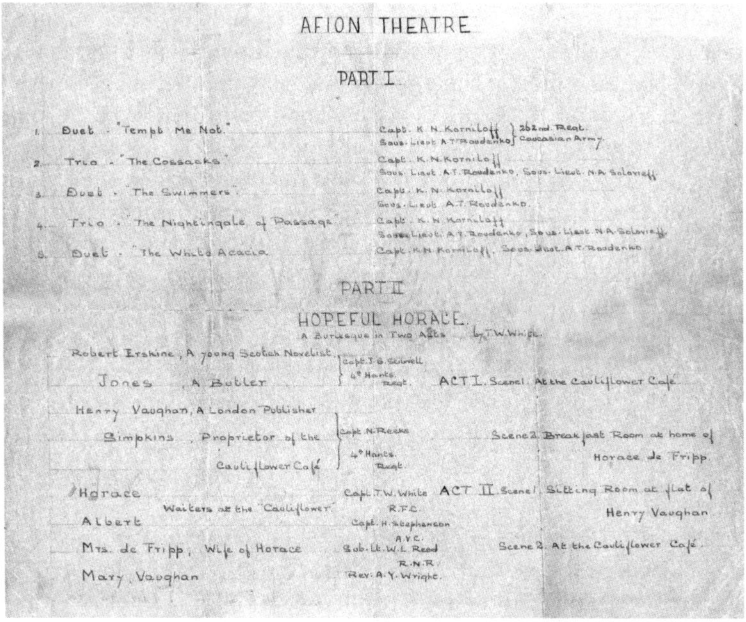

AFION THEATRE

PART I

1. Duet - "Tempt Me Not." — Capt. K. N. Korniloff, Sous-Lieut. A. T. Roudenko } 262nd Regt. Caucasian Army.
2. Trio - "The Cossacks" — Capt. K. N. Korniloff, Sous-Lieut. A. T. Roudenko, Sous-Lieut. N. A. Solovieff.
3. Duet - "The Swimmers". — Capt. K. N. Korniloff, Sous-Lieut. A. T. Roudenko.
4. Trio - "The Nightingale of Passage" — Capt. K. N. Korniloff, Sous-Lieut. A. T. Roudenko, Sous-Lieut. N. A. Solovieff.
5. Duet - "The White Acacia — Capt. K. N. Korniloff, Sous-Lieut. A. T. Roudenko

PART II

HOPEFUL HORACE.

A Burlesque in Two Acts by T. W. White.

Robert Erskine, A young Scotch Novelist }
Jones, A Butler } Capt. J. G. Stilwell 4th Hants. Regt.

Henry Vaughan, A London Publisher }
Simpkins, Proprietor of the Cauliflower Café } Capt. N. Reeks 4th Hants. Regt.

Horace — Capt. T. W. White R.F.C.

Waiters at the "Cauliflower"

Albert — Capt. H. Stephenson A.V.C.

Mrs. de Fripp, Wife of Horace — Sub-Lt. W. L. Read R.N.R.

Mary Vaughan — Rev: A. Y. Wright.

ACT I. Scene 1. At the Cauliflower Café.

Scene 2. Breakfast Room at home of Horace de Fripp.

ACT II. Scene 1. Sitting Room at flat of Henry Vaughan

Scene 2. At the Cauliflower Café.

Copy of theatre programme with William playing Mrs de Fripp.

Sunday 14 October 1917

My dearest Dad,

All's well. Pleased to say we recvd several letters this week, if you have sent me out a statement of my accounts, send out another one in case the first goes astray. Pleased to hear that you are getting on so well, much love to yourself, Ma, Edie & all at home.

Sunday 21 October 1917

Dear Mrs Thornton,

Thank you very much indeed for the money which I have just recvd. Would it be asking too much of you to send me out a suit of uniform & cap with badge (size 7). You can get my measurements from H. Tuffs, Tailor, Greenwich Road, Greenwich, London SE. I have nobody else that can do this for me.

My dearest Edie,

All's well. Last week we recvd several letters I also recvd another parcel cigars, soap etc. they arrived in a very good condition, in future whenever you send me any parcels you might sew them up in canvas. You might send me out some books now and again I believe you can do so through W. H. Smith, Strand by book post. They seem to come through very quickly. I believe I told you before that we have started amateur theatricals we had our first show about a fortnight ago. I took the part of a woman fairly brought the house down when I appeared nursing a baby (Little Willie) you should have seen me washing and doing the usual things. We have started to rehearse a new piece I am taking the part of a woman again. Please send me out two suits of pyjamas some gillette razors and plenty of tea. Don't think I have any fresh news for this mail. Send as many parcels as you can. Trust you Ma, Dad & all at home are well. Write to different friends about parcels.

4 November 1917

Dear Mrs Chitty.

Thanks very much for your very interesting letter. Letters are one of the things we look forward to most. Your son & I are keeping very fit. We are both taking part in our next theatricals which takes place on the 10th. Wishing you & yours a very Merry Xmas.

My dearest Betty.

All's well we recvd a lot of letters about a week ago several from you thanks very much indeed. You seem to have had a good time on your holiday. We are starting our second theatrical show on the 9th & 10th of Nov. I am taking the part of a woman again, a landlady. You might try & send me out a book or two now & again. I believe you can do so through W. H. Smith, Strand by book post they seem to come through very quickly.

We are still allowed to play football three times a week which passes the time away quickly. You might tell my Ma that in future when she sends me parcels to sew them up in canvas. I recvd my parcel of cigars, soap etc in very good condition. Tell her to send me two suits of pyjamas Gillette razor blades & plenty of tea. Don't forget to ask Ray & Florrie to send me out the photos you were speaking to me about. Well Betty dear I expect you will receive this letter about Xmas so must wish you all a very Merry & Happy Xmas. Don't get eating too much plum pudding & drinking too much wine. Kindest regards to your Ma, Ray & Florrie. Much love to yourself.

4 November Xmas Letter

My dearest Ma.

All's well. We are allowed to write an extra letter this week as a Xmas letter. So must start off by wishing you, Dad, Edie & all at home a very Merry Xmas.

Don't get drinking too much wine & eating too much plum pudding. In future when you send me any parcels you might sew them up in canvas. I recvd my parcel of cigars & soap in quite a good condition, you might send me out some books now & again. I believe you can do so through W. H. Smith Strand by book post they seem to come through very quickly. Don't be surprised if you hear that I am signing cheques now & again, I signed one last week. We are still allowed to play football three times a week which helps to pass the time. We are having our second theatrical show on the 9th & 10th Nov. I am taking the part of a woman, a landlady. If Dad has sent me out a statement of my accounts you might ask him to send me out another as I have not recvd the first it may have gone astray. We had several letters from home last week thanks very much don't forget to write often. You might write to Auntie Giles, Mrs Ford & several other old friends (Mrs Firman) & wish them a very Happy Xmas for me. Don't think I have any more to say this mail so wishing you, Dad, Edie & all at home also Betty a Very Happy Xmas.

Sunday 11 November 1917

Dear Mrs Firman,

All's well. Thanks very much indeed for the parcel you sent me which I recvd safely last week, really very kind of you. Wishing you & yours a very Happy Xmas. Kindest regards to you all.

18 November 1917

Ladies Emergency Committee

Thank you very much indeed for the parcel you sent me last April. I recvd it a fortnight ago, in very good condition it was really awfully good of you, tea is a good thing to send. We are allowed to play football tree times a week. Kindest regards.

My dearest Edie,

All's well. We have recvd several letters lately also some parcels. I recvd the parcel you sent me in good condition thanks very much indeed the tea was a treat. I also recvd one from Mrs Firman for which you might write & thank her very much indeed in future when you send parcels sew them up strongly in canvas send as many as you can.

26 November 1917

Dear Mrs Firman,

All's well, thanks very much indeed for the parcel you sent me which I recvd safely. It was really awfully good of you. Wishing you & yours a very Happy Xmas & a bright New Year. With my kindest regards to you all. Should like to hear from you.

Sunday 2 December 1917

Dear Aunt Millie,

Thanks very much indeed for your letters, letters are one of the things we look forward to most. I was most awfully sorry to hear of poor Arthur's death. We are still allowed to play football three times a week. Much love to yourself Uncle & all.

My dearest Betty,

All's well, we have not recvd any letters for some weeks but hope to shortly. Xmas will soon be on us again we are having a dinner party in the evening, you would have laughed if you had seen all twelve of us sitting down stoning the plums & stirring the puddings. We hope to have a very good time. We have two fine turkeys & two geese. Tell my people not to be surprised if I sign a cheque now & again also ask them to send me out a statement of my accounts send more than one in case the first goes astray. I believe my Dad sent me one some few weeks ago but I have not recvd it yet. Dear Betty you might send me out a book or two now and again cheap ones. I believe you can do so through W. H. Smith, Strand by book post they seem to come through quickly. Don't forget to let me know what you get up to Xmas & Boxing days, guess you will have a jolly fine time, I should just like to put my ear to the keyhole, expect I should hear some chatter. You might ask my people if they have heard anything further about my pay if not they might write up and point out that it was only fixed provisionally pending receipt of information from owners of the ship as to my rate of pay. How is Ray & Florrie getting on I should be very pleased to hear from them both, ask Ray from me as to how fairy feet is getting on what about Florrie has she got off yet. Don't forget to send me those photos you promised me taken whilst you were away on your holidays. Well Betty dear really don't think I have any more fresh news. Kindest regards to Ray, Florrie, Ann & your Ma. Much love to yourself.

Sunday 9 December 1917

My dearest Ma,

All's well. We have not received any letters for some weeks. This week I am sending home a photo, a group taken outside our house, hope it will arrive home alright. Don't be surprised if I sign a cheque now & again. All parcels you send me sew them up strongly in canvas & address them well more than once. Much love to yourself, Dad, Edie & all at home, keep smiling, best of luck

16 December 1917

Dear Billy,

All's well, thanks very much indeed for your letter, am very pleased to say that I am keeping very fit indeed, it is very cold indeed here now, about a foot of snow. We are still allowed to play football three times a week. Try & write me now & again also get Muse to write we look forward to letters. Kindest regards to Pelly.

My dearest Ma,

All's well, we have not recvd any letters for some weeks, it is very cold indeed here now about a foot of snow. You write to the old firm & thank them very much indeed for what they are doing for me. Please send me out two pillow cases, two pair of khaki stockings for football, a grey flannel shirt, medium thickness, a dozen soft white collars, 6 silk khaki handkerchiefs, some toilet soap & as many food parcels as you can, as can assure you they are very welcome, sew them up strongly in strong canvas & write the address more than once the best way is to sew on a piece of linen with the address on, you can't be too careful in addressing them. We are still allowed to play football three times a week, but this last fortnight there as been too much snow, about a foot deep. If you write to Mrs Chitty she will be able to tell you a lot about parcels, as to where she buys her cardboard boxes. How is Dad getting on how does he like his new job have you been down to see him yet. Sincerely hope

Edie is keeping very fit give her my love, how are Bert, Kit, Eileen, Syd & Gertie getting on tell them I should be very pleased to hear from them get them to write me often as letters are one of the things we look forward to most. Well Ma really don't think I have any fresh news for this mail. Trusting you, Dad, Edie & all at home are in the best of health & spirits. Kindest regards to Wilkinsons.

Sunday 23 December 1917

Dear Rev. Bateson

I have just recvd a letter from you, thanks very much indeed letters are one of the things we look forward to most. Am very pleased to say that I am keeping very fit indeed. We are fairly well treated & allowed to play football three times a week. We have the Rev. Wright with us he holds a service every Sunday morning for Officers and orderlies, which is largely attended. Would be very much obliged if you would let the Deptford Mission know my address & tell them that I should be very pleased to hear from any of them. Trusting you & yours are in the very best of health & spirits.

Dear Billy,

How goes it, after all this long time I am very pleased to say that I am keeping very fit we are allowed to play football three times a week. We are looking forward to Xmas day when we hope to have a really good time. What are you and Billy doing expect you will be going home, bye the way are you married yet. I should be very pleased to hear from you, as we long for letters write more than once as letters easily go astray was most pleased to get a letter from Coxon some weeks ago. Remember me to any old friends & tell them I should be very pleased to hear from them. Trusting you, Billy, will have a good time at Xmas with my kindest regards to you both.

My Dearest Betty.

All's well, We have not received any letters for five weeks, it is very cold indeed here just now about six inches of snow, twenty degrees of frost. We are still allowed to play football three times a week but we have not been able to play on account of the weather. You might ask my Ma to send me out two pair of khaki stockings for football also six khaki handkerchiefs. We have just had a service this morning and are going to have one early Christmas day don't get drinking too much wine & eating too much pudding. Really don't think I have any fresh news on account of receiving no letters. Send me out some of the photos you had taken on your holidays.

The Ladies Emergency Committee of the Navy League.

This afternoon I have received a food parcel from you for which I thank you all very much indeed it is really awfully good of you, can assure you they are most welcome & needed. Again thanking you all.

30 December 1917

My Dearest Edie,

All's well, we have not received any letters for about six weeks. We had a very good Xmas indeed a top hole dinner. Xmas eve I received three parcels from the Navy League containing provisions you might write and thank them for me, also recvd 100 francs from the ASE. Have also recvd clothes and boots from the Embassy. We are still allowed to play football three times a week but the weather has been too bad this last night fortnight, you might send out two pairs of khaki football stockings, six silk khaki handkerchiefs & some shaving soap & as many food parcels as you can.

How is Dad getting on have you been down to see him yet, if so hope you had a good time. We had another Theatrical show last night & shall again tonight it went off very well. Well, Edie dear really don't think I have any fresh news. So trusting you, Ma, Dad & all at home are keeping very fit. Get them all to write. PS Love to Grace.

Dear Charlie.

All's well, we have had a very good Xmas had a top hole dinner; on Xmas eve I received 100 francs from the ASE for which I wish you would thank them very much indeed for me. I would write to them myself only have forgotten the address of the head office you might point out to them that my name is spelt Louis & not Lewis. We have a fairly good time here we are allowed to play football three times a week. How is the club getting on I should be very pleased to hear from any of them tell them to write more than once as letters easily go astray. Letters are one of the things we look forward to most. Trusting you are keeping fit Kindest regards.

Dear Mabel,

All's well, thanks very much indeed for your letter. We had a very good time at Xmas had a top hole dinner and plenty to drink. We gave our third Theatrical show last night & hope to give another tonight it was a great success. Still allowed to play football three times a week and taking everything in we have a fairly good time. Have you been up to see Gertie lately I expect she spent her Xmas at Oxford. I shall be very pleased to hear from you whenever you have time, write more than once as letters easily go astray. Trusting you are keeping very fit. With my kindest regards

Dear Mr Parry,

I am very pleased to say that I am keeping very fit, we had a very good Xmas considering the circumstances. Would be very much obliged if you would thank the firm for what they are doing for me, it is really awfully good of them can assure them that I appreciate it greatly. Trusting you & yours are keeping in the best of health.

6 January 1918

Dear Mr Ford,

All's well, I am very pleased to say that we had a very good time Xmas Day plenty of plum pudding, turkey & lots of drink. We are allowed to play football three times a week and taking everything into consideration we have a fairly good time. Have started amateur theatricals. I always take the part of a woman, we have had three shows & they have gone off top hole. How is Mrs Ford, Frank, Walter & all the girls tell them I should be very pleased indeed to hear from them, tell them to write more than once as letters very easily go astray. It is very cold here just now about 25 degrees of frost, but we manage to keep warm enough. Trusting you, Mrs Frost & all at your home are in the best of health & spirits.

Dear Mr Juniper,

No doubt you will be very surprised at hearing from me, only I thought perhaps you would like to know how I am getting on. I am very pleased indeed to say that am keeping very fit, we are allowed to play football three times a week & taking everything into consideration we get on very well, had a very good time at Xmas plenty to eat &

drink. We have started amateur theatricals I always take the part of a woman, have had three shows & they have gone off very well. Remember me to Tal & Nell, tell them I should be very pleased to hear from them, write more than once as letters easily go astray. Trusting you & Mrs. Juniper are in the best of health & spirits. With my kindest regards to you both.

Dear Syd & Gertie,

All's well. I am very pleased to say that I am keeping very fit indeed. We had a very good time at Xmas day plum pudding, turkey & plenty to drink, taking everything into consideration we had a very good time. Still allowed to play football & three times a week only lately there has been too much snow, it is very cold about 25° of frost. How are the dogs getting on have you still got Billy if so tell Ma to take a licence out for him is Jack as good a dog as we thought he would. Tell Ma to send me out two pairs of khaki football stockings & six silk handkerchiefs. Well really don't think I have any fresh news as we have not had letters for seven weeks. With my kindest regards to you both.

There follow two notes to say that he has sent further copies of his letters to the ASE and to the Ladies Emergency Committee.

13 January 1918

Dear Mr Parry,

I am very pleased indeed to say that I am keeping very well. Must again thank the firm very much for what they are doing for me, it is really awfully kind of them, don't know what I should do without their help living is very expensive indeed here, can assure the firm that I appreciate their kindness greatly. Trusting you & yours are in the best of health.

My dearest Betty,

All's well, this week we have received a few letters, two from you but none from home, these are the first we have recvd for eight weeks. I was very surprised indeed to hear that Ella and you have quarrelled, I thought you were such great chums, was it because you could not have your own way, don't be offended but I know what a bounder you are. Remember me to Ann tell her that I shall have to come and visit her in the flat. She appears to be of the same opinion as myself and intends to bring her children up the same. Was surprised to hear from you that my people are staying at Leicester they seem to be having a good time shifting about all over the place sight seeing. We had a very good time Xmas day considering, we had plenty of plum pudding, turkey and quite a lot of drink. I also received three very good parcels on Xmas eve. You might ask my Ma to send me out two pairs of khaki football stockings & six silk khaki handkerchiefs & two pillow cases. Well Betty dear, really don't think I have any fresh news for this mail so trusting you & Ray, Florrie & your Ma are in the best of health.

With much love.

My dearest Ma,

All's well, we recvd a few letters this week. I got two from Betty but none from home, these were the first we had recvd for eight weeks. We had a very good time Xmas day, plenty of plum pudding, turkey etc. On Xmas eve I recvd three parcels from the Navy League containing provisions etc. You might write and thank them for me, send me out as many food parcels as you can also two pairs of khaki football stockings & six silk khaki handkerchiefs & some shaving & toilet soap. Don't be surprised if I have to sign cheques now & again. You might write up to the old firm & thank them very much for what they are doing for me. I have written them several times but am afraid my letters have never reached them as have had no reply. How is Dad getting on I heard from Betty that you were down staying with him. How do you like Leicester is it a nice place, is Mr Jeffery also there. You might take out a licence for both the dogs for which I will pay. How has Jack turned out, does he look smart. Well Ma dear, really don't think I have any fresh news for this mail. With much love to yourself, Dad, Edie & all at home.

20 January 1918

Dear Cleverly,

How goes it after all this long time? I have written you & Barlow several times but have had no reply, expect your letters have gone astray. I am very pleased to say that I am keeping very fit indeed, we are allowed to play football three times a week & taking everything into consideration we have a fairly good time, it has been very cold indeed here seventeen degrees of frost, but it has been much warmer these last few days. I should be very pleased indeed to hear from you let me know all the news, often wonder how you are all getting on, write more than once as letters easily go astray & letters are one of the things we look forward to most, Furneaux is here with me wishes to be remembered to you pleased to say he is keeping very fit. Remember me to Barlow, Gostling, King, Seulz & all old friends, tell them I should be pleased to get a line from them Kindest regards to yourself & all.

My dear Edie

All's well. This week we have recvd several letters. I got four from Betty & one from you at Leicester, was very pleased indeed to hear that Ma & you like Leicester very much. I suppose you couldn't find out where my old friend Hatton lives at one time he lived in Melrose Street but have not heard from him for several years. Yes, I recvd one box of sweets, also the cigars & cigarettes quite safely. Have also recvd several parcels from the Navy League. It is a great deal better to send parcels than money, send as many food parcels as you can, also stockings, handkerchiefs and pillowcases. I was awfully sorry to hear that Aunt Millie had been so queer, remember me to her & tell her that I sincerely hope that she is better by now. I was pleased to hear that you have found a new friend is she a nice girl if so, give her my love. What is her name? We are still allowed to play football three times a week but spend most of our time reading books, we have quite a large library here made up of books that people have had sent from home.

You might write to the old firm & thank them very much indeed for what they are doing for me, have you ever written up and pointed out that my pay was only fixed provisionally as I have asked you to do several times to the Admiralty. Ask Dad to send me out a statement of my accounts send it more than once in case the first goes astray have only recvd one since a prisoner. Much love to yourself, Ma, Dad & all at home.

Dear Mrs Firman

All's well, on Xmas eve I received two parcels which I think must have come from you. I thank you very much indeed can assure you they are most welcome, it is a great deal better to send parcels than money. We are still allowed to play football three times a week & had a very good time at Christmas considering everything. Sincerely hope you & yours are in the best of health with my kindest regards to you all.

The Manager
Dear Sir,

I would be very much obliged if you would send me a statement of my accounts, send more than one as letters easily go astray. I shall most probably be signing a cheque now & again, send a cheque book.

27 January 1918

My dear Nell

All's well, thanks very much indeed for your letter, letters are one of the things we look forward to most, was very pleased to hear that Tal & you are getting on so well. Tell Tal to save me a few bottles of whisky, it is a long time since I have tasted any. We are fairly well treated here and are allowed to play football three times a week. I notice that you say that Floss is staying with you, is her husband in France? You might remember me kindly to her. Am looking forward to the time when I shall be able to pay you a visit again, the same as when I was home on leave. You ask me if I have forgotten the Lent Lectures, no fear shall never forget the good old days. I wonder what has become of Wilson. Don't forget to send me a Photo of the Pub. Well, Nell, really don't think I have any fresh news for this mail shall be very pleased to hear from Tal or you write more than once as letters easily go astray. Kindest regards to yourself, Tal & Floss.

My dear Dad,

All's well, this week we have recvd several letters, one from you & one from Edie was surprised to hear you say that you have not heard from me as have written you a lot. Was very pleased to hear that you were getting on well at Leicester and that Ma & Edie like it as well. Was very sorry indeed to hear that Ruby had lost her husband, I expect she will be getting married again don't you. Have you written up about my pay & pointed out that it was only fixed provisionally, pending receipt of information from owners of the ship as to my rate of pay, if so what answer did you get, you might also send me out a statement of my accounts. I believe you sent me one some time ago but have never recvd it, so you might send me another, send it more than once in case the first goes astray. I have recvd several parcels on Xmas eve got two from the Navy League, send as many food parcels as you can it is a great deal better to send parcels than money. You might write to the old firm & thank them very much indeed for what they are doing for me. Well

Dad, really don't think I have any fresh news so trusting you, Ma, Edie & all at home are well.

My dearest Betty

All's well, this week I have recvd several letters two from you & one from my Dad your letter was most interesting, it is really awfully good of you. I notice that you are now writing two & three times a week for which I thank you very much indeed, as whenever there is a mail I get one or two from you. I was glad to hear that Florrie was keeping herself busy, it is far better to mend them than have holes. She never knows when she might fall down & then what a sight. Was very surprised to hear that you has quarrelled with Ella always thought you were such great chums, what was the trouble about. I had a letter from Edie last week, she told they had heard from you, they seem to like Leicester very much indeed. We are playing a football match against the other camp next week, we hope to beat them. Well Betty dear, I really don't think I have any fresh news. With my kindest regards to your Ma, Ray, Florrie much love to yourself.

Dear Annie,

All's well, thanks very much indeed for your letter. I am very pleased to say that we are fairly well treated here & are allowed to play football three times a week. We have the Rev. Wright here with us so we have a service every Sunday morning for officers & orderlies which is largely attended.

I was very glad to hear that you liked Malta so well & that you had a nice garden, you asked me if there was anything you could do or send me, well some cigarettes would be very nice & if you have any funds that send food parcels to Prisoners of War you might put my name on their list but mind I don't want you to spend any of your own money on me, all parcels should be sewn up strongly in canvas. Remember me kindly to your husband & tell him I hope to have the pleasure of meeting him some day. We spend best part of our time reading books have got quite a large library, over three hundred books. Really don't think I have any fresh news, shall always be very pleased to hear from you & yours write more than once as letters easily go astray. With my kindest regards to you both

3 February 1918

The Ladies Emergency Committee

Five days ago I received a food parcel from you dated Aug 8th for which I thank you all very much indeed it is really awfully good of you, can assure you they are most welcome it is far better to send food parcels than money.

Again thanking you all.

There follows a list of letters he has sent that are exact copies of ones already written to a Mrs Barnes, his Dad, Mrs A. Reed, Mrs Firman, Mr Webber and the Ladies Emergency Committee all written between 3 and 9 February.

9 February 1918

My dear Aunt Millie,

All's well thanks very much indeed for your letter. I am very pleased to say that I am keeping very fit indeed, we are still allowed to play football three times a week, last week we played the lower camp a rugby match and after a very interesting game beat them easily. We spend most of our time reading. We have a very fine library here over four hundred books, which people have had sent out to them, believe this can be done through W. H. Smith Strand by book post. Was very surprised to hear that Dad had shifted to Leicester but was very glad to hear that Ma & Edie liked it very much. Remember me to Percy & tell him I should be very pleased indeed to hear from him, letters are one of the things we look forward to most. With my kindest regards to yourself & all.

My dear Edie,

All's well, we have recvd several letters this last week. I was very pleased indeed to hear that Ma & you like Leicester so well, it must be a nice change for you all. We played the lower camp a rugby match last week & after a very interesting game we beat them easily. Was very sorry to hear that Ruby had lost her husband, expect she will get married again don't you.

I have written Aunt Millie again this week. About a fortnight ago I recvd a food parcel from the Navy League, send me as many parcels as you can & sew them up strongly in strong canvas. We are still allowed to play football three times a week, but we spend most of our time reading books we have quite a large library here over four hundred books, you can send them through W. H. Smith Strand by book post. Much love to yourself, Dad, Ma & all at home.

16 February 1918

Dear Billy,

Thanks very much indeed for your interesting letter. I am very pleased to say that I am keeping very fit indeed we are fairly well treated here and are allowed to play football three times a week, last week we played the lower camp a rugby match and after a very interesting game we beat them easily. How are you getting on at the old firm, remember me to all old friends and tell them I should be very pleased to hear from any of them as letters are one of the things we look forward to most. Write more than once as letters easily go astray, also remember me to May Smith. I thought she would have been married by now there is still a chance for Billy. I am pleased to say that my people at home are keeping very fit, my father has got a very good job at Leicester so they are all living there for the present but we are still keeping on the old house as well. Am looking forward to the time when this is all over & I return home then I hope to spend a short time in Southampton. We shall have to spend one of our old nights at the Hippo. Kindest regards to you & Billy.

My dearest Betty,

All's well we have not had any letters for this last week or two last week we played the lower camp a rugby match and after a very exciting game we beat them rather easily. About a fortnight ago we felt a earthquake here it shook our house a lot we all rushed for the street, but am pleased to say no damage was done. We spend most of our time here reading books we have quite a large library over four hundred books which various people have had sent them. I believe you can send us books through W. H. Smith Strand by book post, why not try and send me out *Milestones*. How are you getting on, have you made it up with Ella yet.

Dear Syd & Gertie.

All's well, am very pleased to say that I am keeping very fit indeed we played the lower camp a rugby match last week and after a very interesting game we beat them rather easily. About a fortnight ago we felt an earthquake shock here, it shook the house a lot, we all rushed for the street, but am very pleased to say no damage was done. We spend most of our time here reading books we have quite a large library over four hundred books which various people have had sent them. I believe you can send us books through W. H. Smith Strand you might let them know this at home.

How are you both getting on after all this long time, was very pleased to hear that Ma & Edie liked Leicester so well, I expect you miss them don't you. How are the dogs getting on? Has Jack turned out as good a dog as we thought he would if you like to buy a bitch of the same breed I will pay for it, only whatever you do buy a good one.

Well really don't think I have any fresh news for this mail. Trusting you are both in the very best of health.

From this point on, the record William keeps of his correspondence becomes sketchy and is reduced to the briefest of notes. The letters continued in much the same vein and show the concerns and anxieties that were constantly on his mind from the health and well-being of his family, his wish to reassure them about his health and his money concerns, to his desire to keep in touch with everyone he knew. He continues to tell them of the events of his daily life; food parcels received, more amateur dramatics, cricket or football matches and minor earthquakes. He also mentions climbing the rock and being able to go there for walks and to sit and read. This would have been the rock that is the dominant feature of Afion Kara Hissar to this day. An ancient Seljuk fortress is at the top of the rock where the Turkish flag flutters in the breeze.

Afion Kara Hissar is surrounded by great flat plains from where the nearest towns are at least five hours' drive away over mountain ranges, winding round hairpin bends then on through flat plains and alongside salt lakes of brilliant turquoise. Kara Hissar means 'black rock' and around the base of this dramatic landmark sprawls the old town, a gem of Ottoman architecture. The cobbled streets are so narrow that even a small car can only just get through. The houses are square in a curving kind of way and vertical in a sloping, sliding way. Constructed round courtyards, they are timbered in the manner of Tudor houses and their upper storeys overhang the ground floors. They are brightly painted and have lattice-work shutters, so windows can be left open without anyone catching a glimpse of the women inside. One could imagine lovers passing secret notes and tiny gifts through the gaps in the woodwork.

The mosques in this part of town go back centuries. One in particular, the Ulu Cami, was built by the Seijuks in 1272 and restored a century later. It has no dome and a pitched roof. Huge intricately carved wooden pillars support the roof from the inside.

The town came to prominence after the war when Mustafa Kemal Atatürk chose it as the place from which to make his last stand in the war for Turkish independence. One result of the First World War was the complete destruction of the Ottoman Empire – one of the most extensive and long lasting of empires. Territories were carved up and allocated to the victorious allies. France got Syria and Lebanon, Britain got Iraq and Palestine and Greece got Turkey.

Atatürk was the hero of Gallipoli and as such emerged as leader of the nation after the war. He led his country into further fighting against the allied forces in a bid for Turkish independence. Afion had been a garrison town since the time of the Seljuks, so it was therefore an ideal place in which to keep prisoners of war. It, or at least the Zafer museum in it (*zafer* means victory), was the building from where he planned his last battle in 1922.

On gaining independence, Atatürk began a modernization campaign that radically changed Turkey, catapulting it into the modern world and drawing it nearer to Europe than to the Middle East. He is seen as the father of the nation and is still revered. He introduced the use of surnames to simplify identification and extended the franchise to women. Although 95 per cent of Turkey's population is Islamic and the country remains in effect Muslim, his secularization drive did curb the influence of the imams.

He replaced the Arabic script with the Roman alphabet and encouraged the use of new words, many of them borrowed from French, which was at that time the international language of diplomacy and politics. For example, the word *koafür* for hairdresser is taken from the French *coiffeur* and *otogar* (coach station) is from the French *auto gare*.

Today Turkish tourists visit Afion to pay homage to Atatürk and to climb the rock, which rises abruptly from a flat plain to a height of 226 metres and is the town's most outstanding feature. But all that was to come later. In 1918, being a prisoner of war trapped in the small streets of the town for two years, William must have enjoyed climbing the rock from where he could see the wide open space of the plain and the distant mountains where only four years later Atatürk would fight his last battle.

On 24 April 1918 William noted that it was the second anniversary of his capture and, although he had grown tired of keeping his diary, one or two letters were still copied out in more detail.

22 June 1918

Chief Writer,

I would be very much obliged if you would let me know if I am getting any allowances if so what. Also would be pleased if you would tell me whether I have got my Lieutenancy or not yet, have been a Sub over 2 years am pleased to be able to acknowledge your postcard of 23rd Sept which reached me today.

30 June 1918

Dear Lady Wemyss,

I have received several parcels lately for which I wish to thank the Navy League very much indeed it is really awfully good of them. It may interest your husband to know that myself & what are left of the crew of our ship are keeping very well. I meet some of them occasionally. We are treated fairly well here & get a fair amount of walks.

Again thanking you all.

6 July 1918

Dear Miss Thornton,

Thanks very much indeed for your letter of March 15th it is really very kind of you to send me out the suit of uniform, must also thank you very much for the parcels, I have received several lately. Could you find out for me if any other awards were given besides the two VCs for our stunt on the HMS *Julnar* as I am the only surviving officer & there are several men. The senior military officer is Lt. Col. Warren & the senior Naval officer Lt. Commander Warren RN. Am very pleased to say that we are having a much better time here now, get very fair number of walks. Again thanking you very much indeed for the many favours you have done for me. With my best wishes to you all.

He sent a postcard of the rock to Edie followed by a letter in which he talked of the exchange of prisoners. The Allies were finally winning through and Turkey was beginning to withdraw from hostilities. Rumour, speculation and the desperate hope to be included in the exchanges ran like an epidemic through the camp. Meanwhile, the men continued to put on variety shows and to get together for picnics, cricket and dinners. After reading *The Importance of Being Earnest*, William wrote to both Betty and Edie to tell them to be sure to read it too as it was most enjoyable. The last letter in the diary refers to the *Julnar* and its sad end. Then, on 5 October he wrote to Cleverly:

Letter to Cleverly, 5 October 1918

You can hardly tell how pleased I was to read your letter to Furneaux, but at the same time was very sorry indeed to hear that you had been so ill. Sincerely hope you are quite your old self by this time. You mention that the ship was destroyed was that our dear old friend, hope so as never want to see her again. Do you know what happened to Charlie C. he was very fit when I last saw him. When you write to Barlow or King I wish you would remember me kindly to them both. Should very much like to hear from them have written to you all several times but have had no reply, so expect my letters had gone astray. We have an Amateur Theatrical show here as a rule I take the part of a woman. Trusting you are now in the very best of health.

13 October 1918

Copy of my letter to Cleverley.

The diary ended there, except for lists of names and addresses, so he was either exchanged along with the other prisoners or remained in the prison camp until after Armistice Day.

11

Report on the *Julnar*

With them the Seed of wisdom did I sow,
And with my own hand labour'd it to grow.
And this was all the Harvest that I reap'd –
'I came like Water, and like Wind I go.'
(*Rubáiyát of Omar Khayyám*, verse 28)

My grandfather sent the following report to the military authorities in Baghdad. He wrote it a little more than three years after the events described in the prisoner of war camp at Afion Kara Hissar. Military intelligence was presumably seeking confirmation of the events and trying to find out what had happened to the various crew members, in particular Lieutenant-Commander Cowley.

After the failure of the attack on 22 April 1916, the navy made a useless attempt to get food into the garrison with a view to extending the period of time that General Townshend and his men could hold out. This would have allowed the relieving force to continue trying to repel the Turks and take Kut.

Since from the outset everyone considered it to be a hopeless venture, volunteers would man the *Julnar* and only unmarried men were asked to apply. The enterprise was meant to take place in secrecy, but the ship had been loaded in Amara where a crowd of curious onlookers gathered to watch each day. Also, many of the officers and men at Falahiyah discussed it openly. On top of that it was impossible for the *Julnar* to travel in silence. In the quietness of the night its engines and propellers could be heard from miles away. And the Turks were waiting for them.

c/o The Euphrates & Tigris Steam Navigation Company Ltd
Baghdad, 5 August 1919

To: The General Staff Intelligence
GHQ Baghdad

With reference to your memorandum No. 1(b) 5390 dated 28th June, I have the honour to submit the following reports on the circumstances attending the loss of his majesty's ship *Julnar* in an attempt to reach Kut-al-Amara with stores for the besieged garrison of that town in April 1916.

The *Julnar* was a twin-screw shallow draught oil-fuel steamer of 750 tons formerly belonging to the Euphrates and Tigris Steam Navigation Company, Baghdad. The normal draught of the vessel was 4 feet 5 inches, but it could be loaded up to 5 feet if necessary. The *Julnar* was employed in transport work on the Tigris from 6th August 1915 to 14th April 1916, under orders of the Principal Marine Transport Officer. 'Captain' Cowley of the Euphrates and Tigris Steam Navigation Company commanded the ship. I was Chief Engineer, the crew at that time being entirely native.

On 14th April 1916, Lieut-Commander Cowley received orders while at Falahiyah to proceed at once to Amara with his ship. On the way downstream, I was informed by Vice-Admiral Wemyss Flag Captain, who came aboard at Falahiyah, that an attempt was to be made to run the *Julnar* through Kut-al-Amara with provisions for the garrison.

I asked him that I might be allowed to go as engineer of the steamer during the attempt. On the arrival of the *Julnar* at Amara on 15th April, a volunteer crew of unmarried men was asked for and obtained from the war-craft lying there. Lieut-Commander Cowley volunteered to navigate the ship and I was given naval rank in order that I might take part in the enterprise.

The *Julnar* was six days at Amara, and during that period all cabin woodwork was removed from the inside, and the mast and top-deck stanchions were cut away. The ship was plated with armour •' thick round the bridge and over the boiler and engine rooms, bags of atta (flour) being placed between the armour and the ship's sides to give additional protection against bullets and shell splinters. A cargo of 250 to 280 tons of foodstuffs and hospital comforts was then taken aboard, and on 21st April the *Julnar* left Amara for Arab Village.

The full complement of the ship was as follows:

Lieut. H. Firman RN (Commanding)
Lieut-Commander C. Cowley RNVR
Engr. Sub-Lieut. W. Louis Reed RNR
Engine-room Artificer Murphy RNVR
Petty Officer Rowbotham RN
AB Seaman Williams
AB Seaman Veal RN
AB Seaman Ledger
AB Seaman Blanchard
AB Seaman Featherbee
AB Seaman Bond
Stoker Petty Officer Cook
Stoker Fox
Stoker Fourshere
Stoker Thirgill

The *Julnar* made a good passage up the river, which was in flood, and on 23rd April arrived at Arab Village. The original intention was that we should proceed to Kut-al-Amara that night, but our departure was postponed for 24 hours.

The *Julnar* left Arab Village at 6.45 p.m. on 24th April. The sky was slightly overcast and the night was dark, there being no moon. The river was in flood, and with a draught of 4 feet 9 inches owing to plating and cargo, the steamer did not attain a greater speed than 6 knots. About five minutes after the start we passed through the pontoon bridge over the Tigris at Arab Village. The ship had been under way for about a quarter of an hour when the Turks some distance ahead let off a number of flare lights. I could not see whether we had been observed or not, as I was below attending to the engines, and did not leave the engine-room that night until after the ship had been surrendered.

We steamed upriver without further incident until the enemy trenches at Sanna'iyat were reached. Here very heavy rifle fire was opened on the *Julnar* from both banks of the Tigris, and before we had gone much further the ship was riddled with bullets. They kept penetrating the engine-room and falling down among the engines. Stoker Petty Officer Cook and Seaman Blanchard were slightly wounded by bullets.

After we had passed Sanna'iyat, the enemy fire slackened off considerably, although there were occasional bursts of rifle fire and sniping from both banks. The *Julnar* made a good run until we arrived opposite the Turkish position along the Sinn Bank, where the ship again came under heavy fire, this time from the artillery as well as from rifles. A fragment of shell penetrated the boiler-room and put the oil burners out, but otherwise did no damage of any consequence. Hostile fire still followed us upstream and at about 11.40 p.m., five minutes after passing the Sinn Bank position, I could hear the Turks, during a lull in the firing, bringing down guns to the riverbank some distance ahead. Three or four minutes afterwards the enemy opened a heavy and effective fire on the *Julnar* from guns on the riverbank at Maqasis Fort. A shell hit the bridge, piercing the armour plating with ease and instantaneously killing Lieut. Firman RN. Lieut. Cmdr. Cowley and Seaman Williams, who were also on the bridge, were slightly wounded. A second shell hit the *Julnar* astern but did not cause any serious damage. About this time the bags filled with atta protecting the top deck twice took fire. On each occasion Petty Officer Rowbotham came out from under cover and extinguished the flames.

The *Julnar* continued to proceed upstream under heavy fire until soon after 11.45 p.m. when almost exactly opposite the mud fort of Maqasis on the right bank, the ship struck head-on a wire cable drawn across the river. There was a strong current at this point which formed the southern extremity of a sharp bend in the river. It is my opinion that the Turks used the wire for ferry purposes and that it was not laid down with the intention of stopping the *Julnar*. On the ship striking the cable, the force of the current swung the stern round towards the right bank, where it grounded immediately opposite Maqasis Fort. All attempts to get the *Julnar* off by means of the engines failed.

About 5 minutes after the ship grounded the Turkish fire ceased, and a few minutes afterwards I received a message to go on the bridge. There I found Lieut-Commander Cowley with several Turkish officers. He explained to me that finding it impossible to get the ship under way again, he had decided to surrender in order to avoid useless loss of life. He had intimated his desire to do so by showing a white light when it became clear to him that the vessel was stuck fast.

Lieut-Commander Cowley, myself and the crew were then taken ashore, and almost immediately afterwards were ferried across on a raft to the opposite bank. We were placed in a camp about a hundred yards from the river, where Lieut-Commander Cowley and members of the crew suffering from slight wounds had their injuries treated with iodine. About 3 a.m. Lieut-Commander Cowley and I were placed in a tent together, where we spent the remainder of the night.

Next morning we all marched to another camp about 5 miles distant, where we were again placed in tents, Lieut-Commander Cowley and I still being together. About an hour after our arrival Lieut-Commander Cowley was sent for and after an absence of about 20 minutes, he was brought back and informed me that he had been interrogated by a Turkish Staff officer. Shortly afterwards a Turkish officer came to the tent and said that they could not allow two officers to remain in the same tent. I was accordingly moved to a tent by myself a few yards away. Half an hour later I was informed that I had to proceed to Baghdad at once with the crew of the *Julnar.* I requested permission to go and say goodbye to Lieut-Commander Cowley before I left, but I was told by a Turkish officer that that was not necessary, as they were waiting for a horse for Lieut-Commander Cowley, who would probably catch us up on the way. That was the last time I saw Lieut-Commander Cowley. He was walking up and down in front of his tent and except for two very slight wounds, one on his face and the other in his hand caused by shell splinters, he was in perfect health. We left on the march to Baghdad immediately afterwards.

I have to report the following casualties among the officers and crew sustained in the action and during subsequent captivity.

Lieut. Firman VC RN	Killed by shell near Maqasis Fort
Lieut-Commander Cowley VC RN R	Died (cause of death unknown)
AB Seaman Veal RN	Died while prisoner of war
Stoker Fox	Died while prisoner of war
Stoker Thirgill	Died while prisoner of war.

Most of the crew sustained slight injuries from bullets and shell fragments.

I cannot speak too highly of the conduct during this operation of all ranks of the crew, who carried out their duties with the greatest gallantry and devotion under almost continuous fire from near Sanna'iyat to Maqasis Fort. I find the greatest difficulty in singling out anyone for special attention in circumstances where all displayed the highest courage, but I venture to bring to your special notice the names of the following Petty Officer and Artificers for the acts noted below.

Petty Officer Rowbotham RN, for twice emerging from cover in the face of heavy fire and extinguishing flames which had burst out on the top deck; Engine-Room Artificer Murphy RNVR, for general good work under heavy fire.

Signed W. Louis Reed
Engineer Sub-Lieut. RNR

Lieut-Commander Cowley was believed to have been taken out into the desert and shot by the Turks. He had lived in Iraq for many years, working for Lynch Brothers, the company that owned the Euphrates and Tigris Steam Navigation Company. As a result the Turks did not regard him as British but as an Ottoman subject. They did not think that the rules for treatment of a prisoner of war applied. Perhaps they even regarded him as a traitor for the help he had given the British army. At first they said he had been found dead, then that he was shot trying to escape. The truth can only be surmised.

The last communication from General Townshend arrived on 29 April.

> Have destroyed my guns and am destroying most of my munitions, and have sent out officers to Khalil to say am ready to surrender. Khalil is at Madug. I am unable to hold on any more. I must have some food here. I have told Khalil today, and have sent launch with deputation to bring food from *Julnar* I have hoisted white flag over town and fort. I shall shortly destroy wireless.

The men in the fort had been living on a daily ration of four ounces of flour and a slice of horse or mule meat since 15 April. To that extent the journey of the *Julnar* was worthwhile as it brought food to the starving, skeletal men. The incident also marked the final gasp of the rescue. Had it got through the army would have carried on fighting with even more loss of life and no more promise of success. By the end nearly three times as many men had been lost as needed rescuing in the first place.

Among the souvenirs that my grandfather kept is the following poem. He had two copies, both of which are hand-written. It is written from the point of view of a soldier in the besieged garrison. There is no clue as to the author.

Running the Gauntlet: The Story of the *Julnar*

When in years to come the record of the World's Great
War is read
And our children hear the echo of the strife.

When they think with admiration of the blood that has
been shed,
By the men who counted honour more than life;
There's a story that will rouse them grander victories to
win
For the Empire in whose cause their fathers died –
How the *Julnar* ran the gauntlet from Sunnaiat to Essin
While the Turkish guns bombarded from each side.

In Kut the Sixth division and the Thirtieth Brigade
Had been waiting eighteen weeks to be relieved
And many were the efforts the advancing force had made
And many were the promises received;
And many were the valiant men who bravely met their
fate,
And faced the great unknown with fearless eyes –
Yet still the guns of Gorringe hammered loudly at the
gate,
And still the Turk held fiercely to his prize.

With the Spring came greater hardships, for the Tigris rose
in flood,
And the desert's dust and sand were turned to slime;
The relieving force was wading through a wilderness of
mud,
And they knew that their worst enemy was Time,
But the odds were all against them, and although they
fought their best
At Sunnaiyat, where the Turks had made a stand,
The attack was unsuccessful, and it had to be confessed
The relief could never come to us by land.

It was near the end of April, when our chance seemed one
in ten,
That the final great adventure was essayed,

And that Cowley, Reed and Firman, with eleven gallant
men,
Volunteered to bring the *Julnar* to our aid,
Under cover of the darkness they set out with courage
high,
Every man of them prepared to trust his luck;
If the game should go against them, they were not afraid
to die,
And we thanked the gods above us for their pluck.

There were starving men in Kut that night who felt their
strength revive,
There were wounded who for once forgot their pain;
All the garrison was waiting for the glad news to arrive
That our long endurance had not been in vain.
But our watch was unrewarded, the dark hours of vigil
past,
Every hope was rudely shattered with the day,
For the gallant little *Julnar* was a prisoner held fast
At Fort Maqasis, not three miles away.

Up the stream from Falahiyah they had come 'Full steam
ahead'
Past the enemy position at Essin,
Nothing daunted though the skipper on the bridge had
fallen dead,
Un-alarmed by the Inferno's savage din.
Shells might crash and bullets whistle, guns might thunder
left and right,
They would not resign the task they had begun,
Till they smashed into a barrier that was hidden from their
sight,
And were captured when the game was nearly won.

To have failed was no dishonour, they had made the great attempt,
They had offered up their liberty and life:
They had looked on all the danger and the hazard with contempt
And had thrown themselves whole-hearted in the strife.
Of such deeds as this the fabric of our Empire has been made,
Woven slowly by the heroes of our race,
And among the ranks of those to whom the tribute shall be paid
Let the men who 'ran the gauntlet' take their place.

Epilogue

Up from Earth's Centre
Through the Seventh Gate
I rose, and on the Throne of Saturn sate,
And many knots unravel'd by the road;
But not the Knot of Human Death and Fate.

(*Rubáiyát of Omar Khayyám*, Verse 31)

William never saw Cowley again. It is presumed that the Turks executed him on the banks of the Tigris, the river he knew and loved so well. There is a memorial to him in the British cemetery at Baghdad. It is near the grave of Gertrude Bell.

After the *Julnar*'s failure to break through the blockade, General Townshend surrendered to the Turkish commander Khalil Pasha. There was an exchange of prisoners, mostly wounded, but the Turks took thousands into captivity. The Turks executed all the Arabs of the town, regarding them as traitors. Kahlil Pasha promised to send General Townshend to Constantinople as the honoured guest of the Turkish nation. What a contrast to the sufferings of others who fought alongside him! He spent the rest of the war in a villa on an island off the Turkish coast.

Spot, the only animal to survive the siege, was handed over to Aubrey Herbert to be taken care of and sent home to England. A welcoming committee received Townshend in Turkey and gave a reception in his honour. The Turks greatly admired his courage in holding out for 165 days, one of the longest sieges in military history. He was given a comfortable house in which to stay, with staff to look after him, though of course there were also guards.

The Turks even asked if he would like to bring his wife and daughter over from Britain to stay with him in the British embassy. Townshend was naturally enthusiastic about this idea, but the British government did not want its embassy turned into an internment camp and the Austrian government refused permission for them to cross its territory. Later, in 1918 as the tide was turning in favour of the Allies, Townshend offered to help the Turkish government negotiate its terms of surrender with the British. On 18 October he was sent to Smyrna where he advised the Turkish delegates in negotiations aboard the British warship *Agamemnon*, but was not party to the negotiations. In one part of his diary he writes 'The Turks promised to allow Arabs autonomy ... but you know as well as I do that the Arabs are not capable of ruling themselves.' From Smyrna he returned home.

In the second half of 1916 the army's fortunes turned. The British forces advanced steadily, taking all the Turkish positions for which they had fought so hard and suffered so much the previous year. The navy, moving steadily upstream, assisted them in all their efforts. In February 1917 the British forces under Lieutenant-General Sir Stanley Maude finally recaptured Kut. On 11 March they entered Baghdad and soon afterwards took control of the whole country.

Once the tide had turned everything seemed to go their way. And not just in Mesopotamia. Lawrence arrived in Akabar with gold and promises of freedom to buy the loyalty of the Bedouin and other desert tribesmen and the war in the Middle East turned in favour of the British and their allies. Armistice was declared on 31 October.

After his release from prison William Louis Reed's diaries became very sketchy. The final entry was dated 13 October 1918, so he was not one of the prisoners exchanged early, as he had hoped he would be, but for his freedom had to wait until the Armistice with Turkey on 31 October. He also abandoned his prison diary and reverted to using the diary he had had with him during his travels in Persia and while working on the Tigris and Euphrates before his captivity. Perhaps he was excited at the fact that it had been returned to him. It seems almost incredible in the circumstances that all his belongings or 'gear' were returned to him from the captured '*Julnar*'.

From his diary we know that he went back to work in Iraq, arriving in Basra on 22 April 1919. There followed several entries relating to the comings and goings of Lynch Brothers personnel and then on 23 December he writes: 'Heard today that I have been awarded the DSO announced in the *London Gazette* of November 12th 1919 [or 11th].' More comings and goings were listed. Several of the goings detailed people as 'sacked for drinking'.

A one-line entry stated 'Became engaged Wednesday 21st September 1921.' This was to my grandmother Mary Alouta. In 1890, the first shipbuilder set up in Baghdad 60 years after the first steamship had arrived there. His name was Yusef Alouta, the same as Mary's father, so it is possible that this was her father. Mary had been married once before at the age of 16. When William met her she was the widow of a doctor, Dominic Francis who had also worked in Persia. The Shah of Persia had awarded him the Order of the Lion and the Sun. The document was also signed by King Edward VIII.

Mary and her family were Catholics of the Chaldean rite. This sect of the Catholic Church has existed in Iraq since the time of Christ. Mary and William married in the Chaldean Church a month after their engagement. In 1922 their daughter Muriel, my mother, was born. She grew up in Basra and went to school with the Sisters of Mercy there.

Although I never knew my grandfather, I have vivid memories of my grandmother. In the 1930s she moved to Blackheath in London to enable Muriel to attend the Ursuline Convent in

William with his wife Mary and daughter Muriel.

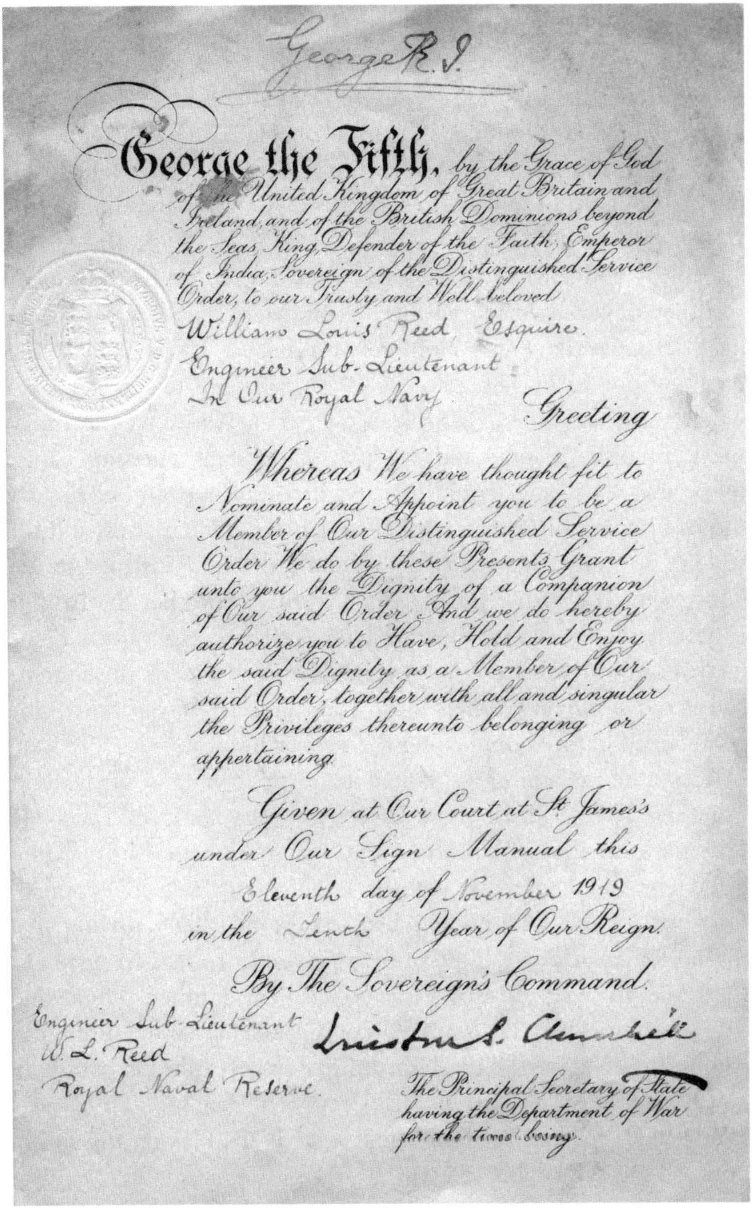
George R.I.

George the Fifth, by the Grace of God of the United Kingdom of Great Britain and Ireland, and of the British Dominions beyond the Seas King, Defender of the Faith, Emperor of India, Sovereign of the Distinguished Service Order, to our Trusty and Well beloved William Louis Reed, Esquire. Engineer Sub-Lieutenant In Our Royal Navy Greeting

Whereas We have thought fit to Nominate and Appoint you to be a Member of Our Distinguished Service Order We do by these Presents Grant unto you the Dignity of a Companion of Our said Order And we do hereby authorize you to Have, Hold and Enjoy the said Dignity as a Member of Our said Order, together with all and singular the Privileges thereunto belonging or appertaining.

Given at Our Court at St James's under Our Sign Manual this Eleventh day of November 1919 in the Tenth Year of Our Reign.

By The Sovereign's Command.

Winston S. Churchill

Engineer Sub-Lieutenant W. L. Reed Royal Naval Reserve.

The Principal Secretary of State having the Department of War for the time being.

Copy of William's DSO (Distinguished Service Order) signed by Winston Churchill.

Greenwich. They were also close to William's family there. Mother and daughter never returned to Basra. William continued to work in the oil industry in the Middle East and was well known in Basra. He died of a stroke in Haifa in 1938 while still working in the oil industry. His body was flown to Baghdad for burial. Obituaries appeared in both the London papers and the *Baghdad Times*.

Sadly, neither Mary nor Muriel were able to go to the funeral and they never saw their country again. Mary stayed on in Blackheath. It may have been difficult for her to travel as war was breaking out again. Later, in the 1950s, we used to stay with her when we were on leave from West Africa. She never learnt to speak English fluently and we played constant guessing games over what word she would next want to retrieve. In her heyday she had hired a tutor to teach her to dance the Charleston and she smoked so much that she had a cigarette machine installed in her house, which a man regularly came to fill, saving her the trouble of going to the shops. Even so, she was over eighty when she died. London was a culture shock. Her first trip to the cinema had so overwhelmed her that, according to my parents, she genuflected before going along the row to her seat.

The other relations we visited regularly were my great aunts Edie and Kit. William must have been very close to Edie. He shows a great deal of concern about her in his letters from Afion Kara Hissar and offers to pay for a cabinet for her collection of Goss figures. He also bought her a diamond ring knowing that she no longer had any hope of being given one as an engagement ring. She always promised to leave it to my mother. Then, one day when she was ill, Muriel's cousin, Eileen visited Edie and admired it as it caught the light on her finger. Edie, in a rush of kindly feeling, rashly promised to leave it to her too. To avoid a family feud she eventually left it to me. It sparkles on my finger now as I tap the keyboard.

William's silver cigarette case escaped the attentions of the Turks. He must have hidden it well and carried it with him throughout his long journey into Turkey and his years of imprisonment. It is now proudly displayed on a coffee table in our sitting room.

As for the *Julnar*, some sources state that it was sunk in Tikrit in 1919. However, it was still registered at Lloyds in 1923 and its name only disappeared from the register the year after that. By 1929 the Euphrates and Tigris Steam Navigation Company has also disappeared from the register. Presumably it was sold or taken over by another company.

After the First World War, Mesopotamia or Turkish Arabia began to be called Iraq. The name was originally used in the seventh century when Islam first became established there. It means 'the country that is firmly rooted'. It is symptomatic of the change of outlook on the area; the move away from the classical Greek name follows the move away from seeing the Middle East in terms of classical history and mythology.

Britain was obliged to set up an administration to impose stability and prosperity in the wake of the Turks' departure. It established three departments – revenue and customs; health; and post and telegraph. Judicial administration was implemented through the Iraq Occupied Territories code based on the Indian civil and criminal code. A military governor controlled each town and the surrounding territory was divided into districts each with its own political and assistant political officers. Their duties were to maintain order, settle disputes and collect revenue. As General Maude's announcement on the capture of Baghdad in 1917 shows, the British were keen to be seen as liberators rather than conquerors. They had had no plans prior to the war to annex any part of the Middle East beyond ensuring that their route through the Persian Gulf to India was secure and that they could maintain control of their oil supply. Their promise, to liberate the Arabs from the Turkish oppressors and to permit self-rule, was what persuaded the Arabs, especially the tribes, to support the Allies and to fight for the British under T. E. Lawrence. He famously led the Bedouin in a guerrilla campaign against the Turks.

The British authorities' first priority was to establish and maintain law and order and to set national boundaries. The boundaries of the country and of its neighbours were set the under the leadership of Sir Percy Cox, or Supposi Kokus as the Arabs called him. In a prewar agreement Britain and France divided the Middle East between them. The Sykes-Picot Agreement of 1916 established that Syria and Lebanon went to France while Mesopotamia and Palestine came under British jurisdiction.

Sir Percy Cox and Gertrude Bell attended the 1919 Paris Conference to put forward Iraq's case and to ratify the boundaries they had set. Gertrude Bell had travelled extensively throughout the Middle East before the war and was a gifted linguist who spoke Arabic fluently. She knew the tribes and the terrain better than anyone of her time. From her travels and work in British administration during the war, she was well known to the people of Iraq and held in high regard. Decisions about national boundaries were based on her work mapping the area and recording the tribes. Drawing the boundaries of the separate states involved a long slow process of negotiation and discussion with all the tribal leaders and politicians. Gertrude Bell was at the forefront of these and so was thought to be the best person to represent Iraq's interests at the conference.

T. E. Lawrence was also at the conference, still full of his romantic notions of desert life and Arab culture. He had been the go-between for the British government in negotiating with the Arabs and had promised King Faisal, the leader of the Arab revolt, freedom and self-government. Paris was a betrayal of all these promises. Lawrence's disappointment was as keen as that of the Arab leaders and led to his eventual nervous breakdown.

The promises made were threefold. First, territories that were free before the war would remain so. Second, any territories the

Arabs liberated would be granted complete and sovereign independence. Finally, the Anglo-French declaration heralded the setting-up of governments chosen by the Arabs.

Some wily Arab nationalist politicians had warned that helping the British and French in the war would mean exchanging one foreign power for another, but few listened to them. When America joined the war in 1917, these fears were pushed aside, for the USA was believed not to favour imperialism. President Woodrow Wilson announced his 14 points advocating freedom and self-determination for races under the thumb of the old imperial powers; however, the need for oil and the rise of Zionism overrode Wilson's points.

There had been a change of attitude to imperial projects among politicians in America and Britain, brought about by the new style of men entering politics. Previously, Britain's politicians had been public school educated and steeped in the classics. They saw the Middle East in terms of Alexander, Xerxes, Darius and Cyrus. The newer type of politician came from a wider range of backgrounds and often from a non-conformist religious upbringing. They saw the area in terms of the Old Testament with a strong belief in the Promised Land and Chosen People.

A trickle of Jews escaping the pogroms in the European states had already begun to move into Palestine before the war. With support from the new style politicians in the West, the idea of a homeland for the Jews began to take shape and British Zionists, led by Dr Chaim Weizmann, began to lobby MPs. Arthur Balfour's declaration of 1917 promised a home to Jewish people in Palestine and protection for the indigenous Arab population. A British Palestine could help secure the Suez Canal and so it became a British protectorate. No one consulted the Palestinians.

In 1920 the League of Nations set up mandates that allowed Britain and France to govern the territories they had divided up between them, but for a limited period of time. They were supposed to work towards establishing independence. Many politicians, including General Maude, believed that the Arabs were incapable of ruling themselves. It had taken a great deal of persuasion to make him sign and read the declaration of 1917, which Sir Mark Sykes had in fact penned. The San Remo conference ratified earlier agreements and the whole of Arabia between the Mediterranean and the Persian frontier was placed under mandates to suit the ambitions of Britain and France.

The nationalists saw the mandate in Iraq as imperialism in disguise and grew impatient to gain autonomy, but the British were looking for a regime that would favour them. Riots broke out later that year. Each faction wanted its bit of power.

As a nation, Iraq had not known independent government for 500 years. Then, under the Abbasid dynasty its empire stretched from Tunisia to the borders of China covering most of modern-day Pakistan. Later, under Ottoman rule Iraq did not thrive. It had not been a nation, merely a collection of provinces under imperialist rule. The tribes, particularly the Bedouin, never succumbed to Turkish rule. They stayed away from the cities; they kept to the land they knew so well – the desert, mountains, marshes and flood plains. They had no concept of nationhood, only of loyalty to the tribe. Gertrude Bell wrote to her parents: 'The truth is that there is very little patriotism in this country.' Then, as now, there were disparate groups that had to be united, Sunnis, Shiites and Kurds, as well as numerous tribes. Many of these different groups rebelled and violence frequently erupted. Gertrude Bell stated that the Kurds had been included within the boundaries of Iraq to try to maintain some kind of balance of power between the Sunni and Shiite communities.

Wilson who occupied Sir Percy Cox's post for a while explained it like this.

> The warlike Kurds numbering half a million will never accept an Arab ruler. The Shia, numbering one and three quarter million in Iraq, would not accept Sunni domination. ... Then there were substantial Jewish and Christian minorities to be considered. Three-quarters of the popu-

> lation was tribal with no previous tradition of obedience to any government.'

To this day not much has changed.

The British saw the Shias and Kurds as potentially mutinous and too hidebound by tradition to form any kind of practical modern government. The Sunnis were a minority who could be easily swept out of power. When the British realized the possible cost of maintaining order in Iraq in the face of frequent rioting, the government opted to put a monarchy in place.

Three choices were before them – Ibn Saud of Saudi Arabia whom the Indian government favoured, Sayid Taleb, the nationalist leader who threatened rebellion, and Faisal, the man who led the Arab revolt alongside Lawrence. He had also been king of Syria under the postwar arrangements but the French threw him out. He left ignominiously, carrying his own suitcase and without ceremony. In Palestine British officials were waiting for him. One man described the scene, 'We mounted him a guard of honour a hundred strong. He carried himself with the dignity and the noble resignation of Islam ... though tears stood in his eyes and he was wounded to the soul.'

As a direct descendant of the prophet, Amir Faisal of the Hajaz probably had as good a claim as anyone to be the first king of the new Iraq. To ensure that this happened, at the crucial moment the British whisked Taleb off onto a ship that took him to Ceylon for an extended holiday and he spent the rest of his life in exile at the British government's expense. He had threatened revolt if the British denied the Iraqis freedom of choice in their selection of a leader. Ibn Saud was given a handsome payoff of £100,000 a year.

Faisal was voted in with a suspiciously large majority, 96.8 per cent, equal to Saddam Hussein's in 1995. Neither ruler faced any opposition. Faisal's brother Abdullah was made king of Jordan to create a buffer zone to protect Palestine, which, under the Balfour Declaration, would become the new homeland for the Jews.

Abdullah was supplied with money and troops to suppress anti-French and anti-Zionist activity. Hussein, the sharif of Mecca and father of Abdullah and Faisal, was rewarded for his part in starting the Arab revolt against the Turks with a similar stipend to Ibn Saud's.

Faisal was crowned on 23 August 1921. Gertrude Bell was his constant adviser in state and family matters. Just as the military administration in Iraq now feels obliged to use men who formerly served Saddam Hussein's government, so King Faisal had to rely on Sunnis who had been prominent in the previous Turkish regime. But it took seven years before Iraq could truly be said to be a federal state.

The king and his Ottoman officials took over the administration when the British departed, leaving 'advisers' in the new ministries to retain Britain's influence, protect its access to India and safeguard the oilfields. Britain also retained two major air-bases. In this way the British were able to cut costs without losing sight of their aims. Even Lawrence regarded these arrangements as sufficient to meet the promises he had made to the Arabs, but the Arabs did not. Revolts were frequent and resentment of the Jewish influx into Palestine grew.

The revolts were ruthlessly quelled. In Iraq the British army burnt to the ground any village from which an attack had been mounted. Winston Churchill, then secretary of state for war and air said, 'I am strongly in favour of using poisoned gas against uncivilized tribes.' And chemicals were used against the rebellious Kurds during the 1920s. America was too interested in the progress of the Zionists in Palestine to be bothered with these events and did not protest, much less intervene.

King Faisal did achieve some measure of independence before his death in 1932, the year the British Mandate ended. The following year, under the orders of General Bakr Sidqi, the Iraqi army persecuted and exterminated hundreds of Assyrians, the ancient Christians of the Chaldean rite. In 1936 he declared a *coup d'état*, but was murdered the next year.

Five years later it was the Jews' turn. In 1942, when Rashid Ali's pro-German government was voted into power, Britain intervened again and restored the monarchy under Faisal II. France stayed in Syria and Lebanon until 1946. The same year Britain gave up its claim to Jordan and Abdullah took over until he was assassinated at the El Aqsa mosque in Jerusalem in 1951. Abdullah's killer was one of those who accused him of betraying the Arabs over Palestine.

In the 1930s, as Jews fled from Nazi Europe, immigration to Palestine increased. In 1936 the British finally crushed the Arab revolt and in 1947, unable to cope with the constant rebellions, they gave up their mandate in Palestine. The UN voted to split Palestine into two separate states, but the Arabs rejected that plan. A year later the State of Israel was established and this immediately led to the first Arab-Israeli war in 1948. America, driven by postwar sympathy for the Jewish people and a strong Jewish vote in the United States, was the first country to recognize the new state and became its greatest ally.

The 1950s were troubled times in the Middle East. Britain, France and Israel went to war to protect their interests when Nasser toppled the monarchy in Egypt and nationalized the Suez Canal, and America intervened to protect its oil interests. Saddam Hussein first entered the political arena in 1956 when he assisted in a failed coup against the monarchy and, a year later, joined the Baath Party, a tiny political entity at the time but promoting radical nationalism. In 1958 a group of non-Baathist nationalist army officers led by General Abdul Karim Qassim perpetrated an extremely bloody *coup d'état* in which Faisal and his family were massacred. Barely thirty years after it had been established the regime the British government favoured and its political officers like Sir Percy Cox and Gertrude Bell so carefully nurtured was swept away.

In 1937, while the British were suppressing the first Arab revolts against the Jewish occupation of Palestine, Saddam was born near Tikrit to a poor, landless peasant family. Tikrit, famous for the pyramid of skulls Tamerlaine left behind, had prospered in the nineteenth century through making *kalksas*, a kind of round raft made out of inflated animal skins, but when the demand for these declined Tikrit lapsed into poverty. The village in which Saddam grew up consisted of mud huts and dirt roads; there was no running water or electricity and people used dried cow dung to fuel their fires.

At the age of ten Saddam, who had an absent father and cruel step-father, was sent to Baghdad to live with his uncle, Khayrallah Talfah, and it was only then that he started school. His uncle, who was a school teacher with pro-Nazi anti-British sentiments, had an immense influence on Saddam's life. Saddam did not do well enough at school to be accepted for army officer training, which had clearly been a disappointment to him. In fact, he was the only political leader to take power in the 1950s and 1960s without a military background. Later, in 1976, he managed to acquire the rank of lieutenant-general and three years later, when he was president, he promoted himself to field marshal.

After Faisal II's death there was a great deal of plotting, counter plotting and jostling for power. As a minor member of the Baath Party at the time, Saddam had helped carry out an attack on Qassim, which failed. Saddam was slightly wounded in the assault and a sympathetic doctor treated him along with the other wounded, but party propagandists tell a different story. They say that Saddam played a vital role in the incident and was badly wounded. Bleeding profusely, he ordered a comrade to dig the bullet out of his leg with a razor blade and the pain was so great that he fainted. He is then supposed to have dressed up as a Bedouin tribesman, swum across the Tigris, stolen a donkey and fled across the desert to Syria – *et voilà*, Saddam, the hero! He did, however, take refuge in Syria, from where he went to Cairo and, supported by the Egyptian government completed his high school education and embarked on a law degree. He never completed it, but was awarded an honorary degree much later, after he became second in command in the regime. In 1961 he returned to Iraq and the Baath Party finally succeeded in killing Qassim, whose body was displayed on television against a backdrop of scenes of devastation in a palace littered with the mutilated corpses of his supporters. Saddam's first job in the new regime was as an interrogator in Qasr-al-Nihayyah, the palace in which Faisal II and his family had been gunned down and which the Baath Party now used as a torture chamber. When the party was ousted nine months later, it was found to be full of gruesome relics.

In 1963 the Baath Party split into two factions. Saddam supported Michel Aflaq, a French-educated Syrian and the party's co-founder and principle ideologue. Aflaq in turn sponsored Saddam in his bid to join the Baath regional command, the highest decision making body. His older cousin General Ahmed Hassan al-Bakr, a top military figure in the party, further supported his position and Saddam's career was launched.

At about this time Saddam married his cousin, the daughter of his Uncle Khayrallah Talfah. Sajida then persuaded al-Bakr's son to marry her sister and two of his daughters to marry two of her brothers, thus creating a powerful, tight-knit dynasty. When General al-Bakr became secretary general of the party in 1965 he promoted Saddam to be his deputy. Following a bout of political upheaval within the party, Saddam was imprisoned and, on pondering his fate while serving his sentence, he came to the conclusion that different factions within the Baath Party had destroyed the revolution of 1963. Unity, he decided, was vital and when he came out of prison he followed his idea to the letter. Anyone who could not be trusted had to be killed and his reputation for terror grew.

When the Baathists seized power in 1968 General al-Bakr became president, commander in chief, secretary general of the party and chairman of the Revolutionary Command Council. Saddam was appointed deputy chairman of the council and put in charge of internal security. Once again he placed his trust in his family and appointed his relatives to key positions in his security service. There followed a period of denunciations, accusations and executions. The persecuted were first the Jews then the Christians but soon Muslims found themselves falling foul of Saddam too as the Baath Party secured its power in blood. Through the security services Saddam took control of the party. While al-Bakr lived modestly, Saddam and his henchmen lived extravagantly as if making up for their years of deprivation and indignity. Little by little they eliminated all political rivals in their reign of terror. By July 1979, after 11 years of working in harmony with al-Bakr, Saddam had achieved absolute power.

When Ayatollah Khomeini ousted the Shah of Iran, who had enjoyed strong American support, Shiite riots broke out across Iraq. Although al-Bakr was keen to make compromises, Saddam wanted the riots put down and the perpetrators punished. Al-Bakr and his supporters also wanted to unite with Syria on the grounds that it would reduce Egypt's influence in the Arab world, which Iraq and other Arab nations wanted to see happen because they opposed Egypt's decision to sign a peace treaty with Israel. Saddam was against unity with Syria as it would have curbed his power so he called on all his family members to support him and al-Bakr was forced to resign, leaving Saddam at the head of the Baath Party. He thus became president, secretary general of the party, head of government and chairman of the Revolutionary Command Council.

On his assumption of power an extraordinary party meeting was held at which all who ever had or were likely to oppose him were denounced and taken away for torture and execution. This purging of opposition and the reign of terror that followed led to Saddam's absolute power. Since party membership was a requirement for most jobs and certainly for government posts, most of the population became party members.

Throughout Saddam's rise to power there was little criticism from the United States of politics or politicians in Iraq. Its interest in the Middle East was purely economic and stemmed from its thirst for oil. In 1931 Charles R. Crane brought in an engineer to survey the region for oil and the following year the Standard Oil Company of California expressed an interest in the prospect; commercial production began in 1938. It was to protect its oil imports that America supported the Shah of Iran's government against the popular uprising.

Since the 1940s America has always had an enemy. It is as if a nation composed of people who have fled persecution or destitution in their own countries suffers from a collective paranoia; so disparate a population with such a wide cultural mix perhaps needs a common enemy against which the citizens can unite. First there was the McCarthy witch-hunt for reds under the bed; then came the cold war and the Cuban missile crisis, Korea and Vietnam. It was just as the USA was recovering from the disastrous Vietnam War that the Ayatollah deposed the Shah of Iran and declared a holy war on Westerners. America was despised as the supporter of a government that the Iranian people hated. There were anti-American demonstrations in the streets and attacks on American embassies with hostages being taken as well as many deaths. As oil prices shot up, Iran took Vietnam's place as public enemy number one in the American nightmare. With hatred for America and terrorist attacks becoming widespread in the Middle East, the USA saw Israel as its only ally in the region and increased its aid to the new state, a move guaranteed to intensify its problems.

Ayatollah Khomeini, who emerged as the leader in Iran, was keen to spread his ideas across the Islamic world and he started with his nearest neighbour. Iranian infiltrators in Iraq encouraged Kurds and Shiites to rebel against Saddam's Sunni-dominated government and, as a consequence, many Shiites were exiled. In the ensuing war between the two countries, America armed and supported Iraq. In 1988 Saddam Hussein sent aircraft over the Kurdish area of northern Iraq to deliver a lethal cargo of chemicals; 5000 of Halabja's 50,000 inhabitants died in agonizing pain. A further 20,000 were severely injured with searing, blistering, permanent lung damage and blindness. By the end of the year he had killed 200,000 Kurds.

Not one Western government spoke up and the world largely ignored what was happening. Worse, the United States tried to blame Iran for the attack and, given that the Americans saw Iraq as a bulwark against Islamic fundamentalism, they continued to pour money into it. Nevertheless, its eight year war against Iran severely damaged Iraq economically. The attack on Kuwait arose directly out of these financial difficulties.

Kuwait refused to lend Saddam the $10 billion he requested to write off debts incurred during the war. In addition, Kuwait was overproducing oil, driving down world prices and so reducing Iraqi profits. The Kuwaiti government refused to change its policy. Saddam also accused Kuwait of slant drilling, which is drilling for oil across the border, so in fact extracting Iraqi oil.

The claim that Kuwait was in fact part of Iraqi territory had been made several times since the British drew the boundaries of the Middle Eastern nations just after the First World War. During the Ottoman Empire, Kuwait had been part of a vilayet or province that covered most of southern Iraq. In 1899 the Ottoman Turks appointed a sheikh to sign a deal with Great Britain, the terms of which were that he would agree to accept British protection in return for becoming ruler of Kuwait. In 1914, Britain gave Kuwait independence. While both the Arab League and the United Nations had rejected all Iraq's previous claims to the sheikhdom, this did not stop Saddam using it as an excuse for his invasion.

It was for these three reasons that Saddam invaded Kuwait, but only after he had consulted the United States. The US ambassador told Saddam that they had no interest in inter-Arab squabbles. This response, coupled with America's previous support and lack of censure when he used chemical weapons against the Kurds, made him feel invincible and confident that US support would continue. Even after Saddam gave several major speeches in which he made blistering attacks on the United States for its policy on Palestine, the American government continued to support him with loans and aid and to import 675,000 barrels of oil a day from Iraq. Only when the USA discovered that Saddam had chemical weapons ready to use against Israel were the loans withdrawn.

Saddam's invasion of Kuwait was in direct contravention of international law. America and its allies had to respond. Saddam moved from being a friend of America to public enemy number one. The Americans looked for support to fight Saddam within the Arab community. The Arab states were worried at the idea of bringing 'infidel' troops onto Islamic soil. Of the many states only three joined the coalition. Egypt was persuaded to back the USA with promises to write off their loans. Syria hoped that the removal of Saddam would leave them as the most powerful state in the region. Saudi Arabia believed, along with everyone else, that they would be invaded next, so wanted American protection.

Onto this scene came Osama Bin Laden fresh from supporting the Mujahaddin in Afghanistan. He proposed a jihad against the Iraqis since he was a Wahabi-influenced fundamentalist Muslim. The Wahabis are a fundamentalist sect dating back to 1740. Propagated by Muhammad Abd ibn al-Wahhab, this theology declared that Muslims had a religious duty to kill those who did not follow the teachings of Islam. Bin Laden abhorred the Iraqi government's secular policies and the secular way of life of the people. His proposal was to use Islamic troops to prevent the ignominy of having infidels fighting on Saudi Arabia's sacred soil, which contains Mecca, the most holy place to all Muslims. His offer was ignored so he sat out the war on the sidelines becoming increasingly enraged at the sight of Christians and Jews polluting, as he saw it, Islamic territory.

The other states, especially Palestine, were pro-Saddam because they saw him as a bulwark against Israel and American Zionist policies. King Hussein of Jordan dared not join the coalition for fear of reprisals at home from the large Palestinian population.

Israel was asked to stay out of the conflict to avoid it becoming an Arab-Israeli war. This it did despite being targeted by Saddam's Scud missiles on several occasions.

After the Americans and the coalition had decisively defeated Saddam's troops, rebellions against his regime broke out in Shiite and Kurdish areas of the country and in the southern marsh area. Instead of supporting these, America simply withdrew its forces. The rebellions were viciously crushed in Saddam's usual manner. Thousands of Kurds were killed, many fled to Iran or Turkey. It was the plight of these refugees seen on television across the Western world that forced the UN to impose a no-fly zone over northern Iraq's Kurdish area. Saddam's revenge for the rebellion in the south was to drain the marshes, which put to an end a way of life that had existed for thousands of years. Iraqi troops also napalmed the towns and dumped chemicals into the water killing hundreds of thousands of fish and birds.

There were two major outcomes of the war and the American victory. One was that the Kurdish territory in the north of Iraq was given some autonomy and became a no-fly zone enforced by the USA. The other was that sanctions were put in place against Iraq as well as freezing its assets to force the government to give up its arsenal of chemical weapons and weapons of mass destruction. It is presumed that these were not used in the Gulf War through fear of reprisals in kind from America, even though it was the threat of chemical attack that hastened Iran's capitulation in the Iran-Iraq war.

Lack of understanding of the outside world led Saddam to make many mistakes, not least the wars against Iran and Kuwait. Now he believed that sanctions would be over in a few months because the world could not manage without Iraqi oil. Iraq holds 20 per cent of the world's oil supplies. He had reckoned without American paranoia and tenacity in the face of its enemies. He agreed to allow the United Nations' weapons inspectors to investigate.

UNSCOM, as the United Nations Special Commission on

Iraq came to be called, met with constant deceit, prevarication and bare-faced lying. This led to the American position becoming even more entrenched. Instead of stating that sanctions would remain until all weapons of mass destruction had been surrendered, they said they would be maintained until Saddam had been removed from power. So when Scott Ritter, a UN inspector announced that a 90–95 per cent level of disarmament had been achieved, there was still no change to the sanctions policy.

US bombing raids during the Gulf War had devastated power stations, oil installations and waterworks throughout the country. These were hastily repaired using cannibalized parts. When these wore out there was nothing with which to repair them so the electricity failed and, without power, clean water could not be pumped. In addition, chlorine could not be imported to purify the water as it was a dual purpose substance that could be used to manufacture chemical weapons.

Iraq's economy was built on oil. Oil revenues paid for clean water, a good and free health service, salaries and food. Now imported foods were no longer available, inflation ran at 2000 per cent and even the middle classes were forced to live at subsistence level. A stable, well-educated, generally well-ordered society had begun to break down. The civil service became corrupt, crime levels soared and people started to sell off whatever they had to buy food. Hospitals were functioning without water, mosquito nets, medicines or surgical equipment. Rationing staved off starvation, but it gave the government ever more power over its people.

By 1995 some 500,000 children had died from disease and malnutrition: one in eight was dying of gastroenteritis or cholera before his or her first birthday. The Iraqi people felt they were being punished. Saddam and President Bush were equally intractable and the innocent Iraqis were caught in the middle. A population that had been largely secular began to turn to religion. Suddenly, Wahabism, which the Iraqis had previously despised, was spreading.

Many people left the cities to work the land again so that food could be brought in from the countryside, but without spare parts for irrigation plants, animal feed, pesticides or fertilisers – all dual purpose commodities – their success was limited. Smugglers and bootleggers prospered while the rest of the country succumbed to hunger and disease.

Meanwhile, UNSCOM carried on its work to uncover weapons factories and installations hidden anywhere from chicken farms to loyal supporters' gardens. Ali Jenabi, an Iraqi economist, is quoted in *Saddam Hussein: An American Obsession* as saying:

> Do you think that Britain and the US are really afraid of our biological weapons? Of course they are not. The sort of things we have, any country could make in a bathtub. A single religious maniac in Japan was able to make nerve gas. They just want to keep Iraq weak and divide up its oil.

Throughout all this, there were constant conspiracies against Saddam and he relied more and more on his family for loyalty and support. However, even they let him down. His sons-in-law escaped across the border to Jordan, though not for long because he brought them back to face torture and execution. All other conspiracies failed, so tight was his grip on security and so efficient his intelligence operations. Some attempts were made to form an opposition to Saddam's government in the free Kurdish area, with support from the Americans, but their intelligence was flawed because very few of their intelligence officers spoke any Arabic, which somewhat hampered communications. In-fighting between the different Kurdish factions held back progress and Saddam's agents infiltrated much of the organization. Saddam sent his tanks into the no-fly zone, but because he was driving and not flying, there was no reaction from the allied forces. He routed the opposition and took back control of the area.

Then came 9/11: it was known almost immediately that the group responsible for the outrage was Al-Qaeda led by Osama

Bin Laden – angered at American power and the fact that the United States retained forces in Saudi Arabia even after the Gulf War was over, as well as its continuing support for Israel. Despite investigations by intelligence officers, there was never any suggestion that Saddam Hussein had anything to do with it. Some information came from defectors from Saddam's government, military personnel and civil officials, but they obviously had a vested interest in implicating the dictator and all their statements were unproven. One defector, the former head of Iraq's military intelligence General Wafiq al-Samarrai, asked how these people could possibly know about such things in a society so murderous and secretive that 'the way to stay alive there was to show no interest in information that did not relate to your job'. Furthermore, Saddam's secular government was such anathema to the fundamentalist Bin Laden that he had offered to lead a jihad against Iraq, which is hardly the basis for a close partnership.

Yet, the USA decided to attack Iraq, allegedly because of 9/11. With Saddam accused of having weapons of mass destruction, we were told that the war was for the greater safety of the West. Iraq was already crippled by the years of war in which it had suffered massive financial losses as well as the destruction of a great deal of its infrastructure. Back in Kuwait in the Gulf War it was already apparent that the Iraqi army was no match for the superior forces of the coalition and not nearly as well supplied or trained as Saddam's boasting about the 'mother of all battles' made the world think. Now, with 90 per cent of their weapons disposed of, according to UNSCOM, they were even less prepared for war. We now know that Iraq had no weapons of mass destruction at this time. But Saddam was not going to lose face, least of all in the eyes of his fellow Arabs. His country was broken, its people living in fear, poverty and misery yet he continued to play his game of brag. American paranoia found itself face to face with Arab machismo and went to war.

Regime change was the other reason given for going to war. Saddam's brutality against his own people was well known and yet not condemned when it suited the USA to have him as an ally. Why pick on him just now? To show the 'folks back home' that Bush's government was responding to the 9/11 attacks? Fewer than 4000 people died in the Twin Towers. In the war that America waged against Iraq it is estimated that 150,000 civilians were killed in the bombing raids. They did not even pay them the courtesy of counting them properly.

If they had read anything of the history of this country they would have known that with the antagonism that exists between Kurds, Shias, Sunnis and tribes it would fracture in the way that it has. Any man who can use the term 'Crusade', as Bush did in his axis of evil speech, unaware that to Muslims the term invokes invasion and massacre by Christian forces, has little grasp of history or of what drives people. The power struggle to fill the vacuum left by Saddam will go on for decades and Britain and America are now the most hated nations in large parts of the world, which is hardly conducive to our greater safety.

In Iraq, initial euphoria at the toppling of Saddam and his cruelty soon gave way to resentment at the new invader and the total destruction of the country's infrastructure. The lack of any peace keeping in the early days after the invasion led to an influx of terrorist groups stirring up further trouble. And why should we think that bombing the hell out of a country is any more likely to endear it to democracy. Perhaps President Bush and Prime Minister Blair should have been warned by the words of Winston Churchill in the aftermath of the First World War when he was head of the British Colonial Office coping with the riots and rebellions in the newly formed country of Iraq. 'I feel some misgivings about the political consequences to myself of taking on my shoulders the burden and odium of the Mesopotamia entanglement.'

In much the same way as General Maude's declaration of 1917 told the people of Baghdad that Britain had come as a liberator, so too did the Americans in 2003. In both cases liberation was to mean rule by a foreign power to suit its own need for oil and security and to put a regime in place that followed the pattern of government in its own country. Bush's commitment to democracy was shown to be lukewarm recently when the Palestinians voted Hamas into power. He is now pursuing policies against them that are making it impossible for them to govern effectively. Some 75 per cent of all financial aid has been withdrawn, and the US government and other Western powers are refusing to have any dealings with the new Palestinian authority. All this means that the Hamas government is unable to pay its civil servants, policemen, doctors and teachers and, consequently, the society is disintegrating.

Will the government currently being set up in Iraq last any longer than the 30 years the administration the British set up in the 1920s lasted? Bush and Blair seemed to take no account of the country's history, which could have shown them how things would turn out. Perhaps they should have the grace to admit the failure of their policies, as Gertrude Bell did after the rebellions in the 1920s when she said: 'In the light of the events of the last two months there's no getting out of the conclusion that we have made an immense failure here.' Can the politicians truly say that they went in as liberators not conquerors? It does not look like it. Can they truly say that their behaviour has been better than Saddam Hussein's? In the wake of the events at Abu Graib prison and the killing of more than 150,000 innocent people, it does not look like it. Unlike Britain in 1917, America did not immediately set up an administration to keep order in the country and to restore the infrastructure, thereby allowing the society to descend into looting and chaos. Now they have replaced one form of misgovernment with another and all for the sake of oil and prosperity for America, not for Iraq.

Now America has a new public enemy. This time it is Iran. And again the accusation concerns weapons, namely the possibility of Iran building a nuclear bomb. Jonathan Porrit of Friends of the Earth stated in a recent talk that America's animosity towards Iran has more to do with the fact that Iran is threatening to sell its oil in euros instead of dollars. This would have a devastating effect on US power in the oil industry and on the value of the dollar and its position as the standard currency in the global market.

And now Israel is bombing Lebanon while America and Britain stand by. What a pity that no one heeded the words of Martin Buber, Jewish philosopher and writer. In 1921 he wrote:

> The Jewish people, who have constituted a persecuted minority in all the countries of the world for 2000 years, reject with abhorrence the nationalistic domination under which they themselves have long suffered. We do not aspire to return to the land with which we have inseparable historical and spiritual ties in order to suppress another people or to dominate it … our return to the land of Israel … will not be achieved at the expense of other people's rights.'

So much blood has been spilt on both sides that bitterness now runs fathoms deep.

Not only did the war destroy Iraq's modern infrastructure but it also destroyed many of the fragile remnants of its history going back 4000 years to the dawn of civilization. In a BBC radio interview, Donny George, head of the Archaeological Foundation, spoke of the damage done. American troops camped next to ancient ruins. The trucks of 2000 marines pulverized the ground smashing any archaeological traces. A helicopter pad was built near the Ishtar gate and sandbags were filled with archaeological debris. These sandbags were transported all over the place, mixing up the historical data: 2500 year old roads have been crushed under the wheels of humvees and other military vehicles.

Iraqi requests to respect their heritage have been ignored. In the early days of occupation there was much looting of museums and historical sites, many of which Gertrude Bell and her fellow archaeologists set up by just before and after the First World War.

Little was done to prevent this until there was an outcry in the West about it. Chemically treated and compacted down gravel to accommodate a camp and parking area now surrounds the Lion of Babylon. Barbed wire now surrounds the sites that used to be popular places for family picnics. There has been no apology from the Americans who blame their allies. The importance of these historic remains is vital since an understanding of the past often explains the present. As we can see in the Middle East today, the seeds of current conflict are created by decisions made in the past.

Ninety years after my grandfather William Louis Reed sailed up the Tigris in the *Julnar*, against all odds, his great-grandson, who also holds RNR rank as a sub-lieutenant, is doing the same thing and for exactly the same reason. He too is in the merchant navy, but in 2004 the Ministry of Defence commissioned his ship to carry troops and supplies in the current war. He spent two years sailing in and out of Umm Qasr, the modern port at Basra. Unlike the army in earlier days of the war, they were issued with body armour. Somehow, this and the fact that they had a naval escort and a detachment of commandos on board were not particularly reassuring. They served to emphasize the danger.

> Oh Thou, who Man of baser Earth didst make,
> And who with Eden didst devise the Snake;
> For all the Sin wherewith the Face of man is blacken'd,
> Man's Forgiveness give – and take!
>
> (*Rubáiyát of Omar Khayyám*, verse 58)

Time Lines

1905 Anti-government guerrilla warfare in Persia. It was uncoordinated and unsuccessful.

1908 Tabriz in Persia fell to rebel forces. The army besieged the city.

1911 Russia intervened to protect its investments and income. The Russians took Tabriz from the rebels and deposed the shah. They also captured Tehran. Russian forces occupied much of northern Persia and the British, to protect the interests of the Anglo-Persian oil company held the south.

1912 Titanic sank on 15 April after colliding with an iceberg.

1914 Archduke Ferdinand assassinated on 28 June. Germany invaded Belgium during the three weeks between 3 and 20 August. On 4 September the first Battle of the Marne began. When the battle finished five days later, on 9 September, there were 240,000 Allied dead and 260,000 German fatalities. The race to gain command of the sea through Verdun, Yser and Ypres began, ending on 24 November. Meanwhile, on 18 October the battle at Scapa Flow took place. Turkey declared war on the Allies on 29 October and the British Indian Army swept into the Middle East taking Bahrain and Basra in Iraq.

1915 Between 1 and 3 January the Russians defeated the Turkish forces, which then went on to massacre the Armenians. Between January and February British Forces stopped a Turkish attack across Sinai into Suez. German dirigible bombing attacks on Britain began on 19 January. In this month too, the French inventor Paul Langevin brought out the first sonar system. The Fokker warplane was the first to have its machine guns synchronized with its propeller. On 31 January the Germans used large quantities of poison gas to take the town of Bolimov in Central Poland, ushering in an era of chemical and biological warfare. The fight for Gallipoli and the Dardanelles saw the failure of the Allied attack against the Turkish forces. The struggle lasted from February 1915 to January 1916. Six battleships were lost and there were 250,000 allied casualties. The Battle of the Atlantic began in earnest. There were massive submarine attacks against Allied ships. The second battle of Ypres took place over the month of 22 April to 25 May. Chlorine gas was used for the first time. The *Lusitania* was sunk with the loss of 1198 people on 7 May. On 23 May Italy entered the war on the Allied side. At about the same time British forces pushed up the Tigris River then advanced on Kut in August. The Turks were defeated but there were more than 4000 casualties. Also in August the Russian front collapsed all the way to the Baltic and Bulgaria. German and Austrian forces advanced 300 miles taking Warsaw and Vilna. Having withdrawn to Ctesiphon the Turks came under attack from the British again on 27 and 28 September. They were defeated, suffering 4500 casualties, and forced to retreat back to the garrison at Kut where they were besieged. On 6 October Germany and Austria attacked and defeated Serbia. The Germans executed Edith Cavell as a spy by on 7 October.

1916 February of this year saw the Germans begin a ten-month long attack on the fortress at Verdun. The attack failed but there were a million casualties. The British and French began their attack on the Somme. This too failed but again with a horrific number of casualties. There was a total of 1,250,000 dead and injured. Chemical weapons were used. The Arab War of Independence in the Hejaz began at this time and continued for two years. Hussein Ibn Ali, Sharif of Mecca led a revolt against Turkish rule aided by his son Faisal and T. E. Lawrence. Arab Forces attacked Mecca, took Medina and by 5 June had joined the Allies. The Easter uprising began in Dublin on 24 April and, over a period of five days, 5000 British Regulars with artillery defeated a force of between 1500 to 2000 inadequately armed Irish volunteers and Irish citizen army rebels. On 29 April the besieged British forces at Kut surrendered to the Turks after a last ditch attempt to get food to them had failed. The Battle of Jutland (31 May to 1 June) was the only major naval battle of the war. The British Grand Fleet led by Admiral John Jellicoe consisted of 28 dreadnoughts. They fought the German High Seas Fleet, consisting of 16 dreadnoughts under the command of Vice-Admiral Reinhard Scheer. The British lost more ships but the Germans withdrew. David Lloyd George, Liberal politician, became the wartime coalition prime minister.

1917 Britain defeated Turkey in Sinai early in January. At the same time the Russian revolutionary army mutinies began on the eastern front quickly spreading to other areas. Strikes and demonstrations spread throughout Russia leading to a nationwide insurrection against Tsar Nicolas II in February. He abdicated on 15 March and a provisional government led first by Prince Lvov and then Alexander Kerensky succeeded him. On 3 February the USA broke off diplomatic relations with Germany. On 22 and 23 February a further attempt to take back Kut was successful and the British forces then went on to take Baghdad and move northwards through Iraq. The campaign to liberate Palestine was started on 26 March but the British attack on Gaza was a failure. The USA declared war on Germany on 6 April. Between 31 July and 10 November the third battle of Ypres took place at

Passchendaele. The British and French forces gained a whole five miles. On 15 October the French executed Mata Hari as a spy. Her real name was Margaretha Gertrude Zelle and she was a Dutch dancer. The October Revolution took place on 24 October. Leon Trotsky led the Red Guard and the Bolsheviks to storm the winter palace in Petrograd. They overthrew the Kerensky government and the Bolsheviks took control in all the major cities of Russia. On 31 October the British attacked Beersheba and forced the Turks to evacuate Gaza. Then on 9 December they took Jerusalem.

1918 Russia bowed out of the war on 3 March and on 21 March a major offensive on the Somme began that lasted until 5 April. On 28 and 29 May the first American land engagement of the war took place. The first division took and held Catigny. With the entry of the Americans into the conflict the fortunes of war turned against the Germans. They made several failed offensives especially at the Marne. The Germans retreated before an advance of French and American troops along the Meuse and at the Forest of Argonne between 26 September and 11 November. General Allenby routed Turkish forces at Jaffa on 19 September and the British also took Damascus. By 5 October Turkish resistance was collapsing and the French took Beirut. On 29 October the British took control of Mosul Oilfield and Baku. Turkey declared an armistice and left the war. The battle of the Atlantic German Revolution occurred when men refused to sail from Kiel naval base. The rebellion led to workers' and soldiers' councils and the abdication of Kaiser Wilhelm II on 9 November. The general armistice was announced at 11 a.m. on 11 November – the eleventh hour of the eleventh day of the eleventh month.

Bibliography

Barker, A. J., *The Neglected War: Mesopotamia, 1914–1918*, London: Faber & Faber, 1967

Bell, Lady F. (ed.), *The Letters of Gertrude Bell*, London: Ernest Benn Ltd, 1927

Braddon, Russell, *The Siege*, London: Jonathan Cape, 1969

Brownstone, D. and Irene M. Franck, *Timelines of War*, Boston: Little, Brown & Company, 1994

Buchanan, Sir George, *The Tragedy of Mesopotamia*, Edinburgh: Blackwood & Sons, 1938

Candler, Edward, *The Long Road to Baghdad*, London: Cassell & Company, 1919

Cato, Conrad, *The Navy in Mesopotamia 1914 to 1917*, London: Constable & Company Ltd, 1917

Cockburn, Andrew and Patrick Cockburn, *Sadaam Hussein: An American Obsession*, London: Verso, 2002

Eames, Andrew, *The 8.55 to Baghdad*, London: Bantam Press, 2004

Fromkin, David, *A Peace to End all Peace*, New York: Henry Holt & Company, 1989

Gray, Mackenzie & Company Ltd, 'Steam Navigation on the Tigris and Euphrates, 1892–1924', Oxford: St Antony's College Middle East Archive

Herbert, Aubrey, *Mons, Anzac and Kut*, London: Hutchinson, 1919

Jones, E. H, *The Road to En-dor*, Oxford: Clarendon Press, 1921

Lynch, Henry Blosse *Paper on Travels in Southern Iran*, London: Royal Geographical Society, 1890

Millar, Ronald, *Kut: The Death of an Army*, London: Secker & Warburg, 1969

Moberly, Brigadier-General F. J., *The Campaign in Mesopotamia 1914–18*, vol. 2 *Official History*, London: HM Stationery Office, 1924

Nunn, Vice-Admiral W., *Tigris Gunboats*, London: Andrew Melrose Ltd, 1932

Plant, Captain S. C., 'Unpublished memoirs 1891', Oxford: St Antony's College Middle East Archive

Richards, Herbert Arthur, 'Life in Mesopotamia and Persia, 1896–1909', unpublished memoirs, Oxford: St Antony's College Middle East Archive

Sandes, E. W. C., *In Kut and Captivity with the Sixth Indian Division*, London: J. Murray, 1919

Shepherd, Sir Francis Michie, 'Unpublished Memoirs, Fought at Kut in Tigris Corps', Oxford: St Antony's College Middle East Archive

Sifry, Micah L. and Christopher Cerf (eds), *The Iraq War Reader*, New York: Touchstone, 2003

Simpson, John, *The Wars Against Saddam: Taking the Hard Road to Baghdad*, London: Macmillan, 2003

Snelling, Stephen, *VCs of the First World War: The Naval VCs*, Gloucestershire: Sutton Publishing, 2002

Thompson, Edward J., *These Men, Thy Friends*, London: Macmillan, 1933

Townshend, Major-General Sir Charles, KCB, DSO, *My Campaign in Mesopotamia*, London: Thornton Butterworth, 1920

Wester Wemyss, Lady, *The Life & Letters of Lord Wester Wemyss, GCB, CMG, MVO Admiral of the Fleet*, London: Eyre & Spottiswoode, 1935

Index